# TRADE AND THE POOR

# Trade and the Poor

*The impact of international trade
on developing countries*

JOHN MADELEY

INTERMEDIATE TECHNOLOGY PUBLICATIONS 1992

Intermediate Technology Publications Ltd,
103–105 Southampton Row, London WC1B 4HH, UK

© John Madeley 1992

A CIP record for this book is available from the British
Library

ISBN 1 85339 121 2

Typeset by Inforum, Rowlands Castle, Hants
Printed by BPCC Wheatons, Exeter

# Contents

# Acknowledgements

There are many people I want to thank: the workers of the Satydoya community in Kandy, Sri Lanka, who arranged for me to visit a tea estate, referred to in Chapter 2; also the officials of the UN Fund for Drug Abuse Control project in Bolivia, and the Village Development Project in Mali. Chapter 7 could not have been written without the help of the Baby Milk Action Coalition, the Dutch voluntary organization WEMOS, the Pesticides Trust, and Greenpeace. Chapter 10 relied on the invaluable help of the alternative trading organizations, Oxfam Trading, Traidcraft, TWIN, and the Federation of Alternative Trading Organizations.

I want to say a special thank you to Lawrence Taylor and John Staley, and all who have taught and studied on the development studies course at Selly Oak Colleges in Birmingham. Since 1977 it has been my privilege to visit Selly Oak twice a year to lead sessions on international trade. These sessions are attended by development workers from both South and North; this book was conceived in the late 1980s out of a frustration that there was not an up-to-date book on the subject that I could recommend to students. It has been shaped by the observations of people attending the course from all over the world who have seen the effects of trade, for good or ill, on their area. How much they have learnt from me, I cannot be sure, but I have gained much from them. I also want to thank officials at the GATT and UNCTAD Secretariats in Geneva for their patient handling of my many queries, and Alison for her careful reading of the proofs. Any mistakes are entirely mine.

# Foreword

*'It is generally true that customs are gentler wherever people trade'* –
Montesquieu, *De l'Esprit des Lois*

FOR MOST DEVELOPING countries, international trade in goods and services is a paradoxical mix of the potential it offers to raise living standards and of the low returns that it now yields. Developing countries currently earn around 15 times more from this trade than they receive in development aid.[1] Yet the trade has brought few benefits for most poorer countries; the terms on which they trade have become increasingly hostile and they have to export more to import the same amount. Over 20 years ago the Swedish economist Gunnar Myrdal warned that 'international inequalities of income have been increasing for a long time and are still increasing'.[2] In 1992 the trend was continuing. International trade has done little to correct global inequalities.

Despite its shortcomings, few countries have opted out of the international trading system. Those that have opted out – such as China under Mao Tse Tung, Cambodia under Pol Pot, Albania from 1945 to 1992 – have eventually come back to a system that seems to bring few benefits. Governments of low, middle and higher-income developing countries, whether capitalist, socialist or liberal, whatever their mixture of politics and economic management, continue to stay in a system that often treats them badly. Why do they pin their faith on international trade? Are they so locked into the system that they cannot leave it even if they wish? Do they really want to trade, when the system seems so unfavourable and shows few signs of changing, or does their poverty give them little option? Are reforms possible? Can developing countries act together to get a better deal from the system?

Questions like these require an understanding of how trade affects developing countries. With the gap between rich and poor nations growing ever wider, the issues and the impact of trade are crucial. Even countries with little to trade across borders, which includes many of the poorest countries, can be affected by the activities of the agents of trade, the transnational corporations (TNCs).

Developing countries, even the poorest, choose to stay in a system that is working against them, partly out of despair that there is no other way, and partly through a belief in its potential and through hope that the system can be changed for the better. For despite the problems and the history, the potential for the South of trade with the North is considerable. If the South can organize to find the power to improve its terms of trade (the money a country earns from its exports in relation to its imports), then it can tap the North's considerable monetary wealth. But that potential will only be realized if there are substantial changes in the international trading system, and if developing countries can export on favourable terms, control TNCs and find alternative trading channels.

The need for oil is a further reason why non-oil-producing countries stay in the international trading system. There are a hundred or so developing countries that possess either no oil of their own or only a small amount (i.e. over 80 per cent of all developing countries), and if they want to have vehicles to transport food from rural to urban areas, if they wish to have any kind of mechanical equipment, if they want their fishermen to have oil to power their boat engines, then they need oil. If they have no oil supplies of their own, developing countries need to export goods in order to earn foreign exchange to buy oil.

This book considers not only the economic, but also the environmental and social aspects of trade. International trade could enable the South to earn more money; it is therefore about economics. It could also damage ecosystems in the South; it is therefore related to the environment. But the environment is often disregarded by economic policymakers, even considered as something without value. Yet to talk of development in the 1990s is to talk of development of people and of sustainable development that is in harmony with the environment and which takes long-term sustainability into account. Trade today which damages prospects for development and trade in the longer term is of limited value. Some of the current international trade in primary commodities tends to mitigate against sustainable development in the South, particularly in agriculture.[3] On the other hand, the developing world is not likely to have the resources to achieve sustainable development unless there is a fairer economic system of international trade.

The economics are also closely intertwined with the social; the deterioration in the economic situation of many developing countries in the past 10 years has been very largely due to the continued decline in world prices for the goods they export, especially commodities. This in turn has severe social implications – less export revenue means less money to spend on rural development, food production, education, health services, and so on. International trade clearly has a crucial impact on developing countries and their populations.

In international forums, bilateral and multilateral negotiations, the South is asking the North for an improved world economic order that includes a better deal for their primary commodities, improved access to the markets of the North for their manufactured goods, more control over transnational firms, relief on commercial debt, and reform of the international monetary system. Despite all the failures of negotiations about trade and development issues, as witness the numerous sessions of the United Nations Conference on Trade and Development (UNCTAD) where industrial countries typically concede little, the developing world still pins its hopes on dialogue. At a meeting in November 1991 of the Group of 77, government ministers called on industrialized countries to engage in a comprehensive dialogue for a new partnership for development.[4] But are industrialized nations willing to do any such thing, given that they appear to hold the strings of economic power? Developing countries might have to co-operate more with each other, to realize the potential of their own economic power, before justice will be wrenched from the North.

## Fair trade

This book looks at the many issues involved in the international power relationship over trade between rich and poor countries. It draws on 16 years' experience of travelling and reporting from some 40 countries in the developing world, and from attending innumerable conferences in that time about international trading matters, beginning in 1976 when I reported on UNCTAD IV for the *Observer*. During this time, I have heard the shouts of both free traders and protectionists. Neither group carries total conviction. What developing countries are asking for is *fair trade*.

Chapter 1 takes an overview of the problem, looking at why countries trade, at the 'comparative advantage' theory and why it has not worked, at the implications of trade for the economies of developing countries, and at what they seek from the international system. Chapter 2 takes a deeper look at the problem in a more personal way; it highlights some of the lives of people who earn their living from the world trading system. Very little research has been done on the impact of most aspects of trade on Third World peoples, but people who work in a trade-related activity are often working for a pittance under conditions which any civilized international community should strive to put right. Some of these people I have met and I have tried to communicate their experiences. When a trading activity causes damage to the environment, it also harms people, and this chapter also considers the crucial environmental impact of trade.

Primary commodities are said to be the South's lifeblood. Chapter 3 looks at the problems facing commodity producers, the reasons for the disastrous decline in prices over the last 30 years, and at how the lifeblood is draining away. Chapter 4 shows the problems that developing countries face when they try to diversify away from commodities into manufactured goods. While most primary commodities are allowed into the markets of industrialized nations without restrictions, tariff and non-tariff barriers are levied against semi-processed and fully manufactured goods. The doors of the North are closed to all but a comparatively small amount of Third World manufactured goods. The chapter points out that the removal of all industrial-country barriers to trade would be worth about US$100 billion a year to developing countries, increasing their overall earnings from trade by about 10 per cent.

Trade in services, especially tourism, is considered in Chapter 5. While more developing countries are now exporting services, the importation of certain service industries, such as banking, could be a threat to development effects. The chapter discusses a little-noticed aspect of trade – the high shipping costs that are involved. It points out that for many developing countries, the average tariff on Third World exports is now much less than the average transport rate. The international liberalization of services may prove to be of little benefit to most developing countries, while tourism is hardly the panacea it might seem.

International trade takes place mainly between private rather than state organizations, many of them TNCs. Developing countries have liberalized their economies in recent years and scaled down their own barriers to international trade. But liberalization can allow greater scope for TNCs. On leaving school, I worked for a TNC for 10 years and gained a basic understanding of the rationale and thinking of the large firm that trades across borders. During my travel in the past 16 years, I have often met and sometimes enjoyed the company of people who work for TNCs. That there are some good people working for these firms I have no doubt, but my overwhelming impression of TNCs is that they are the true latter-day colonialists. To them there is a world to be carved up for inclusion in the firm's profit and loss account; their employees may not be expected to be too particular about the methods they employ in that task. I have even been told, with some pride, of how TNCs are fiddling a country and getting round the rules. It is all seen as quite a challenge. The further from home, the more isolated the area, the more these firms seem to think they can take risks. TNCs are often out of control; governments have under-estimated their deviousness. One lesson of international trade is that the world community must control the firms who control much of the trade. Chapter 6 considers the role of TNCs as agents of trade; Chapter 7 looks at their role as potential agents of death, examining North–South trade in potentially deadly technologies – pesticides, drugs, breast milk substitutes, and dirty industries.

If exchanges of goods and services are to take place, then money is usually, although not always, needed. Chapter 8 considers the role of money, the debt crisis, and how the policies of international monetary organizations are often detrimental to the trading prospects of developing countries. Chapter 9 examines international trading organizations, especially the General Agreement on Tariffs and Trade (GATT) and UNCTAD. Carried out under the auspices of GATT, the Uruguay Round of trade talks have dominated international trade discussions since 1990. These talks are considered in Chapter 9 but also surface in other chapters where they relate to the different trade issues.

Chapters 10 and 11 look at promising alternatives that could help the developing world to get a better deal from the system – alternative trade, South–South trade and producer–country co-operation. Chapter 11 shows that the commodity-producing countries have no need to be passive 'price takers' – that, on the contrary, if they become organized, they can substantially increase their bargaining position and economic power. My own conclusion is that this is the way forward with the greatest potential for the developing world.

In June 1992, the United Nations Conference on Environment and Development (UNCED) – or more popularly known as the 'Earth Summit' – was held in Brazil. UNCED agreed a 600-page document, Agenda 21, which is a plan of action for sustainable development. Between 1993 and the year 2000, $600 billion a year is needed for the measures in the plan. Of this, developing countries are expected to find $475 billion a year – around half their earnings from international trade in goods and services, about a fifth of their combined gross national products. Not all the money needs to come from foreign earnings, but unless there are changes in the international trading system that give developing countries a chance to earn more, it is unrealistic to imagine they can raise such a sum. The Earth Summit avoided this issue; in doing so, it signalled again the unwillingness of Northern countries to improve the terms of trade for developing countries, and strengthened the case for producer co-operation.

In leading discussions on the subject of international trade, I have gained much over the years from *Trade and Developing Countries* by Kathryn Morton and Peter Tulloch.[5] Published in 1976, this was an excellent treatment of the economics of international trade. It is a sign of how trade was seen in the mid-1970s that while there are many listings in the index under 'development' there are none under 'environment'. The environment was then considered neutral, it was not a factor; over the past 16 years, awareness has grown of the crucial connections between international trade and the environment.

One of the difficulties of trying to analyse the impact of international trade on developing countries is that the countries are at many different stages of development. Whereas, for example, gross national product per head in Mozambique was $80 a head in 1989, in Malaysia it was over 20 times as much – $2160.[6] Inevitably some of the more general statements in this book will not apply to all countries.

On language – industrialized countries are also referred to as Western countries, richer countries, the West, and the North. Developing countries are referred to as the South, the Third World, poorer countries, or resource-poor countries. All these descriptions have limitations; the main point is that readers will, I hope, understand whom and what I am talking about! Over 90 per cent of South–North trade is more accurately called South–West trade; less than 10 per cent is with China and the countries of Eastern Europe.

My hope is that this book will be useful for students of economics and geography at GCSE and 'A' level, for those studying economics for professional examinations, for development workers, and for all who seek to understand more about how international trade affects developing countries.

JOHN MADELEY
JULY 1992

# 1 Introduction: why countries trade

*'The exercise of trade is the best-known method of achieving universal civilization without resorting directly to moral principles'* – Thomas Payne

*'Let goods be homespun whenever it is reasonably and conveniently possible'* – J.M. Keynes

INTERNATIONAL TRADE HAS the potential to help materially poor countries out of poverty. Poorer nations have seen richer nations increase their wealth by trading heavily with each other. For a resource-poor country the chance of getting a larger slice of world trade offers a chance to earn more in richer markets, and to gain more resources to fight poverty, and even the chance of moving from a peasant economy to a diversified economy that can meet the growing clamour for jobs. Although the returns from international trade to raw commodity-producing countries are low, they are nonetheless judged to be of importance for development efforts. This helps to explain why developing countries stay in a system which seems hostile to them.

In 1990, developing countries of the Southern hemisphere (including petroleum exporters) earned US$951 billion from their export of goods and services; merchandise trade accounted for $738 billion and services for $213 billion of this total.[1] The earnings accounted for just under 40 per cent of the gross national product (GNP) of the developing world. Primary commodities earned $299 billion of trade in goods, and manufactured products $439 billion – the commodities accounted for only 40.5 per cent of merchandise trade compared with 83 per cent in 1966.[2] This is chiefly because of steep price falls, rather than diversification (see Chapter 3).

Four Asian countries – Hong Kong, Korea, Taiwan and Singapore – account for over a third of the developing

1

world's overall exports, and for most of the growth in the export of manufactures. By contrast, the 69 countries belonging to the African, Caribbean and Pacific (ACP) group of countries (consisting of almost half the countries of the developing world, and nearly all the very poorest countries) accounted for $38.7 billion, less than 5 per cent of developing countries' exports as a whole.

During the 1980s the Third World's earnings from merchandise trade fell steeply in real terms. As Table 1 shows, earnings increased in monetary terms from $582.7 billion in 1980 to $691 billion in 1989, which means that after price inflation was taken into account, they fell substantially.

**Table 1    Merchandise exports of developing countries** *(US$ billion)*

|  | *1980* | *1989* |
| --- | --- | --- |
| America | 109.9 | 122.7 |
| Africa | 94.7 | 55.1 |
| Asia | 355.5 | 455.6 |
| Oceania | 2.2 | 2.9 |
| China and socialist countries in Asia | 20.4 | 55.2 |
| Total | 582.7 | 691.5 |

*Source:* UNCTAD, *Handbook of International Trade and Development Statistics, 1990.*

For Africa especially, but also for Latin America, the figures indicate a disastrous situation. They mean that resource-poor countries had less in real terms for development and other purposes. For Africa as a whole the fall was severe, even in money terms – from $94.7 billion in 1980 to 55.1 billion, in 1989. In 1980, the ACP group earned $66.32 billion from the export of goods; by 1989 this had fallen to $38.73 billion. Schemes to compensate for falls in trade earnings – like the ones operated under the Lomé Convention, between the European Community and the ACP group – have proved inadequate; in the meantime, development aid has stagnated.

## The economics of trade

International trade has been going on for thousands of years, and is referred to in some of the earliest books of the Bible. In some Old Testament times it seems that Israel served as a bridge between Africa and Asia; caravans frequently passed between the two continents. The Israeli king, Solomon, controlled the trade routes through Palestine and collected tolls from the caravans. The First Book of Kings, written in about the twelfth century BC, refers to imports into Israel of 'almug-wood'; the country traded with North Africa, Saudi Arabia, Asia Minor, Spain and Syria. Solomon is recorded as having a fleet of ocean-going trading ships that would return every three years carrying 'gold, silver and ivory and apes and baboons'.[3] The book does not record what, if anything, the country exported in exchange. Later, the world's great clipper ships raced across the oceans carrying goods between countries.

While not condemning trading activity, Biblical prophets attacked the evils that were practised in its name – dishonesty, oppression of the poor, indifference to the plight of the unfortunate.[4] Well over 2000 years after such warnings, the international trade scene seems little changed, still being marred by the practices that the prophets warned about. The prophet Ezekiel's judgement on the people of Israel – 'by your great skill in trading you have increased your wealth, and because of your wealth your heart has grown proud' (Chapter 28, verse 5) seems particularly appropriate today. Trading skills have led to the amassing of wealth, which can in turn lead to pride, indifference, and the oppression of those whose trading skills, resources and circumstances are poor by comparison.

An international trading transaction takes place because someone in one country has something that someone in another wants to buy. Few, if any, countries can produce everything. For example, Britain does not have the climate to grow coffee or tea, whereas Kenya has such a climate. An exchange enables British people to enjoy coffee and tea, and Kenyans to have the foreign currency that comes from exporting such products, which in turn can buy other goods. Climatic conditions can also help to determine where manufactured goods can best be produced. The British cotton goods industry, for example, thrived in towns at the foot of the Pennine Hills because of the natural dampness of the area, which suited the cotton-manufacturing process.

The existence of natural, physical resources is an important reason for trade. Zambia has the copper that is needed by Britain's vehicle industries – there is very little copper under

British soil. As each motor car contains more than a kilogram of copper, without copper there would be no British-made vehicles. International trade therefore enables countries to make goods they could not make otherwise, and enables people to enjoy a wider range of goods and services than would be available to them if they relied purely on the resources of their own country. In short, trade can raise living standards.

Having a resource endowment gives a country an economic advantage over others who lack such endowments. Furthermore, when a country concentrates on making a certain product, its people become skilled in its production – they develop another type of comparative advantage.

The theory of comparative advantage is one of a very few theories that economists generally agree about, although in recent years the consensus has begun to crack.[5] While it explains the great bulk of world trade, historical factors – especially nineteenth century colonialism – are also a powerful influence. The theory states that output and the increase from specialization and exchange 'will be maximized when each country or region specializes in the production of those goods and services in which its comparative advantage is largest'.[6] For a variety of reasons, a particular country may be able to produce something cheaper and better than others. Country A may be able to produce its own watches, but Country B can make them cheaper and of the same quality – it has a comparative advantage over A when it comes to watch making. It may pay Country A to buy watches from B, and for A to concentrate on making those goods in which it has an advantage over B – and then for A and B to exchange goods.

The theory is generally credited to economist David Ricardo, but his book containing the theory, *Principles of Political Economy and Taxation*, came out a year after the publication of a school textbook by Jane Marcet in 1816. Her book, *Conversations on Political Economy*, used lucid fictional dialogue to explain the subject. In the dialogue, Mrs B and her pupil Caroline discuss a key trade issue of that time, the exchange of tobacco from Virginia in the United States for cloth from the mills of northern England.

**Caroline**: If we send the Virginians £1,000 worth of broad cloth they will send us only £1,000 worth of tobacco in return. The

4

merchants will each make their profit, but I cannot understand how the country gains in wealth from such traffic.

**Mrs B:** Each of the commodities acquire an additional value on arriving at their new destination. The tobacco will be worth more in England because, not being cultivated here, it is more scarce and in great demand with us. The broad cloth will be worth more when it reaches Virginia because, not being fabricated in that country, it is more scarce and in great demand there.

**Caroline**: But if we cultivated tobacco AND fabricated broad cloth, and if the Virginians did the same, then each country would be supplied at home. And the expense of conveyance of the two cargoes exchanged would be saved.

**Mrs B:** Let us say that the broad cloth we send to Virginia cost us the labour of one man for 1,000 days, while the tobacco which we receive in exchange would have cost 2,000 days' labour to produce at home. Do we not save 1,000 days' labour? And is not the advantage to the Virginians of their tobacco similar?

**Caroline:** So it is not possible for any single country to succeed in all branches of industry, any more than for a single individual to excel at a great variety of pursuits.

**Mrs B**: Certainly not. The same kind of division of labour which exists among the individuals of a community is also in some degree observable among different countries. And it is generally the best policy to produce manufactures in which we are nearly on a par with neighbouring nations rather than those in which they are far superior.

**Caroline:** The more I learn about this subject the more I feel convinced that the interests of nations, as well as those of individuals, so far from being opposed to each other, are in the most perfect unison.[7]

Kathryn Morton and Peter Tulloch explain another aspect of the theory by using an example of two countries, A and B, which both produce wheat and cloth.

Country A is more efficient than B at producing both cloth and wheat. However, while it costs the same in productive resources to produce one unit of cloth or one unit of wheat in country A, in country B twice as many productive resources go into the production of a unit of wheat as into a unit of cloth. Country A is therefore relatively more efficient, or has a comparative advantage, in producing wheat while country B has a comparative but

5

not absolute advantage in producing cloth. This being so, there is scope for both countries to benefit from international trade and specialization as long as country A can exchange one unit of its wheat for more than one unit of cloth and B can obtain more than half a unit of A's wheat for a unit of its cloth. In other words they can gain so long as the terms of exchange allow them each to end up with a combination of cloth and wheat which is greater than they can produce domestically. It will then pay each country to specialize in production for export.[8]

The theory can be personalized by imagining a carpenter and a gardener who live next door to each other and who excel in their own job but in little else. If they had no contact with each other, the carpenter would have superb furniture in her home but her garden would resemble an overgrown jungle. The gardener, on the other hand, would have a beautiful garden, but as for her furniture, it would be a case of 'pull up a plant pot and sit down'. If, however, the two agree to an exchange – to trade carpentry for gardening skills – then both could have lovely furniture and beautiful gardens. Both gain from trade and exchange with each other.

One problem with the theory of comparative advantage is that it assumes full employment of resources – that everyone is working and that natural resources are fully utilized. If there is unemployment, then putting resources to work even if they have no comparative advantage may be more important to policymakers than economic theory. More seriously, the theory suggests that all countries gain from international trade. This has obviously not happened; some have clearly gained a great deal more than others. Swiss economist Paul Bairoch has estimated that in 1750, GNP per head of people in North and South was about the same; in 1930 it was four times higher in the North; 60 years later it is around eight times higher.[9] Under the theory of comparative advantage, such imbalances were not supposed to happen. For one thing, wages in the North would have become so high that manufacturers would have all moved their factories to the South to take advantage of cheaper labour. At the very least they would open their new factories or locate their new services in the South. But this has not happened to any substantial degree.

A World Bank survey of foreign direct investment (FDI) found that 'during the 15 years from 1970 to 1985, inflows of FDI to developing countries as a whole grew at the same pace as those going to industrialized countries'.[10] The behaviour of financiers and businesses in the North with money to invest appears, at first sight, difficult to understand. As average wages in Britain are around £250 a week and, for example, in Sri Lanka wages average less than £25 a week, why do businesses not put all their money in Sri Lanka and reap the higher profits that come from the lower wages?

There are numerous probable reasons. A firm making clothing could set up a new factory in Britain and be able to export products to other industrialized countries without barriers. If they set up in Sri Lanka, they may be able to export only a limited amount, because of international trade restrictions. Businessmen and investors like political stability; they may feel that their investment is safer in Britain than in Sri Lanka. There may also be administrative problems; it is easier to set up a factory in your own country where you know the rules, rather than in a Third World country where administrative hurdles and unknown factors may have to be surmounted. Whatever the reasons, the theory of comparative advantage has not led to a flow of venture capital that would equalize wages and living standards between countries. But it has also failed to raise living standards in the South for deeply entrenched historical reasons.

The present pattern of international trade was largely established in the colonial era of the nineteenth century. The British economist John Stuart Mill said that 'colonies should not be thought of as civilizations or countries at all, but as agricultural establishments whose sole purpose was to supply the larger community to which they belong'.[11] The world was thus divided into a small number of countries in the Northern hemisphere that industrialized and enjoyed cheap agricultural produce, and a much larger number of countries in the South that provided the cheap produce and bought some, but not many, of the comparatively expensive manufactured goods. This pattern has changed little today.

The theory of comparative advantage falls down heavily in the twentieth century because it only works if trade is between countries which are roughly equal. Western nations, however, have continued to export manufactured goods, while countries in the South have continued to export chiefly primary products and produce. North–South trade is not taking place between equals, but between a rich block and a poor block, with the gap between the two growing ever wider.

Throughout the 1980s the Third World's terms of trade – the rate at which exports are exchanged for imports – moved ominously against developing countries. As Table 2 shows, for the developing world as a whole the index fell from 100 in 1980 to 75 in 1990, and for Africa it fell to only 68, a drop of over 30 per cent in a decade. This means that African countries had to pay out, on average, over 30 per cent more in 1989 than they did in 1980 to buy the same quantity of imports. The average figure hides an even worse situation for some producers.

Coffee-producing countries, for example, were receiving around £500 a tonne for the exported raw coffee beans in April 1992, only a small fraction more than in April 1975. But over the same period the prices of some imports of agricultural machinery have risen fivefold. In 1975, African farmers could have bought a basic tractor for around 8 tonnes of their coffee; in 1992, it would cost them around 40 tonnes.

**Table 2   Terms of trade indices (1980 = 100)**

|  | 1980 | 81 | 82 | 83 | 84 | 85 | 86 | 87 | 88 | 89 | 90 |
|---|---|---|---|---|---|---|---|---|---|---|---|
| *Developing countries* | 100 | 109 | 104 | 98 | 98 | 96 | 71 | 75 | 71 | 74 | 75 |
| Africa | 100 | 109 | 103 | 95 | 96 | 95 | 63 | 67 | 59 | 64 | 68 |
| Asia | 100 | 113 | 111 | 102 | 103 | 99 | 68 | 76 | 71 | 73 | 76 |
| Latin America | 100 | 100 | 94 | 92 | 93 | 91 | 77 | 76 | 74 | 75 | 74 |

*Source:* UNCTAD, *Handbook of International Trade and Development Statistics, 1991.*

The terms of trade for developing countries held up well in the very early years of the 1980s because of buoyant oil prices and reasonably strong commodity prices, but fell heavily in the middle of the decade chiefly because of a sharp fall in the price of petroleum. UNCTAD figures show that in 1985 the price index of crude petroleum was 76.1, but that in 1986 it was only 38.9.[12]

One of the problems for commodity-producing countries is that they face a 'perfect' market for their goods. Information about the product, and of its price at any given time, is said to be 'perfect' in the sense that there is general and universal knowledge about them. The price of coffee beans, for example, is known and applied throughout the world. As there is often over-supply of primary produce, the prices are often low; at present the world has a glut of most of the major agricultural products that are traded on world markets. When people become richer in the North they do not generally buy more coffee and tea; demand for these products is therefore hardly expanding.[13]

Companies that make manufactured goods, by contrast, enjoy an 'imperfect' market. It is one of the ironies of international trade that 'perfect' is usually bad for producers, and 'imperfect' good. Manufacturers can claim special features for their goods and fix prices accordingly; the market is not 'perfect', so there is inevitably imperfect knowledge. A manufacturer making radios can claim that this or that gadget is new or different and worthy of a higher price. If potential customers believe it, they pay the price. And, as living standards rise, so the demand for radios, watches etc. also rises.

Industrialized countries have generated enough money from their manufacture of goods to develop services such as transport fleets, banking and insurance, which again are in growing demand. So these countries are in a much stronger trading position than countries whose economies are based on primary produce. And, in practice, over the last 40 years or more, the price of manufactured goods has increased faster than the price of primary goods.

About half of the foreign earnings from merchandise of non-oil-producing developing countries comes from the sale of one or more primary commodity, usually agricultural, but also from minerals such as copper. Over the past 30 years the prices of the great majority of these commodities has been low and unstable. Attempts to develop international commodity agreements have come to little, while attempts to diversify into producing manufactured goods for export have run into problems, both domestic and external.

Protectionist barriers imposed by Western countries make it difficult for the developing world to branch out into manufactured goods. The West employs not only tariffs, which raise the price of imports, but also a growing range of non-tariff barriers. The 1991 *World Development Report* says that the use of protective measures, such as quotas, subsidies, and voluntary export restraints 'has risen alarmingly since the 1960s'.[14]

A small number of developing countries have gained economically from international trade, and have done so in a quite spectacular manner. 'The Gang of Four' – Hong Kong, South Korea, Taiwan and Singapore – have made tremendous economic strides since the early 1960s. They have done so mainly by finding foreign markets that were still open to manufactured goods, and by developing the comparative advantage of their workforce – who were nonetheless paid low wages and often denied labour rights. The four countries 'began with garments and textiles and progressed through a variety of miscellaneous products to electronic components; in the seventies the degree of sophistication in the commodities exported increased steadily'.[15]

Between 1964 and 1973 the four countries grew at 10 per cent a year, and between 1974 and 1983 at 8 per cent a year. The barriers that were imposed against many of their goods hindered but did not stop their progress. Once they had taken a step out of poverty, and had a foot on the ladder, they continued to climb, even if the incline became steeper. The geographical closeness of the four countries to Japan and China undoubtedly helped. And they were helped by being comparatively small countries (their joint population in 1989 was around 70 million people, only three-quarters that of Nigeria) producing goods that the outside world could just about cope with, with some restrictions.

Most of the developing world would find it difficult to follow the route of the 'Gang of Four'; many Latin American countries have tried but not succeeded with export-led policies. Neither the investment nor the domestic purchasing power exists for all Third World countries to industrialize and market manufactured goods in the way the Gang of Four have done it. There are, however, some openings which can be exploited and which offer the chance of diversification from primary commodities (see Chapter 3).

## Dual economy

The costs of trying to gain more from international trade can be high, especially for poorer countries. Trade can make demands on resources that mean there is less for other sectors of the economy – resources which could possibly be used more profitably in other sectors. It can lead to a dual economy, breeding inequality within developing countries as two economies exist side by side – one, a modern-style economy that is receiving abundant funds to help it produce for export markets; the other, a traditional, subsistence economy that is starved of funds.

A free trade zone might be established with the help of government funding, to make goods for export (see Chapter 4). But this means less funding for other economic and social activities, such as agriculture, education and health. Factories in the zone employ and train people who become skilled in a specialist operation and earn high wages in comparison to people in the rest of the economy. A 'dual' economy therefore comes into being: one modern and relatively well-paid, and one traditional, with low returns and poverty. In theory, the benefits of the modern sector might trickle down to the traditional sector or even pull it up out of poverty. In practice this seems not to have happened; the 'spread effect' has been weak.

International trade has helped economic growth in some developing countries, but has not always helped broad-based economic and social development. Citizens of a country that earns more from trade will only benefit if their government has a policy to spread the benefits of that trade. There is evidence that export-orientated industrialization in the four Asian countries discussed above has been achieved at a severe cost to agriculture and rural development. Governments tended to keep agricultural prices low, both to save money for industrialization and to enable workers in the new export-orientated factories to have cheap food and not demand high wages. Again, people had to be attracted to go into the industries. 'The government has intentionally held down peasants' income so as to transfer these people into industry', admitted Taiwan president Lee Teng-Hui.[16]

'When labour is very abundant and there is a significant level of duality in the production system of the South', says Gragiela Chichilinsky, 'an expansion of exports cannot be expected to improve consumption or real wages in the South'.[17] Under such conditions, a higher volume of exports 'is necessarily associated with a lower (relative) price of the basic good, with lower wages and consumption and with lower consumption of basic goods'.[18]

As consumption of basic goods is already low in most Third World economies, and as most of them are marked by duality and abundant labour, the stark implication of

Chichilinsky's finding is that international trade, at least as it is now practised, leads to more poverty. She says these results 'may seem contrary to existing notions of gains from trade and advantages derived from international specialization'. This negative effect of trade is reversed when 'production systems in the South are more homogeneous and the labour supply is less abundant'.[19]

The economic impact of trade on most Third World economies appears, therefore, to have widened inequalities *within* the exporting country. An assessment given by Swedish economist Gunnar Myrdal over 20 years ago has proved increasingly true – 'international trade will generally tend to breed inequality and will do so more strongly when substantial inequalities are already established'.[20] It seems clear that an increase in their country's exports may be of little benefit to most people in a developing country unless accompanied by domestic reforms. But Chichilinsky points out that better terms of trade for the South in their dealings with the North are linked with 'better distribution of income within the South. The international market is therefore an important factor in shaping domestic distributions within each region'.[21] People in the South will gain from trade when the international terms of trade improve and when domestic arrangements ensure a fair distribution of income.

Moral arguments against the present pattern of international trade are also being raised. It is not easy to justify markets that are shut in the face of the poor. Again, how moral is a system where hungry people export food to the over-fed? An important moral argument is that international trade locks the poor of the Third World into a system over which they have no control. When Third World farmers sell in their own country, they are more in touch with the end market and can more easily adjust their sales at short notice to take advantage of trends than if they sell on the international market. Another moral consideration is that 'industrial nations have shaped the pattern of international trade for their own benefit'.[22] The present-day pattern of international trade was shaped by the colonial era, and the gainers, the industrial nations, show little willingness to change it, even though it keeps many millions in poverty.

It is clear that reductions in tariffs and non-tariff measures should lead to a considerable increase in the trade earnings of developing countries. The World Bank estimates that a 50 per cent reduction in the trade barriers of the European Community, the US and Japan, would raise developing countries exports by over $50 billion a year.[23] The *Human Development Report, 1992* points to much larger potential gains for the developing world that might come from the liberalization of trade in goods and services; it estimates that the lack of market opportunities costs them at least $500 billion a year (see Table below). The report points out that 'real interest rates' have been four times higher for poorer countries, costing developing countries some $120 billion a year; that barriers to manufactured goods, technology and other products cost them at least $60 billion a year; and that restricted access to markets for labour costs $250 billion a year[24] (see also Chapter 9).

Another part of North–South trade that could yield more revenue for developing countries concerns traditional varieties of plants: genetic resources. Most plants originate in the South but the way they have been transferred to the North gives a new meaning to the term 'free trade'. The plants have traditionally been made available without cost to Northern-based companies, international research centres and so on,

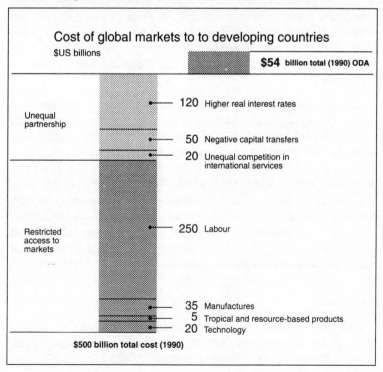

Cost of global markets to to developing countries

$US billions

$54 billion total (1990) ODA

Unequal partnership
- 120 Higher real interest rates
- 50 Negative capital transfers
- 20 Unequal competition in international services

Restricted access to markets
- 250 Labour

- 35 Manufactures
- 5 Tropical and resource-based products
- 20 Technology

**$500 billion total cost (1990)**

to help with the development of high-yielding crops. These resources have often contributed substantially to the profits of Western companies, but neither the governments nor farmers of the South have usually received anything for them. This is now set to change.[25]

With genetic plant resources dwindling, governments are becoming more aware of their importance. They are, in fact, absolutely crucial to the North's food supplies of the future.

'Scientific research papers have calculated that there is no way potatoes could have been cultivated in Europe without the fresh input, the fresh genetic resources, the refreshment of genes coming from countries like Peru and Bolivia where the potato comes from', says agronomist Henk Hobbelink.[26]

He gives as an example a German potato field that gets infected by a new disease:

'What should plant breeders do? They quickly have to look for genetic resources, genes, which could offer resistance against the disease. New diseases occur very often in agriculture; agents of disease, fungi, bacteria, living matter, evolve all the time. Plant breeders might have to travel to Peru or Bolivia to find resistant genes, and they very often find them in fields of farmers who are still using traditional varieties. If these traditional varieties were not around, potato production in Germany would not be possible'.[27]

The nineteenth century Irish potato famine happened because the local potato had no resistance to the blight which struck. Andean potatoes eventually came to the rescue and Irish potato production went on, but too late for the two million people who died. Food production in the North is only sustainable if genetic diversity is preserved in the South. The North's food could ultimately be dependent on the goodwill of the South. Widespread starvation could stalk the North in the twenty-first century if governments of the North do not come to see that it is in their own interests to negotiate a fairer international trading system.

## New order

Developing countries continue to seek changes in the international trading system that are broadly along the lines of the charter drawn up at a Special Session of the United Nations

General Assembly, in May 1974, for a New International Economic Order (NIEO). Seven of the eight key proposals in the charter relate to trade:

1. *Increased prices for primary products.* Prices should increase immediately and be tied directly to the prices of exports of manufactured goods. A new fund should be set up to finance commodity agreements.
2. *Tariffs and other barriers to trade.* Industrialized countries should remove tariffs and other trade barriers imposed against the manufactured goods of developing countries.
3. *Technology.* Arrangements should be made for technology to be transferred from Western to developing countries by other channels than transnational corporations.
4. *International monetary arrangements.* Developing countries should have a larger role in the International Monetary Fund and in other arrangements which affect trade and development.
5. *Foreign debt.* Debt should be cancelled for the very poorest countries, rescheduled for others.
6. *Countries have the right to national sovereignty over their resources.* They can nationalize foreign interests with fair compensation.
7. *Developing countries' share of world industrial output* should rise to at least 25 per cent by the year 2000.[28]

The charter was drawn up – and agreed to by all member states of the United Nations – in the wake of the oil price rises of late 1973 and early 1974 which shook Western governments and convinced them that they had to agree to a better deal for the developing world if they were to enjoy a guaranteed supply of raw materials. But when it gradually became clear, later in the 1970s, that the oil price shock had given rise to something of a false alarm, and that the developing world was not in a strong bargaining position, the Western world lost interest in the new order. They have ignored the 1974 NIEO charter ever since.

With industrialized nations showing little willingness to change the system, developing countries may be unwise to rely on the goodwill of the West for a new international trade. A better option would be to harness the potential of their own resources. Some economists and politicians have argued that the South would be better off 'delinking' from the 'logic of the global system', in the words of one of the

15

most powerful advocates, Egyptian economist Samir Amin. Such a strategy does not mean 'autarky' – the cutting of all South–North trading links. Rather it involves what Amin calls 'submitting external trading relations to the logic of domestic development priorities', with more concentration on national and regional development. He calls it 'polycentrism', and it would, believes Amin, help to neutralize the effects of international trade on a developing country's internal choices.[29]

In Amin's view the present international trading system confines Africa to an 'agro-mineral specialization based upon a destructive, extensive exploitation of land'. He also points out that technological developments in Western countries mean that the West buys fewer of the Third World raw materials and that 'a process of passive delinking is taking place'.[30]

Especially if the terms of trade do not improve in the early years of the 1990s for the developing world, there is likely to be increased interest in delinking, polycentric ideas. It is clearly important that governments do not let international trade become too dominant in their development policy. The words of John Maynard Keynes, 'let goods be homespun whenever it is reasonably and conveniently possible', are a warning against over-emphasis on trade. Both urban and rural communities are likely to be healthier if they have an economic base that provides a high proportion of their needs. Local economics that are too dependent on either exports or imports may be too dependent on outside factors beyond their control – which could in turn threaten their survival. The right balance between production for trade and for local use needs to be struck.

For the international trade that developing countries do, they still want a new order, a better deal. The 1990s may see growing interest in producer co-operation, South–South trade and alternative trade. The spread of democracy in the developing world can be expected to lead to more debate about the future and direction of international trade. With people in the South increasingly seeking more control over their destiny, so their governments will be seeking ways of exercising more control over trade, rather than just being passive recipients of a system that maintains their peoples in poverty.

# 2 Trade effects

*'Live all you can – it's a mistake not to. It doesn't much matter what you do in particular, as long as you have your life'* – Henry James, *The Ambassadors*

## People

The dawn light has yet to arrive as a line of women make their way from the huts where they live to walk to tea fields near Kandy in Sri Lanka. At 6 a.m. they report for work at the muster shed; the overseer gives them a basket each and tells them which hillside to go to, which may be several miles away. Here the women start their daily routine, picking the 'two leaves and a bud' destine ' for the world's tea auctions and the breakfast tables of the Western world.

The work is back-breaking and hot. By mid-morning the temperature is often around 90°F, and the baskets are heavy; at midday the women take an hour's break and then work on until 5 or 6 in the evening. A typical day's pay is equivalent to little more than 50 pence. Back home, there is no water or electricity to help the women cook the family meal. Home is a hut, consisting of two rooms, standing back to back with other huts; the inner room is in total darkness. These 'lines' are much the same as they were a hundred years ago when they were built by British planters. When the women have prepared the meal, they tend to their children's need, wash and clean – until they fall into bed exhausted. In a few hours, it will be time to start again.

Meanwhile, back in England, people are starting breakfast. 'Ceylon' tea will be spooned into a pot, a kettle boiled and a refreshing drink will start the day. With hot water, milk and sugar, the cup of tea will cost no more than three pence. And should the packet be empty, or the kettle leaky – disaster, no cuppa! Rudyard Kipling may come to mind – 'we had a

17

kettle, we let it leak, our not repairing it made it worse. We haven't had any tea for a week, the bottom is out of the universe'. The drink that is so highly valued in the West is produced in conditions in the Third World which mean that those who pick it live in poverty. Talk to the tea pickers and they are too tired and bemused to make any sense out of it all; they just shake their heads with the bewilderment of the defeated.

If people in the West value tea so much, why are they not prepared to pay a price for it that enables the pickers to make a decent living? All but a very small number of tea drinkers will never see the people who make their drink possible. If they could see them, it could be a different story. But unaware of the facts, drinkers barely give the pickers a thought. And, in any case, market forces rule. The world price stays low because, in most years, more tea is produced worldwide than is bought.

The current level of commodity prices on world markets has just one implication for most Third World farmers – poverty. The tea pickers of Sri Lanka are not untypical of commodity growers worldwide. The restrictions to trade in manufactured goods limits the number of jobs that could be created in the manufacturing sector; under the present trade system, this again appears to offer little escape from poverty. The lack of control over the activities of the TNCs means that it is the companies not the host countries that take most of the benefits.

So millions of people throughout the developing world are left struggling to make a living from growing crops for the international trading system – like Juan Diaz, for example, who picks coffee in El Salvador. 'He and his three daughters spend long hard days in the coffee fields of Montenango. On a good day Juan picks enough coffee to earn $1.44; his daughters make a total of $3.35. With $1.24 of these wages, Juan and his wife Paula, are able to feed their family for one day. In bad times, Juan and his daughters make as little as $0.56 a day, less than half the money they need to eat . . .'.[1]

## Coca and coffee

In the Yungas region of Bolivia, Sergio Romero faces an even more serious problem with his coffee. Until 1986, he grew coca, potatoes and beans on a steep hillside plot of about half a hectare. The food was needed for his family, but the coca he sold to a local merchant at the going rate – which varied widely. Coca has been cultivated on these Andean slopes for thousands of years and is important for local people; its leaves are rich in nutrients such as calcium and phosphorus, as well as vitamins A and $B_2$. Local people know that chewing the leaves dulls the appetite and, in this region, people are often hungry. The coca leaves can also be used to make a refreshing cup of tea, as well as a local anaesthetic in the hospitals.

Sergio Romero had no idea what happened to his coca after he sold it. Most of it would probably have been used for perfectly legitimate purposes, but some of his crop might have gone to a hidden and illegal cocaine factory to be treated and turned into paste for the drugs cocaine and crack. The end product of some of Romero's crop might have found its way onto the streets of the world's cities.

In an attempt to persuade coca growers like Romero to grow other crops instead of coca, in 1985 the Bolivian government and the United Nations Fund for Drug Abuse Control (UNFDAC) launched a $65 million project. Under the project, farmers were paid $2000 per hectare to stop growing coca and plant coffee and fruit bushes in its place. For every hectare of land the farmers diversified, another $4000 was put into the Yungas region to develop a more modern infrastructure, with roads, water and new small-scale industries.

It takes three years for a newly planted coffee bush to yield its first beans, so the $2000 per hectare was in part compensation to the farmers for lost earnings. In 1986 Sergio Romero decided to make the switch; he uprooted his coca bushes and planted coffee bushes. By doing so he was taking part in an international effort to reduce the supply of coca coming on to the world market, and therefore to reduce the supply of dangerous drugs on the streets. Little did Romero know in 1986 that a development on the international scene was going to undermine his plans.

At first Sergio Romero was enthusiastic about his coffee bushes. 'Coffee is hardier, it needs less attention than coca', he told me.[2] His eyes were fixed on 1989, when he would harvest his first beans. Romero was optimistic that the coffee would yield more money than coca. He had been assured that the world price of coffee was high enough to give him a good return – and, in 1986, so it was. In January 1986, coffee was fetching £3000 a tonne on world markets. What Sergio Romero did not know was that a slow time-bomb was ticking away under the International Coffee Agreement (ICA) which helped to regulate supplies and keep prices high (see Chapter 3). In 1989, the same year that he was harvesting his first coffee beans, the coffee agreement collapsed. By mid-1989 the world coffee price was down to £1000 a tonne and, by the end of the year, it was a little over £600 a tonne – *barely one-fifth of the price* it had been at the start of 1986.

The world price was reflected in the price that Sergio Romero received. Instead of getting a price that would leave him better off than when growing coca, he received a price for his first beans that left him *worse off*. He had switched crops because he was told he would be in a better financial position, and that he would be playing his part in an international attempt to combat drugs. But there was no corresponding international effort to stabilize prices of the new crops he was growing. Romero felt betrayed, let down by an arrangement he had trusted. His problems have continued; the world coffee price has stayed low; his life is now even more precarious than it was.[3]

People grow export crops to earn money to buy goods and services that might not otherwise be available to them. But returns may be so meagre that they do not cover the cost of production or give growers an adequate standard of living – the return may not enable them to buy other goods. The trade does not give Sergio Romero, the Diaz family or the Sri Lankan tea pickers an adequate living. Would growers do better to opt out of world trade and grow a food crop for their own consumption? Would they be better off if no international trade took place? Switching to other crops may be difficult within existing structures, and the standard of living of people in developing countries who grow crops for export is often not dissimilar to that of people who grow crops for local markets or for their own consumption.

Judging the effects of trade on the Third World peoples who are involved in the trade is difficult. To find out whether they would be better off with domestic food crops rather than export crops would mean comparing a hypothetical situation in which there is no world trade with the actual situation that now exists, which is not easy.

Millions of people in the developing world grow a combination of export and food crops. Demba Diallo and his family, for example, grow cotton, millet and vegetables on their 1.6-hectare farm near Segou in Mali, West Africa. Like nearly all their neighbours, they are poor; they have little or nothing to fall back on if they receive an unexpected blow. Food shortages are never far away if things go wrong. At the start of each year the Diallos weigh up how much their cotton fetched the year before, what their return was after maintenance and so on, and then decide how much cotton to plant for the current year. (Cotton is unusual for an export crop in that it is grown as an annual crop – although growth can continue for a number of years.[4]) When the Diallos plant cotton they know it is taking up land that could be used to produce food for themselves.

If their judgement is right, and the cotton fetches its hoped-for price, the Diallos have enough money to buy other foods, and pay for the children's education. But when the cotton price plunges, as it did in 1985 when it touched its lowest point for 10 years, then the Diallo family has problems. Farmers in Africa, like farmers the world over, make judgements about the mix of crops to grow, depending on current and likely prices. But if farmers want to grow export as well as food crops, in order to earn money to buy other goods, they are likely to have to accept low prices, and those prices may be too low.

In 1985 Demba Diallo temporarily left his farm and headed for the town to look for work that would pay enough to help keep his family alive. The problem is that although the family can make judgements about the mix of cotton and food to grow, sometimes helped by local agricultural extension officials, they usually lack enough accurate information about prospects for world cotton trade. The Diallos, like the tea pickers and the coffee growers, are at the mercy of international factors beyond their control.

In one sense, the Diallos are lucky. It is not always possible to switch to other crops. Farmers who rent land may be compelled under the terms of their land tenure to grow a certain crop. In some countries – Kenya for example – a government decree forbids coffee bushes to be cut down. The tea estate in Sri Lanka is owned by the government; the pickers are landless labourers who may not switch to another crop. Their earnings are not enough for them to buy land; they are effectively trapped. They could lobby their government for land reform so that they could own land, but their long working day makes that difficult. On the tea estate a nearby church organization, called Satydoya, helps to inform the women of their rights. Changes in the international tea trade would help the women, as would changes in the policies of their government.

Government policy is clearly an important factor in determining whether export or food crops are grown. Development workers from Gambia, Fiji, India and Tanzania have spoken of the way growers find it easier to get loans for export crops than for food crops. Rural banks have been asked to ensure this policy is carried out – presumably because exports earn a lot more foreign exchange than food crops. 'We are forced to produce coffee for foreign exchange that is of no benefit to our own local economy', said a worker from Tanzania. In the view of these development workers, the money received from the sale of export crops is not enough for growers to feed their families throughout the year.[5]

Changes in government import policy can clearly have a profound effect on local communities. In 1986, for example, the Filipino government's Ministry of Agriculture announced that it was suspending support for the country's smallholder dairy farmers, in favour of imported dairy products. The government presumably took the decision because it believed that imports would be cheaper; the availability of imports gave the government the opportunity to do that. For Filipino milk producers that was bad news. But if the Filipino people, as a whole, could in future enjoy cheaper milk, then for them the move was good.

In the Filipino case there were losers and gainers, and an uncertainty factor was added because imports may not be as reliable as home produce. If the debt-afflicted Philippines were to run out of foreign exchange to pay for imported milk when local facilities had been severely run down, then a severe milk shortage could result. The Filipino government's action stimulated a number of local co-operatives to compete with the imported milk; in 1990 there were 30 dairy farmer co-operatives in five regions. This indicates that domestic producers can produce efficiently if there is the right stimulus.

## Pesticide effects

International trade in export crops usually means that chemical pesticides have to be used. Most chemical pesticide used in developing countries goes on export crops (around half of total use is on cotton). Such use kills insects, good or bad. There are at least a million species of insects, only a few thousand of which have become pests. By killing the pest the chemical kills far more non-pests and upsets the ecological balance; the natural protection to food crops is therefore lessened. Residues of chemicals in export crops has encouraged some countries to limit pesticide use for fear of their product attracting a ban on health grounds. In Sri Lanka the Tea Research Institute has developed an integrated pest management strategy which makes maximum use of natural methods of pest control and minimum use of chemicals.

But, in many areas, such a strategy is non-existent. Barbara Dinham of the Pesticides Trust speaks of the effects of pesticide use on the Cordillera region of the Philippines:

'The area grows most of the country's vegetables, especially beans, peas, carrots, cabbages, mainly for export. It also grows potatoes – a crop expanding recently to serve the market for McDonalds French fries in the Philippines. Vegetable growing was introduced originally into the area early this century with the onset of the American colonial period. . . . The region grew vegetables, mainly for its own consumption, and was then self-sufficient in rice. Vegetable production was previously concentrated in the valleys, and the pine forests on the mountains provided some animals from hunting. When a US military road was built through the mountains, it drew vegetable production up to 8000 feet for easy access to the distribution routes. Farmers in the valleys still grow some rice, but are opting to grow vegetables as this yields two harvests a year. One of the two main vegetable-growing provinces, Benguet, has the highest rate of consumption of fertilizers and pesticides in the country.

'One and a half provinces of Cordillera is now dominated by small vegetable farmers. This was a poor subsistence farming region, and the cash income offered by vegetable farming is needed. However, while cash incomes have increased to the level where people earn just sufficient in most years, if they lose everything in a bad year, they are impoverished, in debt, and never earn enough in good years to break out of the cycle. They are beholden to the traders, who buy all produce, and who both introduced and have a monopoly on pesticides, fertilizers, and also seedlings. Agrochemicals are almost exclusively from three transnationals: Ciba-Geigy, Bayer and Hoechst.

'Farmers have increasingly recognized the harm caused by pesticides. They have observed animals dying from drinking water from the streams and rivers on the mountains, especially after spraying. For their drinking water, mountain communities now run hosepipes from springs higher up the mountains to villages. Water is an increasing problem, especially in the valleys where all water is now contaminated with pesticides. Communities are beginning to document the pesticide problems: they note an increase in skin rashes, poisonings, and contaminated water sources. In one instance in 1991, in the village of Cadad-Anan, Mountain Province, seven children in one family died after eating Chinese lettuce given by a nearby farmer, who forgot he had sprayed the day before harvesting.

'It is common to repackage all pesticides into small containers: so although the original containers may be labelled, when repackaging, only the name of the pesticide is on the package: this may be the common name or only be the brand name. This means there are no instructions, no warnings, nothing'.[6]


## Fish

One of the developing world's most notable food exports is fish. Such exports earn money but mean that less fish is available for people in low-income exporting countries; many tonnes of fish are exported every year from developing countries that could be consumed by local people.

Coastal developing countries view the sea as a promising source of export revenue. They now account for 45 per cent of the total world fish trade; their earnings from the trade shot up from $4500 million in 1983 to $10000 million in 1988. With many countries under pressure to export more to repay their foreign debts, the trade is likely to increase. The trade has put certain species out of reach of local people; protein consumption is declining as a result. 'Demand for fish is growing faster than supply', says a recent FAO report, 'and this gap is predicted to widen further'.[7] But the widening gap is likely to be at the expense of nutrition and health in Third World fish-producing countries. This raises crucial questions about the ethics of the world

24

fish trade; it means that Third World peoples eat less fish and have less protein.

Those who catch the fish are also affected. Small-scale fishermen in developing countries suffer from the world fish trade in a number of ways. Sea fishermen who cannot afford motors for their boats, or have only a small outboard, are effectively restricted to an area within a mile or so of the shore. With their large dragnets, trawlers fishing mostly for export often overfish waters that are just outside the small fishermen's range, damaging spawning and feeding grounds resulting in fewer fish flowing into the shore areas. Fish-workers organizations claim that government policies are geared to helping the larger boat owners to catch fish for export, at the expense of the small boats who are catching for local consumption. There is also the question of the sustainability of the fish export trade. The FAO report admits that increased demand for fish has put pressure on fishing fleets to step up their catches 'which in turn threatens the sustainability of certain stocks, leading to serious concern over high seas fisheries'.[8]

In Asia and Latin America, sea farming (coastal aquaculture) has witnessed a phenomenal growth during the past decade. International aid money has helped to fund the expansion. The World Bank, for example, has invested quite sizeable sums in Bangladesh to promote the aquaculture of shrimps for export. Fishworkers have expressed concern that export-orientated aquaculture 'has created severe problems, which jeopardize the livelihood of local peasant and fishing communities, and in the long term damage the sustainability of the resource base'.[9]

## The women with ruined eyesight

They have been insensitively called the 'girls with the nimble fingers', such is their skill on conveyor belts.[10] The tens of thousands of women who work in low-paid jobs in the electronics industry in the export processing zones that have been set up in developing countries (see Chapter 4) are also likely to be the young women with ruined eyesight.

An International Labour Office (ILO) study has pointed to the 'overwhelming' evidence of the harmful effects of the semi-conductor industry on women's eyesight.[11] In the export processing zones of south-east Asia, nine out of every 10 workers in this industry are female and aged between 16 and 23. Nimble fingers are a great asset in assembling tiny chips, but the process puts an unbearable strain on the eyes. In the process of assembling and testing electronics components, a silicon wafer about 2–4 inches (5–10cm) in diameter might be sliced into about 500 separate chips. Each individual chip is bonded with wire lead; this is a labour-intensive procedure in which each assembler, peering through a microscope or highly powered magnifying lens, attaches a variety of miniscule wires, each the size of a human hair, to a chip using fine soldering equipment.

The eyes cannot cope for long periods with such a process. 'After several years, it deteriorates to the point that the workers cannot continue', says the ILO study. A Korean survey of the effects of microscope work found that about 47 per cent of the operatives were near-sighted and 19 per cent had astigmatism, although all had perfect vision when they were hired. Female microchip workers are also exposed to toxic chemicals and suspected carcinogens that can damage their health in the future. Elfreda Castellano, for example, joined the firm Dynetics Inc. of the Philippines as electronics worker, engaged on soldering and fluxing operations. After doing this for a year, she was taken and confined to hospital with raging fever. She was diagnosed as having cancer of the lymph nodes. Elfreda Castellano faced death, caused by her work.[12]

As production for the home market uses similar industrial processes as production for export, it may seem unjust to blame international trade for health problems caused by those processes. But, especially in the south-east Asian developing countries where electronics factories are producing mostly for export, the scale of the problem is worse than it would be if only the home market were being supplied.

In the manufacturing of garments for export, there is evidence that production for trade can make life harder for workers. 'Garment workers in India are exploited more if they produce for export than for the local market', said an Indian worker, 'because the quality requirements are higher and more difficult to meet. They don't make as many garments and don't get paid as much'.[13]

The overall effect of trade on communities who provide labour for export trade zones is that females rather than males are likely be employed, and this can lead to a skewed workforce. In Taiwan, women account for as many as 85 per cent of the workforce in the country's three trade zones. This is hardly surprising, as female wages in Taiwan are typically less than two-thirds of male wages, even for comparable work. Young people are also favoured because they can be paid less, and again females are more popular. 'Girls do the job as well and don't make any trouble like boys. They're obedient and pay attention to orders', said the manager of an electronics assembly plant.[14]

It is not easy to know the effects on people in the Third World of decisions that are taken many thousands of miles away from them. When Western governments embarked on restrictive monetarist policies in the early 1980s, developing countries had to find a lot more money to service their debts and often had to divert funds away from domestic support services (see Chapter 8). How many people, already battling for survival, suffered in this process can only be guessed.

Changes in the agricultural policies of Western governments can have a crucial bearing on the agricultural trade of developing countries, and again on people. If the European Community (EC) pays its sugar farmers higher prices, world output rises and prices are likely to be lower. More EC sugar might be 'dumped' on world markets at less than the cost of production, again jeopardizing markets and the lives of growers. Changes affecting preferential trade arrangements, such as the Lomé Convention between the EC and the 69 countries of the African, Caribbean and the Pacific (ACP), can also directly affect growers in the South. Under the Convention the EC gives preferential terms to ACP banana-producing countries; a banana protocol obliges the EC to ensure that 'no ACP state shall be placed, as regards access to its traditional markets and its advantage on those markets, in a less favourable position than in the past or at present'.[15]

In 1991 the EC came under pressure to grant unrestricted access to its markets to lower-cost bananas from Latin American countries, where the fruit is grown on large plantations and often under low-wage conditions. But the European Commission decided, in April 1992, to honour its commitment under the Lomé Convention and protect ACP producers. Quotas will be imposed on bananas from Latin America, at least for the foreseeable future, although the preference may eventually again come under pressure.

Many of the hidden effects of international trade are not easy to tease out. Governments of developing countries who are trying to earn more foreign exchange may have little interest in publicizing the downside of such endeavours. The huge tourist hotel complex that is built to earn foreign exchange could make big demands on the water resources of the area and mean there is less water available for local farmers to irrigate their fields. Lower food output could be the result. But government statistics are unlikely to link a fall in food output to the building of a hotel.

International trade that increases incomes could, on the other hand, mean that rural economies receive a stimulus. Again the link may not always be clear. Although trade has helped some people in the developing world, the evidence is that the way it now operates brings little or no benefit to those involved, and that substantial changes are needed in the international system if the people who make it possible are to benefit. International trade *could* play a key role in local economies. If prices were higher on world markets, then enough would be earned to lift the pay to growers and raise rural incomes – always provided that the government wanted that to happen.

## The environment

International trade can have an impact on a country's physical environment which damages the base of development; such costs are often not calculated. Trade barriers that protect an economic activity can also mean that such activity is carried on in a way that causes environmental damage.

The Brundtland Report (published in 1987 under the title *Our Common Future*) stresses the link between international trade and the environment. 'The main link between trade and sustainable development', it says, 'is the use of non-renewable raw materials to earn foreign exchange. Developing countries face the dilemma of having to use commodities as exports (for growth), while also having to minimize damage to the environmental resource base supporting this growth'.[16]

The export of timber to earn foreign exchange causes damage to forests and also has wider environmental implications, both locally and internationally. Forests act like a sponge, releasing water gradually to land around. When forests are depleted, droughts and floods become more likely.

28

There is also concern over the contribution that disappearing forests could be making to global warming and the greenhouse effect. But this concern has not slowed down international trade in timber, although there is now talk of the need for forest areas to be managed on a sustainable basis. The FAO speaks of a premise that 'considerable socio-economic benefits can be derived from environmentally sound and sustainable utilization and trade . . . of forest products'.[17] The big question, however, is whether 'sustainable utilization' is possible. This remains an area of dispute between forest exporters.[18] What is not in dispute is that the area of tropical forest that was managed sustainably in the early 1990s was very low – probably less than one per cent of the total area – and that a rapid increase in this area is unlikely.

International trade has also stimulated the firing of forest to clear land for cattle ranches, particularly in Brazil. Subsidies (now ended) by the Brazilian government encouraged this ranching and, according to former Brazilian government minister, Jose Lutzenberger, EC policies – especially the demand for corned beef – have also contributed. But, as the soil is poor, the ranching only lasts for a few years before it is turned into wasteland.[19]

The crops that are exported by developing countries usually demand the best land; in some countries the crops take almost all the good land. In Central America virtually all the fertile, flat agricultural lands are used for export-orientated crops. If the structure of land tenure in a country is such that large interests dominate, the best land will tend to be used for export crops, as in Central America. If land tenure systems are more diverse, as in most of Africa, then decisions over whether to grow crops for export or for their own consumption will be made by individual farmers on the basis of their needs. This will often include making a judgement about likely prices, both for export crops and for marketable food. Farmers need to grow enough food to feed their families and they need to earn money to pay for goods and services. If they grew cotton last year and the price was lower than they expected they may this year plant either another export crop or food on some of that land.

Governments can encourage increased output of food for local consumption and discourage the production of export crops if they pay farmers more for food and less for export crops. If they wish to help subsistence farmers to get maximum yields from their land, governments can subsidize inputs such as seed, or make sure that necessary inputs are available in sufficient quantities.

Many decisions over the right mix of crops take time to lead to the required outcome. A farmer who plants tea rather than food crops will have to wait several years for the first harvest; during these years the land under the young tea bushes earns nothing. A switch the other way – from export to food crops – brings results more quickly. Pulling up tea bushes immediately releases land in which food can be planted and soon harvested. (A few crops have more than one purpose. Cassava is a food crop in most of the countries where it is grown, but an export crop for others – Thailand, for example.)

A farmer who is growing both for export and for family consumption is likely to use the best land for the exportable crops so as to maximize the potential yields and income. But how long does the 'best' land remain the best? When cocoa first came to the southern Volta region of Ghana it was planted on the best land, and food production moved to less fertile land. Where planned expansion has taken place, encouraged by government policy and perhaps backed by foreign aid, such expansion has often taken place on fertile land that once grew food. When government authorities bring large areas of fertile land under export crop plantations, small farmers are likely to be pushed out to marginal land where yields are lower. Desertification can, however, be the end result of this additional pressure on fragile land. Overproduction of export crops can clearly have severe environmental costs, not least because farmers are forced to cultivate marginal land.

The impact of export crops on the soil varies, but there is evidence that the practices surrounding these crops are more likely to lead to environmental damage than is the case with food crops. Environmental writers Goodland, Watson and Ledec speak, for example, of the 'profound social and environmental costs' of cotton production. Poorly planned irrigation, plus the attraction of pests and subsequent use of chemical pesticides, mean huge problems with growing cotton.[20]

Tobacco's environmental impact is often severe because of the demands of the curing process. 'The damage to public health and to the environment (of tobacco) appears substantially to outweigh the benefits', say Goodland, Watson and Ledec.[21] On coffee and tea, they say that as these 'are typically cultivated on well-drained sloping lands in high-rainfall areas, neglect of soil protection measures can result in drastic soil deterioration and loss'.[22] Other export crops are kinder to the soil. Cocoa exhausts the soil less than annual crops, although continued cultivation can result in gradual deterioration of soil through the loss of organic matter and nutrients. With oil palms, say Goodland, Watson and Ledec, 'the major environmental concerns . . . are deforestation resulting from the expansion of plantations'.[23]

Export crops are usually grown in mono-cropping fashion as opposed to the mixed cropping that is traditional in many Third World societies. Continuous monoculture increases soil deterioration, making it less capable of coping with dry weather. Export crops tend to be also more heavily fertilized and the long-term impact of heavy doses of nitrogen on the soil can be severe. Soil in one of India's 'green revolution' states, the Punjab, is now losing nutrients because of the heavy use of fertilizers. A key question for the 1990s over export crops is, 'can they grow in a way that is sustainable and does not damage the environment?' Unless crops pass this test, there is a case for them to be phased out.

International trade in fish has sizable environmental costs, which in practice are paid by local people. Coastal aquaculture, for exan. 'e, which fishworkers label as the 'blue revolution', has largely taken place in the large mangrove areas which are the natural breeding grounds of numerous species of fish, including shellfish, or in traditional paddy fields which are the source of staple foods for local populations. 'In the case of shrimp aquaculture in tropical countries, we see the destruction of large tracts of estuarian and mangrove areas', said fishworkers at the end of an international conference in 1990; 'often shrimp aquaculture is undertaken at the expense of staple foods'. The fishworkers point out that less intensive forms of coastal aquaculture 'can provide opportunities for fishworkers' communities to manage fish resources in the areas where they live, to obtain new sources of income and to enhance food production and employment. This requires that such communities are given exclusive rights to control the water bodies and the surrounding environment'.[24]

The fish trade has encouraged unwise local practices. The threat to their fishing grounds has led small-scale fishermen

31

in some countries to resort to desperate measures that damage the environment and the chances of sustainable fish catches. To encourage fish to flood out into the sea, fishermen in the Philippines, for example, have blasted coral reefs with dynamite. Their catches increased spectacularly in the short term, but coral reefs are where the fish feed and spawn. Without the reefs, fish catches will be smaller in future.

In a further twist of international trade, this time with a service industry, fishermen can also suffer from the effects of new hotels on the coastline which are built to attract and win the foreign exchange of tourists. Fishermen in the Philippines and in the Indian state of Goa, for example, have been cleared away from their traditional grounds because of new hotel compounds (see Chapter 5, which also discusses other effects of tourism on local people).

The environment of developing countries that have engaged heavily in trade has often suffered. Taiwan's economic success has been at the expense of its environment; the country has been called 'the garbage island'. Damage to the environment was hardly surprising, given the rate of Taiwan's expansion. In the early 1950s, the country set out to raise living standards through exporting, and between 1955 and 1975, the volume of trade tripled every five years.[25] The infrastructure was developed to help a range of heavy and light industries, but the cost to the environment has been colossal. Forests were ripped up as raw material for industry, rivers have been killed by unregulated dumping of industrial and toxic waste, aquifers have been damaged and farmland polluted; 20 per cent of farmland is now polluted by industrial wastewater. 'As a result, 30 per cent of rice grown on the island is contaminated with heavy metals, including mercury, arsenic and cadmium', says an environmentalist, Dr Edgar Lin.[26] Trade has increased the standard of living measured in economic terms; it is by no means certain that the quality of life has improved. Environmental degradation also raises doubts about the sustainability of Taiwan's development path.

In a study in 1992 of trade and the environment, the General Agreement on Tariffs and Trade (GATT) says that increased trade leads to higher incomes and the opportunity to spend more on the environment. 'There is evidence that this is happening', it says. The survey points out that trade liberalization is likely to reduce some protectionist barriers which are encouraging environmentally harmful activities. But it admits that an expansion of trade could have negative environmental effects 'so large that they outweigh the conventional benefits from open markets . . . resulting in an overall decline in national welfare. However, this is only possible if a country lacks a domestic environment policy that reflects its environmental values and priorities'.[27]

Yet the limited amount of money they earn from international trade gives developing countries few resources to tackle the environmental effects of that trade. Measures to protect the environment in developing countries are thus closely linked with changes in the trading system that would generate additional funds (see Chapters 6, 7 and 9).

There is a further and little-discussed environmental aspect of world trade – the cost in terms of fuel resources of shipping and flying goods and people around the world. Most merchandise goes by sea; people (business people, migrant labour, tourists, and so on) travel mostly by air. Consumption of fuel oil by ships in 1990 was 119 million tonnes; a further 22 million tonnes of diesel was used, making a total of 141 million tonnes of oil used in ships carrying world trade. About 175 million tonnes of aviation fuel was used for flying goods and people, making a total of 316 million tonnes for transport purposes.[28]

Overall consumption of oil in 1990 for all purposes was 2485 million tonnes; shipping and flying goods and people therefore took 12.7 per cent of world oil consumption. As oil is a finite resource, this raises questions about the sustainability of international trade. When the oil runs out, what happens then? This is a question that very few people are addressing. But unless aircraft and ocean-going vessels can switch to technologies that use renewable sources of energy, the future of international trade could be in jeopardy.

# 3 Primary commodities: the lifeblood drains away

*'It would have been better if we had received no aid at all, but that the prices of our commodities had not fallen'* – Julius Nyerere

'Commodities are the South's lifeblood', says the Brandt Report, 'especially for the poorer countries, and to know what damage is done by the vagaries of the market is to understand why the South feels so passionately about them'.[1] When these words were written in 1980, the Brandt commissioners could have had little idea how much of the South's lifeblood would drain away during that decade. While real prices of the chief agricultural primary commodities exported by developing countries have fallen steadily since 1960, the fall accelerated in the 1980s.

Between 1982 and 1990 world market prices for coffee, cocoa and tea – three of the developing world's major export crop earners – fell at an average rate of 11 per cent a year.[2] For a wider range of commodities the fall was also sharp. 'The price index of principal non-fuel commodities exported by developing countries fell by a staggering 50 per cent in real terms between 1979/81 and 1988/90,' said the UNCTAD Secretariat in a paper prepared for its 1992 meeting in Colombia.[3]

The international market for most primary commodities, both agricultural and mineral, can be classified as a 'perfect market' in the sense that there is perfect knowledge about the commodities (see Chapter 1). Prices are decided on the basis of supply and demand, on the free play of international economic forces. The problem is that the production and supply of primary commodities are generally out-pacing consumption and demand, which means that prices are likely to be low. Sizeable reductions in the output of commodities would be needed to raise prices.

Export crops have long been the products of poverty. In the nineteenth century the pattern of trade for many countries now classed as 'developing countries' was laid down by colonial powers in the North. Colonies were developed as an arm of the 'master's' economy and encouraged to grow export crops. The snag was that too much was planted. This 'over-supply' combined with slavery, low wages and control of distribution networks to give the North rock-bottom prices and the South a tiny return. The 'over-supply' of most primary commodities has continued to the present day, with the developing world finding it difficult to shake off the colonial pattern. Diversification to manufactured products has been difficult because of lack of purchasing power at home and import barriers in industrialized countries. In agriculture, the export pattern has changed little. Around 14 per cent of all cropland in developing countries is used to grow crops for export – frequently the best land.

Excluding oil, 51 developing countries depend on the export of three or fewer primary commodities for over 70 per cent of their foreign earnings; 15 countries, 11 of them African, are dependent on the export of three or fewer of them for over 85 per cent of their foreign earnings. Such dependence – which is chiefly on agricultural commodities – is generally not decreasing; on the contrary, as Table 3 shows, with some exceptions, it is becoming more pronounced.

Table 3   Share of three primary commodities in total exports

|  | Average 1975/77 | Average 1986/88 |
|---|---|---|
| Niger | 94.7 | 99.0 |
| Guinea | 99.0 | 99.0 |
| Zambia | 93.2 | 99.0 |
| Mozambique | 46.3 | 97.4 |
| Uganda | 97.9 | 97.1 |
| Liberia | 88.4 | 95.5 |
| Comoros | 64.5 | 90.4 |
| Mauritania | 99.0 | 93.9 |
| Somalia | 80.3 | 93.9 |
| Rwanda | 91.9 | 91.1 |
| Burundi | 99.9 | 88.9 |
| Cambodia | 45.3 | 85.6 |
| St Vincent and the Grenadines | 97.1 | 99.0 |
| St Lucia | 58.0 | 88.4 |
| Surinam | 73.8 | 88.4 |

*Source: UNCTAD Commodity Yearbook, 1991.*

Several agricultural commodities are produced almost exclusively in tropical countries, notably coffee, cocoa, tea, rubber, jute and hard fibres. The supply of these commodities to the world market tends to be unstable, chiefly because of varying weather; this also helps to explain why their prices are low. 'The vagaries of the market' in terms of excessive price fluctuations have meant that many commodity-producing countries have had little idea of how much money they would earn in any year from their major earner. This has made it more difficult for them to plan ahead; if earnings seemed likely to be good, then development projects could be started in the hope that they would be funded by the expected revenue. But if prices suddenly fell, and the revenue was less than expected, then projects might have to be postponed.

High world prices can give misleading signals to policy-makers; they might suggest that more of a crop should be planted. Many export crops take three years from planting to first harvest; during that time the world price could have plummeted. Low prices might suggest that a crop should be uprooted; the resultant lower output raises prices, stimulates interest in growing more and the whole cycle of uncertainty begins again. Instability creates havoc and uncertainty for producers, and also to a lesser extent for consumers.

A further cause of commodity price instability is speculation. Speculators, both individuals and companies, buy coffee, cocoa, etc. in the hope that the price will rise in the next week or so, before they actually have to pay for it. They may have close knowledge about market conditions which leads them to believe that such a rise is likely. If they are correct, they sell their commodity at the higher price, pay for it at the lower, and pocket the difference. If the price falls, they lose. It is difficult to estimate how much speculation fuels commodity price instability, but some estimates suggest that as much as one third of the price movement of some commodities are caused by speculation. The speculator makes life harder for commodity growers and for governments of producing countries. Prices fluctuate more than they would if there was no speculation, making it more difficult to plan.

Demand for minerals like copper and tin tends to rise and fall with the level of industrial activity in Western countries. In boom years, world prices tend to be higher; in times of recession they usually drift lower. Greater efficiency in manufacturing processes in Western countries, and also the use of substitutes such as plastics, have in many cases lowered the amount of metal needed.

## Coffee

No agricultural commodity has suffered a steeper fall in its real price, or fluctuated more in price, than coffee (see graph, page 53). This has been particularly serious for the developing world, especially for Africa. World coffee prices have suffered chiefly because the supply of raw coffee beans coming on to the market has outpaced the growth in demand. Coffee is grown in over 50 countries and earns more money for the Third World than any other commodity apart from oil; annual trade was worth around $15 billion in 1987/8 but, because of the fall in prices, dropped to $6.5 billion in 1990/91. Brazil and Colombia are the largest exporters. An estimated 100 million people around the world earn their living from growing the crop, predominantly on small-scale farms. The price the growers receive is related to the world price, although this varies widely. Some countries pay a low price to growers but give them subsidized inputs; others pay their growers a higher price and let them pay the market price for inputs.

Coffee comes in two chief varieties: *Coffea arabica* typically grows in highlands, for example in Kenya and Colombia; *C. robusta*, which thrives in lowlands such as Brazil and West Africa. Arabica is considered a higher quality coffee and usually commands a premium over robustas.

Countries such as Angola, Ethiopia and Uganda depend on coffee for over 60 per cent of their foreign earnings. In July 1975 the coffee price on world markets was just under £500 a tonne (about 60 US cents a pound). Following a severe frost in Brazil, the world's largest coffee-producing country, and other disruptions to supplies, the price soared to over £3000 by March 1977 (see also Chapter 12). By April 1978 it was down to around £1400 a tonne. In the 11 years between 1978 and July 1989 prices rose and fell, sometimes gradually, sometimes with steep twists, but were buttressed for most of this time by the International Coffee Agreement (ICA). The collapse of this agreement in July 1989 led to a free-for-all on world markets, with producing countries freely exporting stocks that had been built up.

Government revenues from coffee fell sharply after the collapse of the agreement and growers began losing interest in the crop; many were no longer receiving enough to maintain their bushes, keeping them free from blight or replacing old bushes. Early in 1992, world coffee prices slumped to their lowest level for 17 years, below £500 a tonne; it is doubtful if coffee can be produced anywhere for such a price. Producing countries reacted differently to the fall. While Colombia cut the price paid to growers by 5 per cent, the coffee marketing board in Ivory Coast, Africa's largest coffee producer, decided to subsidize rather than cut prices to growers. But the country's exchequer took the strain. In some countries, Kenya for example, it is illegal to uproot coffee, but Brazilian farmers started pulling up their coffee bushes and planting fast-growing alternatives, such as trees, which seemed likely to be in greater demand. The economics of coffee means that many growers will neglect their bushes and produce less – until the next upward cycle of prices suggest they produce more.

Coffee's problem is that too much of the crop is grown around the world compared to demand; production has risen steadily over the past 20 years, far exceeding the growth of consumption. Worldwide coffee production in 1991/2 was around 100 million 60kg bags, exports were about 80 million bags.[4] Low prices may stimulate coffee-producing countries into action. A Commonwealth Secretariat study found that if the world's coffee producers jointly agreed to impose a tax on their coffee exports, they could substantially increase their revenues; there is also considerable scope for producers to co-operate on output quotas to raise prices (see Chapter 11).

## Cocoa

Over half the world's cocoa is grown in Africa, chiefly in Ivory Coast, Ghana and Cameroon, but also in Nigeria and Equatorial Guinea. Brazil grows around 15 per cent of world output. In early 1992, cocoa was in an unusual position for a major traded agricultural commodity – consumption was exceeding production. The 1991/2 output of cocoa was estimated by commodity brokers Gill and Dufus at around 2.24 million tonnes, and consumption at 2.39 million tonnes.[5] But world stocks of cocoa are high – around 1.56 million tonnes, eight months' supply.[6] These stocks are likely to keep prices down, which are not high enough to cover the costs of production. World cocoa prices rose only just over half in monetary value between 1960 and 1990, which again represents a sharp fall in real terms. In March 1992 the price was little more than 100 US cents a kilo; production costs are around 110 cents a kilo, the price which the Ivory Coast pays its farmers for their crop. The International Cocoa Agreement operated from 1973 to 1987 but achieved little; attempts to restart it were under way in 1992.

Cocoa's prospects are poor, unless there are reductions in supply. Yet the trend seems the other way, with producing countries expanding output and acting against their own long-term interests. Technological advances such as faster-yielding hybrid plants are being used in a number of Asian countries, including Malaysia and Indonesia, which have expanded production considerably in recent years. As Ghana, once the world's largest producer, endeavours to revive output, cocoa production may soon begin to outpace demand once more and put the world price under further pressure. A comprehensive study by UNCTAD and the International Cocoa Organization speaks of 'grim prospects' for cocoa. It says that forecasts indicate 'increasing over-supply and consequently persistent low prices in the coming years'.[7]

## Sugar

Sugar is an unusual crop in that virtually every country of North and South is both a producer and a consumer. It is grown in two forms, cane in tropical countries, and beet in temperate zones, yet the final products are similar. Most sugar is eaten in the country where it is produced; only around a quarter of the global production is exported. Cuba, Thailand, Brazil and Mauritius are the largest exporters of sugar cane. In March 1992 the world price of just over 18 cents a kilo was below the cost of production for most countries. While Brazil may be able to produce sugar for 18 cents a kilo, the cost of production in many African countries is much higher. Sugar cane-exporting countries are usually able to make a profit from some of their crop because of trade deals with the industrialized world which pay above the cost of production for a given quantity – for example, the sugar protocol of the Lomé Convention between the EC and ACP group of countries. The collapse of the USSR in 1991 brought to an end its agreement with Cuba to buy the island's sugar exports.

Sugar production in 1991/2 was estimated by a leading London commodity broker, E.D. & F. Man, at 113.05 million tonnes and consumption at 111.47 million tonnes.[8] If the Uruguay Round of trade talks reach a conclusion (see Chapter 9), sugar farmers in the EC will receive lower subsidies and this should lead to lower production. This could improve the market for ACP countries, but India is trying to double its exports, while changes in the former Soviet Union make for uncertainties and could lead to lower demand as a result of reduced purchasing power. Sugar is also being affected by the development of alternative sweeteners. A non-caloric sugar-derived sweetener has been developed, for example, which could be as much as 600 times sweeter than sugar. The support given by the United States administration to the country's sugar farmers has pushed up sugar prices and made the development of alternative sweeteners even more attractive. The long-term prospects for sugar prices are hardly good; governments of sugar cane-producing countries cannot rely on the crop fetching enough to cover its costs of production.

## Rubber

Natural rubber in 1992 is alone among the major traded agricultural commodities in that it is supported by an international agreement; it is also unusual because the world market price in the short term tends to rise and fall with economic activity and growth rates in industrialized countries. The real long-term price trend is sharply downward, and shows much less connection. In 1960 the price was 82 US cents a kilo; in early 1992 it was around 92 cents a kilo. Output, during this time, more than doubled. Malaysia, Indonesia, Thailand and Sri Lanka produce around 85 per cent of the world's rubber output. It costs at least 80 cents to produce a kilo of rubber in Malaysia, Indonesia and Thailand; less in Sri Lanka because of lower labour costs.

While output has been rising in recent years by around 2 per cent a year, consumption was depressed in the early 1990s because of recession in industrialized countries. Prospects for natural rubber hinge both on economic growth in industrial economies and on the strength of competition from synthetics. With output continuing to rise at a time when world demand is quite flat, the outlook for rubber hardly seems good.

## Cotton

While cotton prices have nearly doubled in monetary value in the past 30 years, they have not kept pace with inflation. In the early years of the 1960s the price was steady at just over 60 US cents per kilo. In March 1992 it stood at around 116 cents a kilo which was too low for many farmers to grow the crop profitably. Prices and prospects for cotton are expected to remain depressed as large worldwide stocks have now built up. Recent expansion of acreages under cotton in China meant that the country was likely to change, in 1992, from being a net importer to a net exporter. Output has been rising in Pakistan (the developing world's largest exporter), India, Australia and Brazil; this additional output plus a jump in exports from the countries of the former USSR has kept the price depressed. According to the International Commodity Advisory Committee, world cotton output in 1992 was expected to be 93.7 million bales (480 lb each) and consumption 90.3 million bales.[9]

Attempts in the early 1980s to start an international cotton agreement were thwarted largely by the United States. Developing countries, which grow nearly two-thirds of world cotton, formed a Third World Cotton Association in 1983. The countries aimed to 'strengthen co-operation in the development of their cotton economies'. But member countries have not co-operated on cutbacks in cotton output to strengthen their position on world markets, and prices have remained depressed.

## Tea

Global output of tea has more than doubled since 1960 and outpaced demand. India, China, Indonesia, Sri Lanka, Kenya, Malawi and Tanzania produce the bulk of global tea output, over a third of which is exported. In real terms the world price has fallen steeply – from 153 US cents a kilo in 1960 to 135 cents a kilo in early 1992. Few countries can produce tea for 135 cents a kilo. As only seven countries account for most of the world's tea output, the commodity lends itself to producer action. Yet tea-producing countries have differing interests which has so far made agreement difficult; protracted negotiations for an international tea agreement have been taking place, intermittently and without success, since the late 1960s. African producers have expanded their tea output substantially over the past 25 years and have been reluctant to accept restrictions such as export quotas.

The former Soviet Union was a key player in the international tea market in the late 1980s, replacing Britain as the world's largest importer of tea. But USSR purchases faltered in 1990 and continued downward in 1991, putting prices under further pressure. Tea drinking will increase at around only 0.6 per cent a year in the 1990s, according to UN Food and Agriculture Organization (FAO) forecasts. Even though global tea production fell slightly in 1991, 'tea prices are expected to remain depressed', predicts the FAO.[10]

## Tobacco

Grown in most tropical countries, tobacco is the most controversial of the major traded agricultural commodities; when turned into its final product, tobacco damages and can destroy health. Three-quarters of all harvested tobacco is turned into cigarettes and smoked in the country where it is grown; China, India, the United States and Brazil between them produce over half the global output. Worldwide production of tobacco in 1990 was 6.9 million tonnes and stocks were 6.3 million tonnes, almost a year's output, which is far larger than any other agricultural commodity. Of the one-quarter that enters world trade, 70 per cent comes from nine countries – Brazil, Bulgaria, Greece, India, Italy, Malawi, Turkey, the United States and Zimbabwe. Worldwide exports of tobacco in 1990 were 1.436 million tonnes; about 0.78 million tonnes came from the main Third World producers.[11]

The price trend is again downward with the real price dropping substantially between 1960 and 1990; for most Third World growers the crop lacks profitability. At the national level, there is growing evidence that the cost of producing tobacco outweighs benefits. A research study of tobacco's costs and benefits in Canada shows that benefits amount to $3 billion a year and that costs, including physicians' services, hospital bills, drugs and administrative services, come to $2.4 billion. To this another $1.5 billion can be added, say the study's authors, for the loss of productivity caused by smoking-related disease. The tobacco industry therefore costs Canada almost $1 billion a year.[12] The cost of smoking in Egypt was estimated for 1981/2 at $1352.6 million; the economic benefits were only $764 million – nearly $600 million less.[13]

Global consumption of tobacco fell in the second half of the 1980s and, despite picking up in 1990, is likely to drop in the long term as a result of the increased public awareness of the serious health risks of smoking (see also Chapter 6).

## Tropical timber

Trade in tropical timber products is also controversial. Over the last 30 years tropical forests have been felled at an accelerating pace, and trade has risen enormously. Whereas FAO estimates in 1980 suggested that 11.3 million hectares of forest was being felled each year, by 1990 this figure had been revised to 17 million hectares. Between 1961 and 1989, exports of forest products from developing countries rose from $500 million to about $9459 million, an almost nineteenfold increase, which far exceeded the growth of Third World trade in commodities as a whole.[14] Wood for industrial purposes – building and manufacturing, including furniture – is the chief export. About 60 per cent is in the form of logs.

A World Wide Fund for Nature report said in 1989 that exports of timber to Japan will lead to the destruction of the remaining rainforests in south-east Asia within 20 to 30 years if they continue unchecked. Japan controls 29 per cent of the international timber trade, according to the report, and imports 70 per cent of all its tropical hardwood from the two Malaysian states of Sabah and Sarawak. The imports are chiefly raw logs that are cheaper than Japan can produce. Most Japanese plywood is made from tropical timber; at least a third of this is used in the construction industry as panelling for moulding concrete. 'Most of this ends up on the scrap heap after being used, on average, just two or three times', says the report.[15] Forests are often seen by governments as a non-renewable resource and 'mined' to earn foreign exchange – but with careful planning they can be harvested on a sustainable basis. Many trees also produce non-wood products in a sustainable manner, such as fruits, and have more value left standing than cut down.

## Palm oil

Palm oil earns foreign exchange for Malaysia, the Philippines and Indonesia among other countries; it competes with soya bean, groundnut (peanut), coconut, rape-seed, cotton seed and sunflower seed grown in Western countries. Subsidies given to Western producers are therefore a factor in influencing the level of output and prices. The price of palm oil has risen in monetary terms from $144 a tonne in 1960 to $390 in March 1992, not keeping pace with inflation. Output increased over sixfold in this time. Indonesia expanded the area under palm oil in the late 1980s by hacking new plantations out of the jungle. Both Malaysia and Indonesia were heading for bumper crops in 1992, but the additional output was likely to depress prices further. Expansion of palm oil (used for industrial frying, margarine and soap production) has also been encouraged by foreign aid. With aid from Belgium, Britain and Germany, expansion is going ahead in the Amazon region of Ecuador, which involves large tree clearance and damage to native peoples.

## Commodity agreements

Fluctuating primary commodity prices are bad for the North as well as the South. The factory in the North that uses copper as a major component in the manufacture of its goods finds it more difficult to price those goods if it is not certain how much components will cost. If it believes that copper prices will fall, it may price its final product low – but copper might rise in price, leaving the firm facing a loss. Or it could price its end product at a higher price, believing that copper will rise on world markets and its price may be judged uncompetitive. Fluctuating commodity prices are also likely to be inflationary. When the world price of coffee rose sharply between mid-1975 and early 1977, the shop price also rose sharply. But when the world price fell, the shop price was slow to follow suit. Consumers paid more; for them the volatile world price was inflationary.

In order to steady commodity prices for the benefit of both producing and consuming countries, a number of international agreements or pacts have been signed since 1950 and although, by 1992, only one of them existed in any effective form (for rubber), some achieved a modest degree of success for a number of years. Arguably the most successful international commodity pact was the Commonwealth Sugar Agreement (CSA) which began in 1951 and ran until 1974. Under the agreement, Britain agreed to purchase 1.74 million tonnes of sugar cane from Australasia, British Honduras, the Caribbean, East Africa, Fiji, Mauritius and Swaziland. The agreement guaranteed that CSA-producing countries could sell the 1.74 million tonnes to Britain for a basic price of £50 a tonne (this was reviewed every three years). It gave producing countries an assured, stable revenue; they knew how much they were likely to earn from their sugar exports and could plan their economy accordingly. It gave the grower more chance of a stable income, and it gave Britain the guarantee of sugar supplies: two-thirds of its requirements came under the agreement.

While the world sugar price at one stage went as low as £20 a tonne, the agreement held. But in early 1974 the world price soared to around £250 a tonne, chiefly because of forecasts which suggested a shortage of sugar. Producing countries were placed in a dilemma; as low-income countries they needed as much foreign exchange as they could get for economic development. Under the CSA, Britain offered the sugar cane producers £50 a tonne at a time when the world market offered them £250 a tonne. When the British government refused to increase the amount it paid under the CSA by a substantial amount, the producers opted for the world market price and the agreement collapsed.

The CSA worked well when it suited the interests of both producers and consumers. But it showed how the pressure on an international commodity agreement can be intense. When the price is low, consumers may wish to break it; when the price is high the producers may want to get out. Fixed price commodity agreements, such as the CSA, are rare. Most other international commodity pacts have worked on either a quota or buffer stock system.

The International Coffee Agreement (ICA) was set up in 1963 to try to stop the downward drift of prices, and to 'stabilize prices above their free market level'.[16] It did this by

45

regulating the supply of coffee beans coming on to the world market. Producing countries each agreed to export a 'quota', a certain quantity of coffee, which was a little less than they would have normally exported without controls. By exporting slightly less than they might have done, the producing countries received a higher price per bag – and their overall revenues were higher. When coffee prices rose, producing countries were allowed an increase in their quotas; when prices fell their quotas decreased. The ICA's quota system survived from 1963 to 1972 and again from 1980 to 1989, when the agreement covered 50 producing and 25 consuming countries.

The agreement managed the market in a modest way but its biggest problem was that a timebomb marked 'overproduction' was persistently ticking away underneath it – and finally exploded. Coffee producers had constrained their exports but not their output. This led to a huge build-up of stocks that countries could not sell, and it was clear that when the agreement ended, many of the stocks would be released on to the world market and the price would plummet. In July 1989 the ICA collapsed, as it did in 1972, because of a disagreement over quotas and the pressures caused by the world surplus of coffee. Brazil, which had a quota under the ICA amounting to 30 per cent of world trade, would not agree to a cut in its quota to enable other coffee-growing countries to have larger quotas.

The United States wanted larger quotas to be given to the producers of the higher quality arabica coffees. And like other importing countries it wanted action to end the black market in international coffee trade, whereby countries traded their surpluses unofficially, at a price sometimes only half that of the official world market price; half-price was thought better than dumping coffee beans in the sea or letting them rot. The ICA's demise was hastened by this two-tier market – one inside and one outside the pact, the latter with much lower prices. Consumers were reluctant to pay the higher prices governed by the agreement when they could buy cheaper outside it.

The International Tin Agreement, set up in 1956 and made up of 22 governments, worked on a buffer stock system and was generally successful in steadying prices for over 25 years. A stock of around 20000 tonnes of tin was held and managed by the agreement's managers, the International Tin Council (ITC), serving as a 'buffer' against price fluctuations. When the world price was low, the stock's managers bought, so helping to raise the price; when it was high they sold, which brought it down to a realistic level. But after a spell of low prices in the pact's early years, which took the stock up to 23700 tonnes, prices rose and during the period from 1961 to 1966, the stock was practically exhausted. Although it recovered to reach 12400 tonnes by 1972, by 1974 it was again almost flat.

In an effort, successful for a while, to stimulate world tin trade the ITC began building up stocks at an unprecedented rate. In the later stages of the pact, in 1985, it was buying tin for 'forward' delivery with money it did not have. By late 1985, stocks totalled 85000 tonnes and the price was at a record high, some £9000 a tonne, which gave exporting countries a substantial profit – chiefly Malaysia, Bolivia, Thailand and Indonesia, who between them account for around 80 per cent of world trade in tin exports.

But the bubble burst when it was realized that it was governments of exporting countries who were encouraging the ITC to buy tin and that debts of around £400 million had built up. The London Metal Exchange suspended trading in tin and the price halved in months. The attempt to fix the market had not worked; unless demand is keeping up with supply, a commodity price may stay high for a while, with either normal or dubious management, but will eventually fall.

The collapse of the agreement had an unforeseen and disastrous spin-off. Many mines that were profitable when the price was £9000 a tonne were very unprofitable at £4000 a tonne, and were forced to close; this caused particular problems in Bolivia, where many of the now out-of-work tin miners were in the coca-growing area of Chapere. Growing coca to supply the expanding market for cocaine was an option in which former miners seemed to have some comparative advantage. Thus the collapse of the tin agreement helped to fuel the global drugs industry, adding to the supply of cocaine, keeping prices lower and more accessible to potential addicts.

The International Cocoa Agreement also worked on a buffer stock system. With 18 exporting countries, it started life in 1973 and effectively ended in 1987 when the buffer stock operation was suspended. Initially the agreement made use of both buffer stocks and export quotas, but quotas ended in 1980, following opposition to them from the United States. Cocoa prices rose during 1991 chiefly because of the prospects for a new price-stabilization agreement; the Malaysian government and a French trader, Merkuria-Sucden, put forward a plan to halt the expansion of cocoa cultivation until prices rose; to establish a network of national supplies, managed by a central authority comprised only of producers; and to create a joint producer consumer programme. The plan has potential if producer-countries support it. African cocoa producers have put forward ideas for a new agreement based on export quotas but, as this lacks support from consumer countries, it seems unlikely to go ahead.

The International Tropical Timber Agreement was set up in 1984 to develop trade in tropical timber. Unlike most international commodity agreements, it has no purely economic clauses and has never aimed to be a price stabilization pact. Rather, it defines its aims as promoting the expansion and diversification of timber trade, increasing the processing of tropical timber in producer countries, improving marketing and distribution, and encouraging reforestation and forest management. The agreement – which is managed by the Yokohama, Japan-based International Tropical Timber Organization (ITTO) – made little or no contribution during its first eight years to slowing either the pace or the unsustainable nature of forest destruction.

At a meeting in May 1990 the ITTO approved guidelines for the sustainable management of tropical forests for timber production, but there was no mechanism for monitoring these guidelines and they were judged by environmental groups to be far from a code of conduct for loggers. The meeting set the year 2000 as a target date by which all internationally traded tropical timber would be derived from 'sustainable sources'.[17] Friends of the Earth, UK, say that many tropical timber exporters already claim, in contradiction of ITTO's own studies, that timber is derived from such sources. Non-government organizations (NGOs) have called for the scrapping of the agreement as they believe it encourages forest exploitation and deforestation.

By early 1992 the only commodity agreement with economic clauses that was actually working was the International Rubber Agreement. Set up in 1979, the agreement relies on a buffer stock to defend its price, with the stock's managers buying when the world price is low and selling when it is high, to try to reduce fluctuations. While the agreement may have helped to reduce fluctuations, it has not prevented the steady downward trend in the world price. Its failure casts severe doubts about the ability of traditional-style international commodity agreements to help give producers a higher return.

## The integrated approach

In 1975 the UNCTAD Secretariat put forward a proposal for an 'integrated programme for commodities'. This envisaged the setting up, and in a few cases the stepping up, of 18 commodity agreements – for bauxite, bananas, cocoa, coffee, copper, cotton, hard fibres, iron ore, jute, manganese, meat, phosphates, rubber, sugar, tea, tin, tropical timber and vegetable oils. It urged the establishment of a $6 billion Common Fund for Commodities and more help for producers to process their commodities 'on the spot', adding value to them and making more of their economic potential (see Chapter 4).

The integrated programme was approved the following year by industrial and developing nations at UNCTAD IV in Nairobi (see Chapter 9). The final conference resolution said the programme would help to achieve stable conditions in commodity prices, with prices 'remunerative and just to producers and equitable to consumers . . . .Steps will be taken towards the negotiation of a Common Fund'.[18] Lack of money was seen to be a key reason for the slowness to set up commodity agreements, especially when a buffer stock was needed. The UNCTAD Secretariat pointed out that the existence of a fund, financed on an ability-to-pay basis, with countries with the heaviest involvement in world trade paying most, would allow buffer stocks to go forward unhampered by financial difficulties. The resolution said that negotiations over individual commodities should be concluded by the end of 1978. The then UNCTAD Secretary-General, Mr Gamani Corea, described the conference as a 'real milestone'.[19]

'Millstone' might have been more appropriate; the 'integrated approach' proved a failure. By the end of 1978, no new commodity agreements had been set up and negotiations on an effective Common Fund were seriously bogged down. The fund eventually limped into life in January 1989 – more than 12 years after the Nairobi conference, an indictment on the slowness of North-South negotiations. From the envisaged $6000 million, finance from the new fund was slashed to only $750 million, which in real terms was less than a tenth of the original proposal and too small to support an effective organization for commodity price stabilization. In the meantime, most developing countries had become convinced that Western countries were not serious about wanting to make commodity agreements.

The failure of the process was largely due to bad faith on the part of Western countries. Judged by their slowness to negotiate on commodity matters, it seems clear that they had little intention of taking the UNCTAD IV resolution seriously, even in the late 1970s. But the 1980s hammered the final nail into the coffin of the integrated approach, with the coming to power of right-wing governments in the United States, West Germany and Britain, three major actors on the world trade scene. Managing the market had little attraction for them.

At the 22-nation summit meeting in Cancun, Mexico, in October 1981, Tanzanian President, Julius Nyerere pointed to double standards when he said that the market philosophy which the United States applied to the developing world was not applied to US farmers who received many kinds of subsidies and price supports. Nyerere's words struck home, but not quite in the way he hoped for. The following year at a GATT Ministerial Meeting in Geneva, the United States argued for agriculture to be brought within GATT and later in the 1980s pressed for the abolition of government price support to farmers – although it still wanted to retain a way of supporting its own farmers.

Commodity agreements between producing and consuming countries have a poor record and poor prospects. The losers have been the developing countries and the people who grow or mine primary commodities, most of whom have seen the prices of the material they produce go down and down. What should now be the Third World strategy on commodities? What are the prospects for producers to set up arrangements to control production and prices, such as the the Organization of Petroleum Exporting Countries (OPEC), which might be classed as cartels?

For a cartel to work, several factors must be running in its favour. Firstly, a small number of producers must account for a large proportion of overall output, otherwise agreement between them is almost impossible to achieve. Secondly, there must be few or no substitutes or synthetics that consumers can switch to when the price is raised. Thirdly, the primary produce must be a substantial input into the consumer's way of life. The producers of oil have a product which satisfies, at least to some extent, these three conditions. Oil is a major input into the economies of Western countries; many of their industries depend on oil-based technology. But although OPEC quadrupled prices in late 1973 and doubled them in 1979, the 1980s witnessed the limitations of its power. Alternatives were developed, OPEC members disagreed about levels of production, energy conservation was taken more seriously, recession in the West reduced demand for oil, and even the 1991 Gulf War could not rescue a flagging price. Oil prices could soar yet again, however, if industrialized nations are foolish enough not to check energy demands.

The producers of most commodities are in a far less favourable position than oil producers. Beverages such as coffee, cocoa and tea, and metals such as tin and copper can be substituted. There may be scope for a 'joint metal-producers cartel', of copper, tin and bauxite producers, but the large number of countries involved would make this difficult. However, while the economic facts of life mean that the aspirations of commodity-producing countries have to stop short of full-blown cartels, that is not to say that they have no power, especially if they can co-operate on production restrictions (see Chapter 11).

### Alternative commodities

Given the expected sluggish demand for 'major' export crops, expansion would only reduce prices still further. There are better prospects for developing countries to exploit so-called 'minor' crops, perhaps local specialities, which could be significant export earners. Processed fruit and vegetables, cut flowers, canned fish, herbs, medicinal plants and specialist crops like jojoba all have potential. Jojoba, a bushy plant that grows well in dry areas, produces a seed the size of a pea which is 53 per cent oil, and this is used to make high-quality vehicle engine oils and cosmetics, and as a substitute for sperm whale oil. Sudan has been experimenting with jojoba on a site in the Red Sea Hills.

Kenya has succeeded in winning some 80 per cent of the world market in pyrethrum, a daisy-like plant that yields an extract for a natural insecticide. With the dangers, both to the environment and to health, of chemically-based insecticides becoming more apparent, the demand for natural products seems promising. Over 20 per cent of Kenya's export earnings are now coming from new products. Ghana, Mauritius and Zimbabwe are also doing well with 'alternative' products.

Consumption of many tropical fruits and vegetables is rising in Western countries. In France, for example, the consumption of mango has increased by 25 per cent over the last three years. Lesotho is selling canned asparagus to Europe – some 1200 farmers in Lesotho now grow the crop on small plots. Careful research of crops that grow or could grow locally, and of foreign markets, can uncover new export potentials.

## Debt and export crops

During the past 10 years the external debt of most developing countries has grown by massive proportions. Africa's debt, for example, grew more than tenfold between 1974 and 1990 to reach $272 billion. This is equivalent to over 90 per cent of the continent's GDP. The annual cost of 'servicing' this debt – the interest due and the capital repayments – was around $23 billion in 1990, roughly equivalent to the amount of development aid that Africa was receiving.

The need to earn money to service debts of this kind could lead governments to encourage an expansion of export crops even though they are already in over-supply. As seen in Table 3, many developing countries rely on export crops for a sizeable proportion of their foreign earnings. There are signs that some countries have been tempted to try to solve their problems by growing more export crops; this has occurred in Latin America, the continent with the higher overall debts, but not generally in Africa, which has a higher debt burden in relation to its income. Structural adjustment programmes imposed by the International Monetary Fund (IMF) and the World Bank have encouraged such expansion (see Chapter 8) and contributed to the fall in price of many internationally traded commodities.

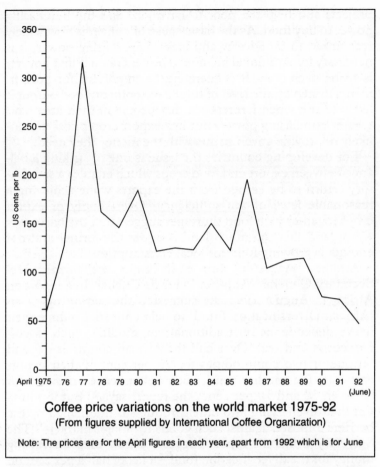

**Coffee price variations on the world market 1975-92**
(From figures supplied by International Coffee Organization)

Note: The prices are for the April figures in each year, apart from 1992 which is for June

What is clear is that changes in the mix of crops grown for export and/or local consumption can have a critical bearing on income distribution and, hence, on the access to food by the poor. If export crops are produced mainly in capital-intensive plantations, and poor crops by semi-subsistence peasants, a shift of resources to the export crop sector can reduce the income of poor peasants. The farmer or country switching to export crops will only be better off if the income earned is greater than the value of the food that could have been grown.

Less food grown locally, because of a switch to export crops, could mean higher food prices in local markets, which in turn could lead to hardship and hunger for poorer people in urban areas. On the other hand, increased export earnings enable a government, if it chooses, to step up development projects and help the poor to have jobs and the purchasing power to buy food. As the basic cause of hunger is now widely recognized to be poverty and lack of purchasing power, it is necessary for additional income to be generated if that poverty is to be overcome. It is therefore be important for governments to step up the level of rural development; food output is likely to rise when farmers see that people in their area have greater purchasing power. But low export crop prices are unlikely to provide governments with the money they need.

For developing countries the issue is one of striking a balance between export and food crops which enables a satisfactory return to be earned from the exports while achieving a reasonable level of self-sufficiency. Over-supply of export crops together with food shortages suggest that the balance is wrong and that too much land is under the former and not enough is growing food for local consumption.

Another suggestion has come from the former UN Secretary-General, Mr Javier Perez de Cuellar. In a report on Africa, in August 1991, he suggested the setting up of an 'African Diversification Fund' to help countries reduce their heavy dependence on traditional commodities such as coffee, cocoa and tea. 'Over half the African countries depend on one or two commodities for 70 per cent of their export earnings; for another third, such dependence accounts for between 50 and 70 per cent', the report says.[20] But it points out that diversifying into other products is not helped by the barriers imposed against such goods by 'major markets'. The Secretary-General's report suggests a new idea for raising money for the diversification fund – a tax of half a per cent on the consumption of all commodities in industrialized countries. 'This would raise considerable sums of money without affecting consumption', the report claims.

Most developing countries and peoples have seen only limited gains from the primary commodities they export to the West. Revenues have not been enough to help them move out of poverty. But while prices have been too low, new technology, such as biotechnology, could lead to additional output and further depress markets. Developing countries need a new strategy to get the most from their traditional commodities (see Chapter 11). Only a sizeable change in the nature of this trade, in particular a reduction in the volume of commodities being produced and exported, is likely to improve matters for the developing world.

# 4 Manufactured goods: the South's obstacle course

Stalled by low prices for their primary commodities, developing countries have turned to the manufacturing sector as a potentially more profitable earner of foreign exchange. The value of manufactured exports from developing countries, as a proportion of their overall exports, has increased from 10 per cent in 1955, to 20 per cent in 1965, 40 per cent in 1975, and 55 per cent in 1990.[1] While this seems an encouraging increase, to some extent the rise reflects the lower returns from primary commodities. Also, most of the South's manufactured exports are coming from a small number of countries.

At a conference in Lima, Peru, in 1975, developing countries agreed a plan of action that was endorsed the same year by the United Nations Industrial Development Organization; this called for an increase in the developing countries' share of world industrial production from 11.6 per cent to at least 25 per cent by the year 2000. By 1992, however, it had reached only 14.9 per cent.[2]

The biggest opportunity for most developing countries to industrialize for the export market lies in two economic sectors: turning their primary agricultural commodities into processed foodstuffs, and developing their exports of textiles and clothing. In 1980 the Brandt Commission included figures which showed the importance of on-the-spot processing of primary commodities. It quoted UNCTAD estimates that on the basis of their 1975 trade figures, 'for 10 commodities local semi-processing could provide the developing countries with gross additional export earnings of about $27 billion a year, more than one and a half times what these commodities now earn'.[3]

Provided the Uruguay Round GATT talks reach a conclusion, tariffs on processed agricultural foodstuffs should be reduced by a third. Textiles barriers should be subject to reductions through the abolition of the Multifibre Arrangement (see below). Beyond the processing of agricultural foodstuffs, and textiles and clothing, lie other manufactured goods that developing countries have sought to make for export. While a few countries have done well from such exports, most developing countries have found the 'manufacturing for export' path a thorny route. In practice it is beset by difficulties, most of which are created outside the country, although there are also some internal obstacles.

External barriers consist of those erected by purchasing countries, that is, constraints on the demand side. Chief among them are tariffs, quotas, rules-of-origin, 'voluntary' export restraints, health and administrative regulations, monitoring and surveillance, and subsidies given by governments of industrialized countries to allow their manufacturers to cut costs so that their goods can compete on price with imports from developing countries. In theory, these barriers run contrary to GATT. The articles of GATT are based on the assumption that only emergency restrictions are allowed, to prevent damage to industry in the importing country, 'to the extent and for such time as may be necessary to prevent or remedy such injury' (see Chapter 9).

Internal barriers are those in the developing countries: constraints on the supply side. These include lack of know-how, skills and training; lack of capital; and lack of export promotion services to exploit the possibilities that do exist despite obstacles on the demand side.

## External barriers

World Bank figures suggest that the trade barriers used by industrialized nations to keep out Third World goods cost poor countries anything between $50 billion and $100 billion a year.[4] External barriers take a number of forms. A *tariff* is basically a tax which is levied on a product at the port of entry into a country; this increases the price of the imported product and is therefore likely to reduce sales. Tariffs raise revenue for the importing country, but that is not the main reason why they are applied; rather they have traditionally been the first line of protection, keeping out goods from the importing country by artificially raising their price, making them uncompetitive.

If, for example, an Indian exporter wants to sell a garment to Britain for £10 which is identical in every way to a garment already on sale in Britain for £12, then provided distribution channels are good and the Indian garment can be made available throughout Britain, it will, in theory, corner the market. Why pay £12 when you can buy the same article for £10? But British manufacturers of garments will not be pleased, and neither will their workers. Facing shutdown and redundancy, they will clamour for restrictions against the Indian goods. And being in a politically powerful position (they have votes in Britain, Indian exporters do not), they will be heard. They might, for example, argue that a tariff of 25 per cent be imposed on the garments. This will mean that its price will rise to £12.50, and why pay £12.50 for a garment if you can buy one for £12? The Indian firm loses the business it would have won without the tariff.

Tariffs between industrialized countries were high until the Kennedy Round of GATT negotiations in 1967, and the Tokyo Round in 1979 reduced them to an average of about 5 per cent. But tariffs imposed against the processed agricultural foodstuffs and manufactured products of developing countries are higher, sometimes well over 10 per cent.[5] Tariffs tend to rise with the degree of processing. While primary commodities are allowed into most Western markets free of any tariffs (although there are some exceptions), if the commodity is semi-processed it may attract a 10 per cent tariff and, if it is fully processed, the product may attract double, or even more.

An enterprising Third World company may be able to get over the tariff hurdle. The manufacturer of garments cited above can increase the efficiency of his factory and get his costs down to a level that still allows him to compete, although there is always the danger of the barrier then being set higher still.

Recent years have seen the growth of non-tariff barriers to Third World trade; just under a quarter of its exports attract these measures.[6] Chief among them is the *quota*, a quantity restriction. Under the quota system a certain volume of a product is allowed into the market of a country, but no more. The Third World manufacturer, with a restricted home market for his goods because of limited purchasing power, is stymied by the quota. Expansion is out of the question, exports are fixed perhaps with a small per centage increase per annum; the business is therefore placed firmly in a strait-jacket. The most infamous and protectionist trading arrange-ment based on quotas is the Multifibre Arrangement (MFA).

## Textiles

Situated in a prominent position close to the centre of Man-chester, one of Britain's chief textile centres, lies an imposing building called the Free Trade Hall. Built in 1865, the name of the hall was inspired by the nineteenth century campaign for free trade which Richard Cobden and John Bright had mounted in the city. The campaign led to the abolition of the Corn Laws, which had put tariffs on grain imported into Britain, and the sweeping away of the mercantilist trade barr-iers of the day. The abolition of these barriers helped the local cotton industry; Cobden's interest in campaigning for free trade was said to be 'the plight of cotton mill operatives in Manchester'.[7]

In the shadow of their well-known landmark dedicated to free trade, textile producers and trade unionists have gathered over the past 40 years to talk about the opposite – how to impose protectionist measures to stop free trade. Textiles and clothing from the developing world have been perceived in Manchester, and in other centres of Western textile activity, to be causing job losses because they are cheaper.

After food, clothes are people's most basic need, and the advantage of exporting textiles is that a country has a domes-tic market for the products; it does not start from scratch. It has expertise, a certain level of activity on which it builds. So it is hardly surprising that textiles has been the first export industry that developing countries have entered – they have been seen to have a comparative advantage in making fibre products.

The constant pressure by both companies and trade unions in the West for import controls resulted in barriers to trade in cotton goods in the 1960s, and eventually in the MFA. First signed in 1974, the MFA provided guidelines for trade in textiles and clothing between countries of North and South. It does not cover North–North textiles trade, which has usually not been subject to restrictions. The MFA was supposed to be a temporary agreement to give countries of the North a breathing space to adjust their economies to

Third World imports. But powerful protectionist interests in the North made the MFA anything but a temporary arrangement.

However, in clamouring for an MFA, the protectionist lobby was attacking the wrong target. Even the stringent protectionist measures of the arrangement failed to stop job losses in the textile industries of the Western world. It became apparent that more jobs were being lost in the textile industries of the West because of the introduction of automated machinery than because of low-cost imports. The advent of micro-electronics enabled Western clothing manufacturers to produce the same volume with fewer workers, making unit costs lower. In a sense, the West seized back a comparative advantage in making these products.

In the many studies that have been conducted on the causes of job losses in Western textile industries, a virtually unanimous conclusion has emerged – exports from the Third World to the West pose only a small threat to jobs in Western countries, compared with losses from increased productivity.[8] But these studies have carried little weight against the protectionist lobbies, even though governments were for the 'free market' on domestic matters. Shoppers on the streets of cities and towns in the West were meanwhile denied the opportunity of buying the goods the Third World wanted to sell – they had a more restricted choice of goods and had to pay higher prices for them. The MFA has been estimated to cost British shoppers £18 a year per person.[9]

Exports of textiles and clothing account for about a quarter of the total manufactured exports of developing countries.[10] While some countries, notably Hong Kong, Taiwan, Macao and South Korea, have succeeded in exporting fibres in spectacular fashion, most countries have been caught in what amounts to a protectionist racket. North–South bilateral negotiations are conducted on the basis of MFA guidelines. When the MFA was first negotiated, it allowed textile products from developing countries to increase at 6 per cent a year but, when it was renegotiated in 1977, the EC insisted on a new clause (called a protocol) allowing 'reasonable departures' in bilateral agreements. In practice, this had the effect of curtailing the growth of quotas. The MFA was next negotiated in 1981 and a new protocol was added which tightened restrictions yet again. Hong Kong, Taiwan, Macao and South Korea were asked to negotiate reductions in their quotas, while growth from other countries was linked to the increase in national income in the importing countries; a global ceiling on the total export of textiles was also imposed. MFA 4, negotiated in July 1986, tightened restrictions yet again. At the insistence of the United States, it was extended to cover sisal, jute and ramie (a linen-like substance). It did, however, offer a small amount of comfort to the very poorest countries, such as Haiti and Bangladesh, allowing them increases in their export quotas.

But the MFA itself was under pressure. As part of the Uruguay Round of GATT talks, consuming and producing countries began talking about its dismantling. When negotiations on its future were concluded at the end of July 1991, it was agreed that current levels of protection should continue for 17 months and that the MFA should end in December 1992. There is, however, a 10-year period for phasing out quotas. It would therefore be 2002 before the MFA finally ends, and its shadow will linger over the world textile and clothing trade. Bilateral agreements will take the 1992 level of exports and imports as their starting point. Producing countries will have to fight hard to get any increase, and even to avoid reductions. For, as the case of Mauritius shows (see below), Western countries have not hesitated to seek restrictions even under agreements which appear to open trade doors, such as the Lomé Convention.

Some Western countries have taken modest steps to restructure their industries to allow them to import more Third World goods without clashing with domestic interests. Sweden, for example, moved 'up-market' in textiles, concentrating more on higher-priced fashion clothes, so as to allow more imports. The Netherlands restructured its furniture industry in similar fashion. 'The crucial issue is whether countries like Britain are prepared to *accommodate* Third World growth by adapting their industries to the relatively new and increasing competition presented by Third World competition', points out Abby Rubin Riddell in a book on restructuring.[11] In practice, the West has shown little such accommodation. High levels of unemployment and the political necessity of getting short-term results seem to rule out longer-term considerations. When Western economies are doing badly and unemployment is high, governments do not want to consider changes that might cause more job losses. When economies are doing well, the restructuring of Western industry to help the Third World still has a low priority.

Some countries, notably Bangladesh, would seem to have bright prospects when the MFA comes to an end. But if the country seems in danger of grabbing too high a share of a developed-country market for textiles and clothing, it may be asked to apply a *voluntary export constraint*. Under this device, developing countries are asked to restrict exports to a certain country voluntarily. As enforcement may follow if the developing country does not agree, it usually agrees. When woollen garments from Mauritius began to capture a sizeable share of the EC market in the early 1980s, for example, it was asked to 'voluntarily' restrict its exports to the EC.

*Rules-of-origin* are a further barrier to Third World manufactured goods. These rules state that all the raw materials used to make a manufactured product must originate in the developing country. A boat maker in an ACP country can sell boats to the EC without barriers; but if a single nut and bolt on the boat is made in Japan, then the boat is barred.

## Generalized system of preferences

At the first United Nations Conference on Trade and Development (UNCTAD), held in Geneva during 1964, a scheme was put forward to help developing countries diversify into manufactured products. It was proposed that a system of preferences be devised under which industrialized countries would lower the tariffs they applied on manufactured goods from developing countries, giving them preferential treatment over other industrialized countries. The idea was accepted in principle at UNCTAD II in 1968. But although the scheme was called the Generalized System of Preferences (GSP), it has, in practice, turned out to be anything but general, and has yielded only modest gains.

A 'general' scheme might reasonably have been a single scheme, embracing all products and applied by all industrialized countries. Industrialized countries, however, did not want anything that was general. They went away from UNCTAD II to work out their own schemes, eventually devising plans which did not have a great deal in common. The first was introduced in 1971 by the European Economic Community (EEC); Britain followed suit in 1972, and the United States in 1976. Australia, Austria, Canada, Finland,

Norway, Sweden and Switzerland also introduced GSP schemes.

Few, if any, of the schemes have kept to the original spirit and intention. 'Industrialized countries insisted at the inception of the GSP that the system should not be prejudicial to their own economics', said a report on the scheme by the Organization for Economic Co-operation and Development (OECD) Secretary-General.[12] This insistence led industrialized countries to exclude from their schemes the manufactured goods in which developing countries had most interest. Goods which developing countries did not make, such as aeroplanes, were given a preferential tariff rate. Others which they did make, like processed foodstuffs and textiles, were excluded. Products that were included were usually subject to quantity restrictions. Industrialized countries could also cancel preferences at a moment's notice if they wished, which was hardly a sound basis for a country to develop a particular business sector. Thus the GSP was turned from a scheme which seemed promising into one of only marginal significance.

'The lists of manufactured and semi-manufactured goods excluded from preferences form a substantial part of the manufactures in which the poor countries have potential comparative advantage', wrote Kam Hameed; 'these exclusions drastically reduce the effectiveness of the agreed Generalized System of Preferences'.[13] By 1990 about half the manufactured exports of developing countries were not covered by GSP schemes and were thus excluded from benefits. Of the remaining exports which could *potentially* receive GSP treatment, only about half actually did so, largely because of quota and non-tariff barriers applied against them, and also because of rules-of-origin. In other words, only about a quarter of developing country exports were covered.[14]

Overall, the value of developing country products exported under the GSP schemes of OECD countries increased from $12 billion in 1976 to over $60 billion in 1990.[15] In real terms, the increase is modest, and most of the benefits have occurred in the few countries which had a chance of making some of the goods that were included for preferences. 'A large part of the benefits of the system have been concentrated among a few of the more advanced developing countries', says the OECD report.[16] For the least developed countries the gains have been minimal. Some positive moves in favour of selected groups of countries are pointed to in UNCTAD's 1991 Trade and Development Report. It says, for example, that both the USA and the EC have improved benefits for four Andean countries under their GSP schemes.[17]

UNCTAD appears to judge the GSP in a favourable light; its Secretary-General, Mr Kenneth Dadzie, said in May 1990 that the GSP 'was an outstanding example of what could be achieved by multilateral negotiations on concrete issues of benefit to developing countries'. But he went on to admit that the experience of the past decade 'showed that these schemes had a number of shortcomings which limited their usefulness'.[18]

If the Uruguay Round leads to tariffs being reduced to around 3.5 per cent on most of the world's traded goods, there will be fewer preferences to give and the GSP will have less relevance. The GSP promised much but delivered little, because the underlying factors which caused industrialized countries to protect their markets from Third World manufactured products did not change. The reverse of the scheme still effectively applies – an industrialized country which imports manufactured goods from other industrialized countries applies lower tariffs against many of their goods and gives them preferential treatment over manufactures from developing countries.

The Development Committee of the World Bank and the IMF calculate that a lifting of barriers would 'increase developing-country income by about twice the general value of official development assistance from OECD countries'.[19] The removal of all industrial-country barriers to trade would therefore be worth about $100 billion a year to developing countries; it would increase their overall earnings from trade by about 10 per cent.

## The Lomé Convention

Under the Lomé Convention the 69 countries which make up the African, Caribbean and Pacific (ACP) group can sell their manufactured goods and processed agricultural foodstuffs to the 12 EC countries without facing any barriers. They are, in theory, exempt from MFA restrictions.

In 1975, the European Economic Community, as it was then called, and the 46 countries which then made up the

ACP group signed their first trade and aid deal in the Togo-lese capital, Lomé, in 1975. This was hailed as a break-through in North–South trade and aid relations, even as an important step along the road of the 'New International Economic Order' called for at the United Nations General Assembly in 1974 (see Chapter 1). But although the deal promised much, it has brought few benefits to ACP coun-tries. The Lomé Convention tidied up the arrangements that Britain and France had with their former colonies, replacing Commonwealth preferences and the Yaoundé Convention. In practice, the five-year deal gave the ACP countries prefer-ential treatment on trade compared with non-ACP coun-tries; it gave sugar-cane producing countries a guaranteed market for 1.3 million tonnes of sugar each year; aid worth 3.4 billion European Units of Account (ecus) – about $3.4 billion – and a compensation scheme that helped countries if their earnings from commodities fell by more than a pre-scribed percentage.

The first Lomé Convention was replaced in 1980 by Lomé II and again in 1985 by Lomé III. In December 1989, by which time the number of ACP countries had grown to 66, Lomé IV was signed for a 10-year period, with 12 billion ecus (nearly $15 billion) allocated for the 1990–95 period. Most of the aid goes through the European Development Fund and actual disbursements have been persistently slow.

But it is over trade where most of the dissatisfaction with the Convention has surfaced. Schemes called STABEX and SYSMIN have helped a little to compensate primary com-modity producers for the drop in prices that have occurred since 1975, but they could not make up for the bulk of the losses suffered. And there is greater dissatisfaction over mar-ket access to the EC.

Although the Lomé Convention gives ACP nations the right to sell most of their manufactured goods and processed agricultural foodstuffs in the EC, the ACP's share of the Community market has declined since 1975. The voluntary export restraint that was imposed against Mauritius (noted above) cast severe doubt on the spirit of the Convention. It shows that EC countries will not hesitate to restrict entry for products that are considered a threat to their own industries. EC countries are only willing to import ACP manufactured goods if quantities are so small that no one is going to notice them very much. Despite the existence of the Lomé Convention, the ACP countries have no guarantee that when their quantities of manufactured exports become too large they will not be severely restricted. Again under the Convention, rules-of-origin have also been used to keep out some ACP products.

Overall, the Lomé Convention has been of doubtful benefit to ACP countries; it has not provided the economic uplift that many hoped for. 'The Conventions have been in existence for 15 years', said an Overseas Development Institute paper in October 1990, 'yet they have not represented a step on the road to a New International Economic Order. Many countries are now in worse shape than they were at the start'.[20]

## Internal constraints

Third World countries who want to diversify into manufactured products for export are likely to face the problem that few of the people have the skills needed to develop the new industries. A foreign company may have to be sought to build and operate a factory, but a price will have to be paid. Capital is often lacking for new industries and, although the TNC may be willing to build a factory and install the necessary equipment, in practice it will expect a good return. Stifling bureaucracy, too much government interference, and lack of any incentives from a government can also be a brake on new industries.

The lack of export promotion services can also hinder plans. Breaking into new markets does not just happen, it requires resources and some very careful market research and preparation. Western exporters have a wide range of services to help them, for example the UK Export Credit Guarantee Department which provides insurance for British exporters who sell abroad. Most Third World country services are underdeveloped and the would-be exporter may not get the help needed at the crucial stage of trying to break into a new market.

But most of the controversy about internal constraints and the negative effect they might have on trade, particularly new trade in manufactures, centres on government policy. Developing countries also impose import barriers – sometimes higher than those imposed by industrialized countries – and the question is whether such barriers hinder the growth of manufactured exports. The neo-classical economic view as stated in a World Bank publication is that countries imposing sizeable restrictions on imports distort the internal market signals and prices and do not help exporters.[21] From this approach, trade liberalization is seen as the answer, with a dismantling of import barriers, often accompanied by a sizeable depreciation of the currency, so as to make exports cheaper and imports dearer.

Trade liberalization can lead to certain gains. Allowing foreign goods to compete with domestic goods can confront inefficient ways of production, and challenge domestic monopolies. Some studies appear to show that high rates of protection are detrimental to the export performance of developing countries. Levels of protection in sub-Saharan Africa 'are substantially higher than in most other developing countries', calculates Dean DeRosa of the IMF, who argues that 'restrictions on imports impose a tax on exports'.[22] His point is that when a country restricts its imports, the import sector increases its use of domestic resources in order to expand output. This causes the cost of domestic resources to rise, making exports based on those resources less competitive and therefore less likely to be in demand abroad. DeRosa calculates that protectionist barriers reduced the combined annual exports of 23 sub-Saharan African countries 'by between about 3.5 per cent and 2 per cent of gross domestic product each year, or between $2.7 billion and $1.3 billion a year in 1985 dollars'.

Developing countries have maintained that barriers against imports are justified because they are necessary to promote 'infant industries', which are just starting and which need time to get established. There is a genuine case for protection from goods from abroad which are produced by longer-established, more efficient producers. But since 1986 more than 50 developing countries have liberalized trade and swept away most import barriers, and the results are mixed.

A 1991 UNCTAD report said that 'in recent years a large number of developing countries have taken measures to open up their economies and give exports a more prominent role in their development strategies . . . the response to these policy changes in terms of investment and growth has been uneven'.[23] Several countries, which had 'well-diversified economic structures', technological capabilities and people with skills, have been able to expand their trade, stimulate new investments and promote economic growth, it said, 'but trade liberalization measures failed to stimulate economic growth and investments significantly in countries lacking flexible and diversified economic structures'. It also pointed out that in 'debt-distressed countries', falling investment was common.

In terms of development, rather than merely economic growth, the effect of trade liberalization has also been uneven. Four developing countries were foremost during the 1980s in liberalizing trade: Chile, Indonesia, South Korea and Uruguay. Although they all increased their exports of manufactured goods, the development benefits have been limited. All four countries have politically right-wing governments who have ruled for a considerable time and have hardly been in the forefront of spreading the benefits of economic growth to their citizens. Trade liberalization does not appear to have led to the creation of many extra jobs. 'The evidence suggests that the effects of trade liberalization on unemployment have been small', says the World Bank report referred to above.

Developing counties have a difficult balancing act; they do not want to pursue protectionist policies that might hinder export growth, but they need to develop a certain level of industrial activity if they are not to be dependent on buying from abroad. And while losses in exports that come from protection are real, they are modest compared to the losses in exports that result from other obstacles, chiefly the barriers imposed by industrialized countries. It seems clear that developing country governments can only achieve so much – in terms of export growth – by their own trade liberalization. It is liberalization in Western markets which stands to help them far more. External factors are a much larger factor responsible for holding back the growth of exports than internal constraints in developing countries.

Some developing countries have partly overcome the trade barriers imposed by Western countries by moving the production of certain products 'offshore' – transferring them to other developing countries which could gain entry to Western markets. Hong Kong business interests, for example, faced with restrictions on the volume of garments they could sell to Western countries, have set up factories in Bangladesh and China in order to export under their quotas. Puerto Rica has done a certain amount of sub-contracting for other

67

Caribbean countries. There are clearly limits to this type of loophole activity; while the ending of the MFA will not sweep away quotas on textiles and clothing, it may ultimately mean less opportunity for 'offshore' operations.

## Exporting processing zones

To try to maximize the possibilities of making and exporting manufactured goods, 63 developing countries have set up export processing zones (EPZs), also known as free-trade zones, which in practice are industrial estates situated near a sea or airport. This has usually involved offering inducements to TNCs to bring in their know-how to make manufactured products and train local people in the necessary skills (see also Chapter 2).

The World Bank describes an EPZ as a 'relatively recent variant of the free-trade zone (FTZ) – a designated area, usually in or next to a port area, to and from which unrestrictive trade is permitted with the rest of the world. Merchandise may be moved in and out of FTZs free of customs . . . saving interest on customs payments . . . orientated to export production'.[24]

By 1990 there were 208 such zones in 63 countries of Asia and the Pacific, Africa, Latin America and the Caribbean. As Table 4 shows, they provide employment for nearly 4.3 million people, with Asia the dominant region.

**Table 4  Export processing zones (EPZs)**

|  | No. of countries with an EPZ | No. of EPZs in operation | Persons employed |
| --- | --- | --- | --- |
| Africa | 12 | 24 | 202 300 |
| Asia and the Pacific | 23 | 99 | 2 991 900 |
| Latin America and the Caribbean | 28 | 85 | 1 073 700 |

*Source:* Starnberg Institute Databank, quoted in 'Employment and Multinationals in the 1990s', ILO, Geneva, 1992 (China is not included).

Employment in EPZs therefore increased more than eight-fold between 1975 and 1990. But 4.3 million jobs in these zones represents at best no more than 5 per cent of total employment in the manufacturing industries of developing countries; it is also small compared with the estimated 300 million people who work in their 'informal sectors'.

Wages for EPZ workers are usually low, and governments of developing countries need to allocate substantial amounts of often scarce funds to attract companies into the zones. A country might typically offer a free building, a five-year 'tax-free' holiday and other perks to an interested company. To develop an EPZ at Bataan in the Philippines, for example, the Filipino government offered companies 100 per cent ownership, permission to impose a minimum wage lower than in the capital, Manila, tax exemptions on imported raw materials and equipment, exemption from export tax, low rent for land, plus other inducements.[25] Wages were low. The first six months of employment at Bataan are a probationary period, paid at 75 per cent of the 'minimum' wage. 'Some plants terminate employment after this period has elapsed and replace workers by fresh trainees', says an International Labour Office (ILO) report.[26]

Despite the World Bank definition, a factory in an EPZ does not enjoy 'unrestrictive trade with the rest of the world'. In practice the goods made in the EPZ are subject to the same barriers to Western markets as goods made outside the zone.

While there may be some exceptions, the zones have proved disappointing. Developing countries set up EPZs to help diversify economies, increasing their exports of manufactured goods, bringing new technology into the country, creating more jobs and skills. 'Apart from a few notable exceptions', says the ILO survey, 'the process of export-orientated industrialization continues to be of rather minor significance . . . despite the fact that a substantial share of available infrastructure and investible funds have been swallowed up by export-orientated production'.[27]

The zones have led to little diversification of economies. the same ILO survey notes that EPZs 'continue to demand overwhelmingly unskilled and semi-skilled workers' and that skills acquired on the job 'are often limited and mostly unusable outside the plant'.[28]

The zones have led to increased exports and more jobs for a small number of developing countries. In Africa, the gains have been concentrated in four countries: Egypt, Mauritius, Morocco and Tunisia. In Latin America, most employment gains are concentrated in central America and the

Caribbean. In Asia, where many countries have started EPZs, the gains are spread more evenly, although the zones of Hong Kong, Malaysia, South Korea, Philippines and Sri Lanka have attracted a sizeable share of the available investment.

Mauritius is often considered to be an EPZ success story – wages in the zone are only about a quarter of those in Hong Kong, making it particularly attractive to investors. Unemployment in Mauritius fell from 14 per cent in 1985 to 3 per cent in 1989, while exports averaged an 8 per cent annual growth from 1983 to 1988. Almost 90 per cent of EPZ investment in Mauritius went into textiles, chiefly sweaters and shirts. Most of the exports go to France, Germany, Britain and the United States. The Mauritius EPZ eventually fell victim to its own success, having to introduce 'voluntary' export constraints. And despite its 'success', an IMF working paper notes that although the economic benefits for the country have been higher than the costs, 'we cannot draw any conclusions as to the superiority of the EPZ concept over alternative development strategies. Losses in economic welfare cannot be completely ruled out. As for budgetary implications, the expenditure for EPZ-related infrastructure will be a substantial long-term burden on the budget without guarantees for a positive return'.[29] An ILO report warns that in spite of the success story of the clothing export sector in Mauritius, there is an 'inherent fragility' which comes from a small country being heavily dependent on commercial transactions.[30]

Such frank assessments raise related questions about, for example, the true costs of setting up EPZs, and the opportunity cost, measured in terms of the benefits that the money invested in them could have brought to other sectors of economies. The success of any zone geared up to export will ultimately depend on the market abroad for its products, and a developing country EPZ is an expendable pawn in that market. Prospects for other developing countries setting up EPZs are limited. 'Only those developing countries that have a relatively skilled labour force or are well situated geographically may pin some hope on export-orientated investment to boost employment', says the ILO report.[31]

Developing countries have tried to diversify from the export of primary commodities to strengthen their economies and improve their terms of trade. But even with EPZs, manufactured exports have not provided developing countries with any major escape from the long-term decline in their terms of trade. In practice, even despite any liberalization that follows the Uruguay Round, industrialized countries could maintain barriers against Third World manufactured and processed exports unless they restructure their industry and move out of those goods the Third World want to sell. The 1980s were decade of 'structural adjustment' for developing countries; a decade of adjustment for the industrialized world appears to be needed if Third World goods are to be allowed access to Western markets. Unless such access is allowed, especially for textiles and processed foodstuffs, then trade barriers against developing countries will continue to deny the peoples of those countries the chance to escape from their dependence on primary commodities.

# 5 Trade in services

*'We have a future ahead of us in services'* – Ugandan Minister of Commerce, 1982

When 88 trade ministers from industrial and developing nations met under the auspices of GATT in Geneva in November 1982, to discuss improvements in the world trading system, they achieved little. But for good or not-so-good for the developing world, the meeting put trade in services very firmly on the international agenda. Commercial services that are traded internationally include tourism, labour, telecommunications, information, mail, radio and television, banking and finance (including foreign investment), accounting, insurance, ideas such as patents and copyrights, maintenance, advice (legal, for example), advertising, transport, shipping, engineering, and construction. Services such as health and education are also subject to a limited amount of trade.

International trade in services has developed in a way that could scarcely have been foreseen, even in the quite recent past. Since the late 1970s the trade has grown at a huge rate; in 1978 the value of world trade in commercial services was estimated by GATT at around $50 billion, whereas by 1990 it had shot up to $770 billion, about 20 per cent of all world trade. Some 22 per cent of the South's exports now consist of services – chiefly tourism, labour (nationals of the South working abroad), and air and shipping services. In 1990 the South earned $213 billion from the export of its services; it imported services to the value of $299 billion.[1]

At the GATT ministerial meeting in 1982, the United States government proposed that services be included in trade liberalization schemes, and vigorously campaigned on the issue throughout the 1980s; GATT had traditionally only been concerned with trade in goods, not services. The

USA even proposed that the words 'and services' simply be added every time that the word 'goods' appeared in a GATT document. Much of the growth in world trade in services in the past 15 years has come from US efforts to develop this sector; this was spurred on by the deterioration in its trade balance in manufactured goods. Since 1985 the USA has refused to be involved in any trade negotiations that did not include services. Ironically, by 1992, when the USA realized that some developing countries stood to do very well by selling services to the American market, it argued in the Uruguay Round negotiations that it should be exempt from around three-quarters of tradeable services (see Chapter 9).

As trade in services is important for many developing countries, the effects of trade liberalization are likewise of considerable significance. For many countries, says the GATT Secretariat, 'services is the fastest growing economic sector and the most vigorous creator of jobs. For a large proportion of those countries, trade in services represents the greatest hope for export success in the future'.[2] But the complete liberalization of international trade in services would almost certainly not be helpful to most developing countries in the 1990s.

The South Commission report, *The Challenge to the South*, points out that recent advances in information and telecommunication technologies have added 'an altogether new dimension to the role of services in the development process'. Business services, for example, are used by companies to produce goods; these services can have 'a profound impact on the competitiveness of a wide range of economic processes and products, for instance by computing inventory management'.[3]

While liberalization could open up new markets, it could threaten existing sectors. Better-off developing countries might gain; the majority of lower-income countries would be worse off, for, while developing countries would in theory be able to sell their services without restriction to the rest of the world, equally they would have to open up their markets and end any protection they give to their service sector. This sector tends to grow as other sectors develop; different services are needed to help the manufacturing industry to have the information it needs, to move goods, and so on. Industrialized countries tend to have a comparative advantage in most services and therefore stand to benefit from trade liberalization. Having been in the service sector longer, they can perform many of them more efficiently than the Third World. Around six out of 10 jobs in the West are in the service sector, only two out of 10 in the developing world.

Fears have been expressed that the United States and other Western countries are keen to have services covered by GATT in order to help the service industries of their countries to win markets in developing countries before service industries in those countries have a chance to become as efficient.[4] There are serious doubts about the appropriateness of GATT rules for service sectors. 'GATT rules, developed . . . in the context of trade in goods, are quite inappropriate for a regime of trade in services', says *The Challenge to the South*.[5] While trade in services has an important potential for developing countries in the future, such potential is not likely to be realized unless they can first develop greater expertise in domestic commercial services. The key issue facing the Third World is 'the extent of liberalization that is desirable (at) their present stage of development and future prospects for further development', says Martin Khor of the Penang-based Third World Network.[6]

Trade liberalization undoubtedly threatens some of the Third World's service sectors, particularly banks and financial services. 'If finance is brought under the GATT, it will be the end of our hopes', Mr J. Aliro-Omara, Ugandan Minister of Commerce, said at the GATT Ministerial Meeting, Geneva in November 1982. Third World countries could then be obliged to allow the giant Western banks free access to their markets. This could be highly damaging to Third World banks, many of whom are now struggling to find their feet, with the help of protection from foreign banks. Martin Khor points out that at the time of Malaysia's independence, foreign banks controlled the overwhelming share of the country's banking business. In 1990, however, domestic banks had the dominant share, largely as a result of restrictions placed on the establishment or expansion of foreign banks.

The issue of 'access' presents particular problems for developing countries, says the UNCTAD 1991 Trade and Development Report. 'Lacking large TNCs with global infrastructures, financial strength, mastery of advanced technologies, and accumulated knowledge and established reputations, developing countries may find it virtually impossible to capitalize effectively on negotiated market opportunities'.[7] Developing countries will be relative beginners competing on equal terms with experienced players.

There are also wider implications. In any country the banking sector can be a powerful instrument for controlling or influencing production and even the pace and character of economic development. It is the banks that decide who has credit, how much and at what price. If a foreign bank, answerable to shareholders abroad, is in charge of such decisions then Third World nationals may feel that they have no way of redressing what they believe are injustices in the bank's lending policy. In this way, foreign-owned banking services are likely to be less democratic.

UNCTAD has warned that the liberalization of international trade in banking services has substantial dangers for developing countries.[8] Its 1990 report points out that commitment to liberalizing cross-border transactions in banking services would entail dismantling significant parts of national regimes of exchange control. In many developing countries these regimes are essential to micro-economic management. Liberalization could reduce the effectiveness of monetary policy in developing countries, which often relies heavily on direct methods of controlling credit and interest rates.

In view of the way liberalization could threaten their service sectors, the South Commission report notes that developing countries only agreed to participate in negotiations on trade in services in the Uruguay Round after a GATT Ministerial meeting in 1986 had agreed that negotiations on trade in services would be conducted in 'an *ad hoc* juridical frame of reference separate from the negotiations on trade in goods'; also that development in Third World countries would be regarded as 'an integral part of the objectives for negotiations'; and furthermore, that any Uruguay Round agreement 'would respect the policy objectives of national laws and regulations applying to services'.[9] Many countries could find that an excessive dependence on imported services is detrimental to development efforts. When key service sector activities are not being run by local people, skills are not being developed, and heavy reliance on imported services means that value is added abroad rather than domestically. Services are therefore more likely to make a contribution to development in the poorer world if they develop locally rather than be imported (see also Chapter 9).

# Shipping

In the Uruguay Round negotiations, the United States, despite its campaign to include services in trade negotiations, urged that three major service sectors were excluded from the trade liberalization – sea transport, air transport and basic telecommunications. Sea and air transport are, ironically, two of the chief services in which the South have an interest as exporters. Some 95 per cent of all the goods that are traded internationally are transported by sea; according to UNCTAD, developing countries were the origin of 47.6 per cent of world trade in 1989 but owned only 21.1 per cent of the world fleet – and over two-thirds of this share was accounted for by 10 countries.[10] Liberia and Panama are the two most significant Third World countries in sea transport, although their share of the trade declined in the late 1980s as a result of competition from other countries. Tonnage registered in Liberia dropped from 94 million tonnes in 1988 to 77 million tonnes in 1989, and in Panama the drop was from 71.5 to 61.3 million tonnes.

One little-noticed aspect of shipping concerns transport and insurance costs. UNCTAD's 1990 review of Maritime Transport reproduces an article from the *Journal of Commerce International*, which says that for many developing countries, particularly those that are distant from Western markets, the average tariff on Third World exports 'is now far less than the average transport rate'. Furthermore, it seems that transportation costs often increase with the level of processing. 'The freight rate for Ghana's exports of cocoa beans runs about 5 per cent, but the rate for cocoa powder and cocoa butter is 10 per cent of their value. . . . There is considerable evidence that this "escalating" structure of freight rates is due to the arbitrary pricing policies of liner shipping cartels that charge what the market will bear'.[11] It goes on to point out that freight rates are frequently more favourable on shipments from North to South than they are from South to South.

Whereas shipping costs account for 11.29 per cent of the value of Africa's imports, they account for only 4.42 per cent of the value of industrial-country imports.[12] The shipping cartels operate in liner 'conferences', of which there are around 400 a year. Shippers meet at these conferences to fix the prices they will apply on their routes. The Europe/East

Africa conference, for example, has 14 member shipping companies, including Cunard Ellerman Ltd, Mediterranean Shipping Co. SA, and the Kenya National Shipping Line Ltd. But whereas the cartels once shipped around 80 per cent of world trade, their share has now dropped to around 50 per cent. They now face more competition from shippers outside the cartel, with the result that prices are under more pressure. (See also Chapter 2 about the oil used in shipping.)

**Remittances**

In 1989, developing countries earned about $25 billion in receipts from its nationals working abroad. Of this, Yugoslavia received $6.3 billion, Egypt $4.3 billion, Turkey $3 billion and India $2.7 billion.[13] Such earnings can be highly volatile. The 1991 Gulf crisis caused tens of thousands of migrant workers to be laid off work in Kuwait and sent back home. While there appears to be little chance of any long-term stability from such earnings, the South would at least have a chance to step up receipts if barriers to the movement of workers were removed. Barriers such as immigration laws and consular procedures 'impede the export of labour services from developing countries'.[14] The potential to increase earnings from remittances is considerable, but dependent on a relaxation of immigration controls. The *Human Development Report 1992* says that even using 'very conservative assumptions, immigration controls deny developing countries income (direct and indirect) of at least $250 billion a year'.[15] A tenfold increase in remittances is therefore possible if immigration controls are relaxed.

The biggest service sector earner for many developing countries, and also one of the most controversial, is tourism. Third World tourism does not have the restrictions that affect most developing country trade; it takes the form of the poor world earning foreign exchange by serving the rich world.

## Tourism – tainted honey?

The roll of drums that echoes at dusk across the swimming pool of the beach-side Regent Hotel in the Fijian resort of Nadi is a signal for tourists to pick up their cameras and walk. Momentarily foresaking the delights of the bar's

'Happy Hour', out they flock like eager sparrows across the still-warm patios to film what is claimed to be a traditional torch-lighting ceremony. As the torch-bearer runs around the pool's perimeter, lighting strategically placed points against a background of the setting sun, the shutters click away and everyone is happy. The tourists, mostly elderly Americans, have their pictures to show the folks back home – who might be so impressed that they are tempted along to the hotel next year.

Many developing countries, Fiji among them, have a comparative advantage in many of the things that tourists like. They have the sun, climate, sea, beaches, scenery, wildlife, history, archaeology, tradition (real or concocted), sometimes sex, that Westerners are willing to pay for. As they have such an advantage, it follows that they exploit it. So while developing countries are net importers of most of the services that are traded internationally, the exception is tourism. Next to oil, tourism earns more foreign currency for the developing world than any economic activity.

Whereas only a limited number of Third World nationals take their holidays abroad, a growing number of Westerners have become tired of holidaying in America and Europe and are heading instead for Third World locations. At home they may not be allowed, because of trade barriers, to spend their money buying Third World goods, but there is nothing to stop them travelling to experience what the Third World has to offer. 'There are far fewer restrictions placed on citizens of the developed world in their choice of vacation destinations than in their choice of clothing, footwear or foodstuffs', says Anne Booth.[16]

In terms of its potential to earn foreign exchange, tourism is the main service sector of most developing countries. It seems a cast-iron way in which poorer countries can cash in on Western affluence and earn much-needed foreign exchange. But although tourism has promised much, it has so far brought only limited benefits to developing countries and there are serious doubts over how it contributes towards overall development.

Some 250 million people from Western countries now holiday abroad each year, of whom some 50 million visit Third World locations. In 1989 developing countries earned more than $55 billion from tourism, over 5 per cent of their earnings from trade. An ILO report predicts that by the year

78

2000, tourism and related activities will surpass all other economic sectors.[17] The benefits are not evenly spread. Around 45 developing countries take the lion's share of the tourist trade, with Kenya, Sri Lanka, Thailand, the Philippines, Hawaii, Mexico, the Caribbean, and parts of India among favourite locations. International aid agencies, such as the World Bank, encourage developing countries to exploit their tourist resources and potential, so as to create new jobs and earn foreign exchange. Some regions now seem to be dependent on tourism for too large a proportion of their foreign earnings, especially the Caribbean which earns around 25 per cent of its foreign earnings from the trade.

The $55 billion of foreign exchange earned by developing countries is by no means net earnings. It is rare for more than 40 per cent of the money that tourists spend on a holiday to stay in the Third World country they visit – and sometimes it is as low as 10 per cent. A large proportion of the price that Western tourists pay for their holidays is for hotels, most of which are owned by Western hotel chains. It is not just hotels that developing countries have to build. Economies have to be adapted to suit tourists' needs. Land, beaches, water, and so on have to be reserved and infrastructure built. New feed-roads will usually be needed; services have to be laid on for holiday complexes. The cost of providing the infrastructure may have to come from host country budgets, causing other items of government spending to be postponed. Nor will the jobs created necessarily make up for the damage caused to people who are displaced by the new tourist industry.

Harvey Perkins, an Australian who has studied the effects of international tourism, estimates that 13 multinational corporations dominate the tourism industry – six from the United States, four from France and one each from Australia, Britain and Canada. 'Four of them', says Perkins, 'operate 97 per cent to 100 per cent of their hotels outside their country of origin and nine of the 13 have more than 50 per cent outside. All six from the US are owned by airlines as also are two from France'.[18]

What the holidaymaker does not see is the way that the tourist industry competes for local resources – and this can mean that local people are cheated out of them. Local people can lose their homes, their land and traditional means of livelihood; survival becomes dependent on serving the wealthy tourists whose demands have upturned their lives. People who live in Third World tourist areas often have little or no power over an industry which can critically affect them. As most hotels are built close to beaches it is Third World fishermen who rank among the biggest losers. Although they may have made their living from a base on a beach, it is common for fishermen not to be consulted about new tourist complexes, and to be cleared away with no compensation. At one location in the Philippines, for example, local fishermen were forbidden to fish within 40 kilometres of a new hotel complex.

The tourist demand which has possibly the most serious implications for developing countries is for water. Tourists expect unlimited water; a hotel guest can use 500 litres of water a day, 10 times more than local people. Yet many developing countries have serious problems with water supplies. Tourists are not usually aware of it but they compete for water with local people, including food growers; water for local people, including farmers, can run dry; farming crops and food for local people can therefore be adversely affected.

Developments to cater for the tourism industry in Langkawi, a Malaysian island, appear to have put a severe strain on water resources. 'Physical development has destroyed catchment areas in Langkawi Island which resulted in decreased water-holding capacity'.[19] Farmers on Langkawi Island are suffering soil erosion and sedimentation due to the development and face water shortages, especially in the island's dry season from January to May.

Food production might be affected as rural people leave the land to cater for the tourist trade. In one area of Fiji, the production of foodstuffs dropped as a number of workers left the fields to work in tourist hotels as firewalkers and in traditional dancing ceremonies. On the other hand, it could be argued that the development of tourism has in this case widened people's job opportunities; a spot of firewalking in the evening may be judged preferable to working all day in the fields.

The tourist trade demands imports which in turn means that valuable and often scarce foreign exchange has to be allocated for such imports. Local industry in a developing country is unlikely to be able to meet the demands for furniture from a new several hundred-roomed hotel. Nor is there much point in a local entrepreneur setting up a factory to make hotel furniture when the business may be of a 'one-off' nature. Local industry may therefore gain little or nothing from tourism. Lorine Tevi, of the World Council of Churches, who has studied the effects of tourism in the Pacific, believes that it would not be unusual for a Pacific island hotel to buy its furniture from Sweden, office machinery from the United States, lighting from Holland, vans from Germany, curtains from France, and food from Australia.[20] In the tourist-popular West African country, Gambia, the manager of one hotel admitted importing virtually all the food that was placed before the hotel's guests.[21]

There is little evidence that Third World tourism has developed sufficient links with other economic sectors of the local economy to benefit development as a whole – the beneficial 'spin-offs' have been few. Dr Ziadi Mohamed, who has researched the effects of tourism in Tunisia, says that tourism has created very few jobs and that little economic development is occurring in tourist areas; 'the lack of connection between tourism and development is very worrying', he points out.

Tourism affects local cultures in many ways, not least by its demand for people to wait on wealthy people, and for economies to be geared up to tourists' needs. 'Tourism is cultural prostitution', believes Haunani-Kay Trask, professor of American studies at Manoa University on Hawaii; 'it is violence against us'.[22] Hawaii has a particular problem; five million tourists descend each year on a local population of only one million. In a number of tourist destinations the trade has led to an increase in sexual prostitution; this is especially evident in countries such as Thailand and the Philippines. Two out of every three Japanese tourists to the Philippines are men on package tours with 'built-in' sex. Around 3000 Malaysian men visit brothel towns in Thailand every weekend. In Sri Lanka an estimated 2500 boy prostitutes, so-called beach boys, earn their living from male tourists. Lesotho and Swaziland have attracted sex-tourists from the Republic of South Africa, in the shape of men who were barred by law from having sex with black people in their own country.

In a report by the Ottawa-based North–South Institute about the role and impact of tourism, E.Philip English says that, for some developing countries, tourism has become an even more powerful economic stimulus than trade in goods.[23] With the prospect of lower travel costs following airline deregulation and falling oil prices, international tourism 'seems well-placed for continued growth, even if there are temporary and localized setbacks due to concern over terrorism'. At the same time, the institute's report documents the doubts that have arisen concerning the lasting economic advantages of international tourism in developing countries. It says that in some cases, Third World taxpayers may even end up subsidizing the holidays of rich Westerners through public expenditure on tourist-related infrastructure such as roads and airports.

Steve Britton, in a study of tourism in Fiji, points out that tourism 'has been grafted on to a once colonial economy in a way that has perpetuated deep-seated structural anomalies and inequalities'. Western companies, he says, have direct contact with the potential customers and, in practice, dominate the international tourism business.[24]

## Goa

The development of Goa, on the western coast of India, is an almost classic case of tourism's detrimental effects on local people. Goa, with beautiful Indian Ocean beaches, was developed in a small way for domestic visitors in 1962. In the mid-1960s it was discovered by Western hippies but, until 1976, tourism in Goa was unorganized and unstructured. In 1976 the first five-star hotel was built, followed by another three over the next seven years. These were co-owned by Indians and TNCs.

In 1983 the Indian government hosted the Commonwealth Conference and selected Goa for a weekend retreat for the 40-plus leaders. Top-of-the-range accommodation had to be built and Goa was firmly on the map as an international tourist location. A hotel complex was built in the south of Goa which blocked the access of some local fishermen to the sea, causing serious disruption to their livelihoods.

On 30 May 1987 Goa became a state in its own right; on 1 June 1987, the new state government announced that tourism in Goa would be an industry. This meant that all future hotels would receive a 25 per cent subsidy and land for hotels could be purchased on a compulsory basis. Five days later a tourism 'master plan' was announced and presented to local people as *fait accompli*. The people most affected, such as the 80 000 strong fishing community, were not consulted. But so incensed were local people about the plan that a protest group, the *Jagrut Goenkaranchi Fauz* (Vigilant Goans' Army), was formed and successfully mobilized opposition. Flights from abroad were met by black flags and banners, urging the tourists to go back home; they were handed leaflets which explained why they were not welcome in Goa. In the face of persistent opposition, the state government dropped its master plan in 1988, although it continued to sanction new hotels.

The development of tourism is unlikely to be 'neutral'; it often involves developing land from which someone has been making a living. Tourism in Goa has led to considerable displacement of local people, often with no compensation; the state's coastline is 105 km (65 miles) long, of which 70 km (43 miles) is beach from which local fishermen have launched their boats for centuries. Many fishermen have had to find other launching sites, an often difficult process. Catches have also suffered from the development of new water sports. Water skiing and high-powered engines are enough to persuade fish go elsewhere.

Small farmers, displaced from their near-shore land to make way for hotels, and also farmers further away from the immediate tourist site and not directly displaced by the new hotels, have been affected by severe water shortages. 'Less than a quarter of a mile from a luxury hotel in Goa, a village's water supply was restricted to an hour a day so that there would be enough water for tourists to use 55 gallons every day', says Roland Martins, secretary of the Vigilant Goans' Army.[25] When local people suffer because of demands of this nature, then tourism appears to be rampant colonialism at its worst.

While jobs for local people are available in the new luxury hotels, few financial benefits seem to be filtering down to local people. The jobs are a mixed blessing. Goans who once had a independent economic activity have become hotel servants to pander to the needs of wealthy tourists. Against their will, their independence has gone. 'Many local people feel that government subsidies could have been better spent on improving the local infrastructure, schools and health facilities and by supporting local industry,' believes Martins. Economic linkages seem to have generally been weak; the growth of tourism has done little to stimulate the development of other local economic sectors.

Local protest was successful in slowing down, though not stopping, the development of Goa, and shows that local people are not without power. Concern among people about the damage that tourism can cause appears to be little shared by Third World governments. Although community groups churches, NGOs and others have presented well-researched evidence pointing to the downside of tourism, their views have been largely brushed aside, even hushed up, in order not to deter the would-be tourist. Many governments are determined to see further expansion; the international debt crisis has made them desperate for foreign exchange no matter what the disadvantages.

## Doubtful benefit

Deals of highly doubtful benefit are beginning to emerge. While most countries oblige foreign companies to co-operate with local interests in new tourist complexes, foreign companies have been allowed, for example, to invest in the Mexican tourist industry since 1989 without being obliged to set up joint ventures with Mexican partners. In 1990 Egypt sold 18 of its most celebrated hotels to British, American and French companies. India offers investors the chance to build hotels with low-interest loans for up to 20 years.

Environments are also taking the strain. From all over the developing world there are reports of quite serious environmental damage caused by tourism. Trekkers in Nepal are causing erosion of the fragile mountain paths in the Himalayas; trees have to be cut down for fuel to cook the trekkers an evening meal and provide them with a hot shower. Hotel chains in Mexico have burnt down parts of the forests in order to construct new complexes for tourists. Some of East Africa's game parks have been turned into dust bowls by tourists' vehicles. Indonesia's head of tourism planning has warned that traditional life on the island of Bali is threatened by environmental damage caused by investment in tourism. In Ladakh, Kashmir, tourism is reported to have led to the complete disruption of the local economy and culture. Hotels have mushroomed, overloading the fragile ecology of Lak town.

The key questions about tourism concern how its worst effects can be overcome, and how it can become a more balanced, just and sustainable activity. 'If tourism is to be based on equal terms with Third World countries', asserts Lorine Tevi, 'it has to take seriously the basic philosophy of life there, which is to approach and live life in its wholeness and fullness – it is this on which village life is based'.[26] Some countries are trying to develop tourism in a way that overcomes its negative impact. In Zimbabwe, for example, the National Parks Authorities are involving local communities in the task of working out strategies for park management. In Senegal and Sri Lanka, 'alternative' tourism is now on offer, with visitors staying with local people rather than in hotels. Costa Rica is trying to develop small-scale 'ecotourism'; a think-tank has been created, comprising representatives of the tourist industry, government officials and environmentalists. Ecuador, Dominica and the US Virgin Islands are also developing ecotourism.

In the early 1990s, debate was growing about 'sustainable tourism development'. Writing in the Spring 1991 issue of the magazine *Tourism Concern*, Edward Niles of Grenada said that several major steps must be taken if this is to be achieved. A way of measuring GNP is needed that takes into consideration environmental and social costs. The correct economic values must be given to tourism resources. An environmental assessment must be made of planned tourism projects. Tourism should also be part of an integrated development plan. But 'the key ingredient' for sustainable tourism development, stresses Niles, is that everyone should participate in the 'planning, implementation and maintenance of plans that profoundly affect their lives' – and institutions are needed to enable them to do this.[27]

Tourism is notoriously unreliable as a foreign exchange earner. The tastes of holidaymakers can change rapidly – a holiday spot they like this year may be out of fashion next year. There are signs that tourism in Hawaii is declining as tourists weary of fighting for a place on the beaches and paying exorbitant prices in souvenir shops. A tourist location depends on satisfied customers. If people like a resort, they are likely to say so – but if they do not like it, they may be even more vocal. Information is all-important; 'countries wishing to expand their foreign exchange and income generation from this sector (tourism) will have to take into account the problems and opportunities arising from the increasing independence of the world tourism industry on the flow of information'.[28]

A more just international economic order that allows developing countries to earn more from other economic activities and to have the power to stand up to the world tourism industry would help them to overcome tourism's damaging effects. At the national level, it is Third World governments that have the responsibility to ensure that tourism is balanced, attracting people from abroad in a way that can be sustained, but not in such numbers as to damage local peoples, cultures and the environment. Governments who put too many eggs in the tourist basket could end up with egg on their faces. The South has a future on tourism, if the beauty that attracts the tourist is retained, and if the negative effects on local people can be offset. Otherwise, popular local feeling could make life for the tourist a little uncomfortable.

# 6 Transnationals: agents of trade

Transnational corporations (TNCs), large companies with subsidiaries in different countries, have a considerable impact on the economies, trade and people of developing countries. TNCs are a powerful adjunct of industrialized countries and powerful agents of world trade. They employ about 65 million people worldwide, 43 million at their head offices, 15 million in subsidiaries in other industrialized countries and seven million in developing countries. What is also known is that they are becoming ever larger actors on the world stage. TNCs increased investments outside their home countries by 29 per cent *a year* between 1983 and 1989, with the United States, Japanese and European companies especially dominant investors.[1]

The effects of TNCs (also referred to as multinational corporations) on Third World economies are extraordinarily difficult to measure. In the continuing debate over their impact, Third World governments usually give them warm support, and NGOs are often fiercely critical, especially those in the South who see the corporations at work. A Malaysian NGO report speaks, for example, of the rural poor of many Third World nations faring disastrously 'because of the evil impact of TNCs'.[2] In probably no other area of development is there a bigger gap between governmental and NGO thinking than over the value or otherwise of these mammoth corporations.

For governments, the attractions of TNCs are clear – the companies have money and skills to help development and trade efforts, especially to earn additional foreign exchange and create jobs. The 'veneer' seems good. But when that veneer is stripped away, a quite disturbing picture emerges in which NGO criticisms are often justified; a picture of companies dealing in trickery and treachery, operating undemocratically with little or no government control, no effective responsibility to developing countries and peoples, and leaving few, if any, long-term benefits through their presence or activities.

TNCs control 'between a quarter and a third of all world production and are particularly active in processing and marketing', says the Brandt Report; 'the marketing, processing or production of several commodities – including bauxite, copper, iron ore, nickel, lead, zinc, tin, tobacco, bananas and tea – is dominated in each case by a small number of transnational corporations'.[3] The overall extent of their activities is higher still. In 1985, 40 per cent of imports into the United States and 31 per cent of US exports were associated with TNCs.[4] One estimate suggests that the biggest 500 TNCs 'control about 70 per cent of world trade, 80 per cent of foreign investment and about 30 per cent of world GDP'.[5]

Many TNCs are larger than some of the developing countries where they operate. The largest 56 TNCs have sales ranging from $10 billion to $100 billion a year, while the biggest each have a larger turnover than the national income of most developing countries. It is size that makes for an unequal relationship between government and corporation, the latter often holding most of the cards and usually getting the best out of a deal. 'The activities of some transnational enterprises have caused suspicion and doubt in the developing countries. The size and character of these enterprises in relation to many national economies are a source of considerable uncertainty for developing countries in negotiations with them', says a Commonwealth Experts Group. It goes on to say that TNCs 'can have a positive role to play in the industrialization process in the developing countries, because of their command over finance, technology and access to markets, and their capacity to plan, establish and manage complex operations'.[6]

But there are doubts over whether TNCs can play a positive role in the trade and development efforts of poorer countries, unless they can be subject to more effective control. Yet control could be undermined by the trade-related investment measures that are proposed under the Uruguay Round of GATT (see Chapter 9). While some of the problems that hold back developing countries from increasing their exports of manufactured goods (considered in Chapter 4) could be overcome if TNCs brought in finance and skills, there remains a major question mark over the appropriateness of the usually large-scale technology these companies like to introduce. The experience of three 'development decades' shows that such technology has little relevance to the needs of the Third World poor, although it may help their government ministers and wealthier urban dwellers. The problem is that many governments still believe that 'big is best' and set out their stall to attract the TNCs with their 'advanced' technology.

When Western-based TNCs invest in the economies of other industrialized countries they do so because they believe they can run profitable operations in those countries. The 1980s witnessed a fast growth in such investment, as noted above, with the United States, Japan and the EC stepping up investments in each other's countries, rather than in developing countries. According to a World Bank report, the years since 1985 have seen a marked decline in the share of foreign direct investment going into developing countries; their share of direct investment dropped from over 30 per cent in 1967 to around 25 per cent in the 1980s. Of the investment going to the Third World, 86 per cent went to 18 countries.[7]

The developing world holds many attractions for TNCs. Mining firms want to be located where minerals are to be found, and companies which produce consumer goods are attracted by the low rates of pay that prevail in most Third World economies, also by the frequent absence of organized labour unions. The government of a developing country may offer to exempt the firm from paying tax for the first five or even 10 years of its operation. TNCs are more likely to invest in countries where the government appears stable, and have concentrated their investment in less than 20 developing countries, often because the governments of those countries were authoritarian and judged to be reliable 'client' states.

A sizeable proportion of the international trade conducted by TNCs takes place within their own organization – a subsidiary in one country selling to and/or buying from a subsidiary in another, or the head office. According to one estimate this 'intra-firm' trade makes up 30 per cent of all world trade.[8]

By having subsidiary companies TNCs are able to make use of a mechanism known as transfer pricing, which operates to the detriment of developing countries. Under transfer pricing, the parent TNC sells materials to its subsidiaries in developing countries at artificially high prices. Such materials are then used in a manufacturing process or service industy. Having to pay these high prices reduces the profits of the subsidiary company, and means they pay less tax in the developing country where they operate – which is therefore cheated out of tax revenues. The difference between the declared profit of a TNC subsidiary and its real profit can be considerable. In Colombia, for example, the overcharging of drugs by foreign-owned drug companies meant that TNC subsidiaries reported a six per cent profit to the Colombian government. The real profit was estimated to be 79 per cent.[9] While the extent of transfer pricing is unknown – TNCs are unlikely to give details of it in their balance sheets, and observers find difficulty obtaining evidence – the practice is probably widespread.

In addition to tax avoidance, a further reason why TNCs use transfer pricing is that profits are often difficult to take out of a developing country – which naturally hopes they will be reinvested. However, with the liberalization of trade, there has been some relaxation of previous restrictions on financial flows, which could lessen the incidence of transfer pricing.

### Investment

The money that TNCs invest in Third World economies seems welcome – but the question is whether it results in a net gain. The money the firms invest is often *not* their own. To make investments they might borrow heavily from banks in developing countries; this reduces the amount of money that the banks have to lend to smaller businesses in their country. Can the TNCs be relied on to stay in a country? Economist Donald Hay points out that TNCs are naturally more concerned about their own profit than they are with the welfare of a host country. This sometimes results in shutting down an entire operation, an action which could have a devastating impact.[10]

Nervousness among developing country governments about the activities of TNCs caused a brisk period of expropriation of their assets in the late 1960s and early 1970s, causing the climate for them to become distinctly murky. Governments of developing countries believed that by nationalizing TNCs they could expropriate for themselves

**Table 5    Expropriation acts by year**

| Year | Number of acts | No. of countries expropriating |
|------|----------------|-------------------------------|
| 1968 | 13 | 8 |
| 1969 | 24 | 14 |
| 1970 | 48 | 18 |
| 1971 | 51 | 20 |
| 1972 | 56 | 30 |
| 1973 | 30 | 20 |
| 1974 | 68 | 29 |
| 1975 | 83 | 28 |
| 1976 | 40 | 14 |
| 1977 | 15 | 13 |
| 1978 | 15 | 8 |
| 1979 | 17 | 13 |
| 1980 | 5 | 5 |
| 1981 | 4 | 2 |
| 1982 | 1 | 1 |

Source: UNCTC Reporter, No. 25.

the profits that were going to the TNCs. But the expropriation period was short-lived. Table 5 reveals the rise and fall of expropriation.

The dramatic fall seems to have occurred chiefly because governments realized that it was one thing to take over a factory, quite another to run it profitably. TNCs are skilled at operating an economic activity at a profit – they would not stay in business otherwise. Governments quickly realized that they could not run the often quite complex, usually Western-style type of TNC operation with the same degree of profitability. The hoped-for gains from expropriation frequently failed to materialize, and nationalization of TNCs was dropped as the answer to the problem; expropriation continues to be a largely abandoned approach.

But developing countries' governments also continue to be in a dilemma. Governments of debt-burdened countries tend to welcome any investment in their country. The deeper problems of TNC activity are often not considered alongside the more pressing economic need to step up activity that will bring in foreign exchange. A further problem for governments is that TNCs are powerful, often have considerable knowledge of the situation 'on the ground' and can pull the wool over the eyes of a government, who may even end up defending TNCs who are cheating them.

One reason why developing countries try to attract TNCs is to create jobs; as discussed in Chapter 4, many exporting processing zones have been set up partly with this aim. Yet according to an International Labour Office report, the role of TNCs in job creation is 'at best marginal'. It says that if TNC employment is growing at all, it is 'due to acquisitions and mergers rather than to new employment opportunities.[11]

## Code of conduct

The United Nations Center on Transnational Corporations (UNCTC) was set up in 1974 to serve as the UN Secretariat's focal point on matters related to TNCs. Its stated objectives are 'to advance understanding of transnational corporations, to secure effective international agreements relating to their activities, and to strengthen the negotiating capacity of host countries, in particular the developing countries'.[12] One of its main tasks has been to draw up a draft Code of Conduct on TNCs. Despite over 15 years of work, however, by 1992 a code had still not come into effect, and the centre had been down-graded and renamed The Transnational Corporations and Management Division (TCMD). This renamed body ceased to be a separate United Nations body and became part of the UN's new Department of Economic and Social Development.

The code of conduct is supposed to 'establish standards for the conduct of TNCs from all countries to protect the interests of host countries, strengthen their negotiating capacity and ensure conformity of the operations of TNCs with national development objectives'. It is also there to 'set standards for the treatment of TNCs by countries to protect the legitimate interests of investors . . . and create a climate for foreign direct investment which is beneficial to all parties in the investment relationship'.[13]

As far as developing countries are concerned, the chief point of a code would be to pinpoint the responsibilities of TNCs to their economies, peoples and environments. But this aspect of a code has received far less attention in the discussions than the issue of how governments of developing countries treat the companies. 'Since 1981, the negotiations on a draft code of conduct for TNCs focused mainly on the provisions dealing with the treatment of these firms by Governments', says an ECOSOC report.[14]

Whereas Western countries urged in the negotiations that developing countries should encourage TNCs and protect their investments, developing countries stressed the need for companies to adhere to the development objectives. When, in the late 1980s, a growing number of developing countries removed barriers to trade and began to offer guarantees protecting TNC investments, so Western countries, very probably influenced by their TNCs, began to lose interest in the code. Yet the need for a code of conduct remains. The same ECOSOC report says, 'The changes that have taken place in recent years . . . increase the need for an international framework for transnational corporations'.[15] A framework in which TNCs agree to keep to certain standards in developing countries seems a long way off. Such is the power of modern-day TNCs that they have successfully influenced the UNCTC agenda and set the pace over the code of conduct. The centre has effectively been turned into a centre *for* rather than *on* TNCs.

Behind the slowness of the centre to finalize a code on conduct, and its downgrading in 1992, lies the very deep influence that TNCs have in the United Nations system. In 1978 a Swiss-based organization, *Association pour un Developpement Solidaire*, published excerpts from internal files which showed how TNCs operate in the UN system. The files show that the corporations have succeeded in 'subversively infiltrating the UN and its agencies and neutralizing them as a potentially countervailing force, or even utilizing them for the corporation's own purposes'.[16] The excerpts show the delaying tactics that TNCs have used over codes of conduct and their strict rejection of any control mechanism – including an independent control body for the code – which means its impact would inevitably be weakened. The policies of Western governments over the negotiations of a code of conduct have been profoundly influenced by the TNCs. It is the companies, not the governments, who are making the running.

All too often the publications of the UNCTC sound like a public relations exercise for the companies. Its 1988 report refers to the companies as a major force for the growing integration of the world economy, through direct investment, franchising, joint ventures and sub-contracting.[17] Perhaps the most disturbing aspect is the way that the TNCs have influenced the wider United Nations organization. The September/October 1991 issue of the UN newspaper *Development Forum*, for example, carries an adulatory, unsigned article, 'Transnationals lead the way'. It begins by saying foreign investment is becoming 'a central determinant of economic growth and competitiveness . . . transnational corporations have, through a host of equity and contractual arrangements, eased the way for developing country firms to enter world markets . . . are also the prime generators of new technology and the leading channel of global technology transfer to developing countries'.[18]

The article gave the impression that it could have been written by a public relations firm of a TNC. It contained not a hint about the downside of such activity. As the article appeared in a UN paper with worldwide circulation, it appeared to show the deep infiltration of the United Nations system by TNCs.

What the UNCTC has done is to highlight the poor record of TNCs on environmental issues. A survey that examined the environmental practices of over 200 of the world's biggest and most 'environmentally innovative' TNCs found that less than half of the firms co-ordinated their environmental policies internationally or published a formal international environmental policy. While the corporations gave importance to such headline issues as atmospheric protection, toxic wastes and freshwater protection, issues such as biodiversity and urban and rural poverty are not yet high on the corporate agenda. Over half the respondents did not utilize any international guidelines in their policy development; many firms were unaware of the nature or existence of particular international guidelines. More often than not, corporate headquarters lacked basic information about the firms' environmental activities. A majority of the responding TNCs are disposing waste outside the country of origin.

While TNC managers are seeking more control over the handling of environmental, health and safety issues in their own countries, they are tending to overlook enforcement in developing countries. Less than a quarter monitor air emissions in developing countries. One third do not know whether their plants in these countries are located near freshwater supplies. In a number of cases, headquarters are not aware whether any formal mechanism exists to monitor affiliates in developing countries.[19] (See also Chapter 7.)

## TNCs in agriculture

TNCs are involved in a wide range of economic activities – mining, manufacturing, banking, transport, road building, energy, power supply – but are often most visible and controversial when engaged in the most basic industry, agriculture. They supply seeds and inputs for farmers, grow crops, give advice, and are engaged in processing and marketing,

The widespread nationalization of foreign companies in the 1970s included many of the large-scale plantations growing export crops. In the late 1980s a number of developing country governments invited foreign investors back into their country, often on a joint-venture basis, but the era of large-scale TNC ownership of Third World land seems to be over, although it still persists in some countries. Consultancy is now more common, with TNCs selling services which might include advice on seeds, hybrid crop varieties and management practice. But the corporations continue to dominate world markets in internationally traded agricultural commodities. Fifteen TNCs control between 85 and 90 per cent of world traded cotton; eight TNCs account for between 55 and 60 per cent of world coffee sales, seven account for 90 per cent of the tea consumed in Western countries, while six firms buy 90 per cent of tobacco leaf.

The TNCs might buy crops for export from commodity marketing boards, or enter into contractual arrangements with farmers. In Kenya, for example, a subsidiary company of the giant BAT group has a contractual arrangement with around 10000 small farmers to buy their tobacco. This activity is not untypical of a TNC contractual arrangement with growers of export crops. The company provides farmers with a package deal that includes seeds, fertilizers, pesticides, and technical advice. Farmers have to 'cure' the leaf – dry it out – before selling to the company. The price the farmers receive for the leaf is totally dependent on the company's evaluation of its quality, and ranges from around 25 pence to £1 a kilo. The return is both uncertain and low, although farmers have the advantage that the company pays quickly, which is not always the case with state purchasing bodies. But the farmers are nonetheless 'price takers'. They are powerless to do anything about the prices the company offers, they have no option but to take it or leave it. BAT (Kenya) Ltd has a monopoly in Kenya over the purchase of tobacco and the production of cigarettes, and the farmers have no other outlets.

To grow tobacco for BAT, a farmer is supposed to plant 1000 eucalyptus trees a year in order to have enough trees to feed into his or her curing barn, which makes heavy demands on timber. As not all farmers grow the trees they need, they are forced to either buy or chop down trees from elsewhere, all of which does nothing to help the local environment.

BAT's monopoly position in Kenya puts the firm in a powerful position. When I enquired in 1982, for example, at the country's Ministry of Health about how many farmers had suffered poisoning because of the pesticide BAT then recommended its farmers to use, dieldrin (already banned in most countries as too hazardous for use), I was told 'ask the company; we don't keep figures like that'. An article I wrote about the trees being felled in Kenya for the curing barns was attacked in the Kenyan parliament as an afront to the government rather than the company – an example of a government siding with a TNC whose activities caused environmental damage, but which was too powerful to stand up to.

Barbara Dinham of the Pesticides Trust points out that 'TNCs need a regular and reliable supply of good quality raw material to feed into the markets, preferably enough of an over-supply to keep prices of the raw materials low'.[20] By their demand for export crops, TNCs effectively encourage farmers to keep on growing them. But over-supply and low prices mean that often they make only a bare return. The best route for commodity-producing countries would be to band together, reduce output and win higher world prices (see Chapter 11). But TNCs are hardly likely to encourage them in this – lower commodity prices are better for company profits.

One of the most concentrated areas of TNC activity in agriculture is in seeds. From the dawn of agriculture until the present day, farmers have had to produce and save seeds for sowing the next season. This necessity contributed to the development of genetic diversity and resulted in varieties remarkably well adapted to very specific conditions. In the late twentieth century, especially in the wake of the 'Green Revolution' of the 1960s, the TNCs moved into the seeds business in a breathtaking way. The reason for their interest lies in the possibility of developing and establishing patents over, for example, higher-yielding seeds, for which farmers must pay – there are even instances of TNCs taking out patents on seeds which are already naturally present in a Third World region.

Farmers need new seed from time to time if genetic diversity and crop yields are to be maintained. The Irish potato famine of the 1840s occurred because existing varieties had become tired and there was no breeding of new varieties. Of the 75 types of vegetables available during the early twentieth century, some 97 per cent of the varieties of each type are now extinct.[21] Many governments in the Third World have neglected investments in national seed research, development and production and have left the door open for the TNCs. Today seeds are a $13 billion-a-year business and plant breeding is a corporate activity. As government involvement in plant breeding has declined, so the giant petrochemical and drug companies have moved in to acquire hundreds of once family-owned seed companies in the Third World.

Among the largest seed companies are Royal Dutch/Shell, Ciba-Geigy and Sandoz of Switzerland; Atlantic Richfield, Upjohn, Occidental Petroleum, Pfizer, and ITT of the United States; Lafarge Coppée, Elf Aquitaine and Rhône Poulenc of France; Volvo and KemaNobel of Sweden; and Dalgetty and British Petroleum of Britain. A number of these are also among the world's largest chemical companies. TNCs have become involved in the seed business because it is highly profitable. Distribution channels are identical to those of their crop chemicals, and there is the possibility of linking chemical and seed development and marketing. This is perhaps the most ominous development of all – the type of seed sown can determine the farmer's need for fertilizer and pesticides. Ciba-Geigy, for example, markets its own brand of sorghum seed which comes wrapped in three chemicals; the integration of these technologies into one marketing package allows the company to sell more seed and chemicals.

The TNCs have therefore come to dominate the commercial seed market especially in countries where laws give corporations patent-like control over new varieties they develop. Often called 'Plant Breeders Rights', these laws allow corporations to own plant varieties and set the sale conditions for them. This has meant that the few companies big enough to have fully-fledged plant-breeding programmes obtain most of the patents, locking up the market on new seed varieties.

Furthermore, these same companies often cease to offer traditional varieties because no patent-like control can be obtained over varieties that pre-date the laws, with the result that many traditional varieties fall out of use.

The extension of patenting laws to the Third World (see Chapter 9 on GATT) means that companies can control and market crop varieties in countries which had donated the genetic material used to breed those varieties. Germplasm donated by the South to the gene banks of the North has made a sizeable contribution to plant breeding in the North. But while the contribution of wild species to the economies of the North is substantial, the South has rarely received royalties, and has been effectively cheated out of valuable resources.

Increased imports of patented varieties to centres of crop diversity in the Third World would result in the wholesale replacement and extinction of traditional varieties. Communities are therefore in danger of becoming dependent on outside sources of seeds and the chemicals needed to grow and protect them. The loss of traditional qualities such as drought resistance can cause real hardship for farmers because seeds bred for large farmers in industrialized countries are rarely bred for such resistance. Self-reliance in agriculture thereby becomes harder for poorer communities. Saving agriculture's genetic diversity does not guarantee self-reliance or development, but losing this diversity reduces options and fosters dependency.

The advent of biotechnology and genetic engineering pose an additional threat. Again TNCs are highly prominent. While biotechnology holds out the promise of large increases in crop yields – as high as 500 per cent for some crops, such as coconut, oil palm and cassava – such developments will alter the structure of these industries, affecting supplies, price, the need for labour and land. Breakthroughs in one crop could affect the fate of other, similar crops, possibly making them more vulnerable to genetic uniformity.[22]

## Forests

Tropical rainforests are being degraded at the annual rate of 17 million hectares, according the UN Food and Agriculture Organization. Forests can be likened to a wet sponge, releasing water slowly to the surrounding land. With deforestation a natural regulator is lost and flooding and drought both become more likely. Food output is therefore put at risk in surrounding areas. The causes of deforestation are many, but one of them is the axing of forests by logging companies in order to sell timber to the West; TNCs play a major role in this production and trade.

Japan is responsible for a great deal of the destruction in neighbouring Asian countries. In order to leave its own forests standing, Japan has systematically purchased the forests of others, and its companies have been the agents who reaped the reward. Since 1945, Japanese companies have logged and brought back to Japan a large slice of the forest of the Philippines. Whereas the Philippines used to have 17 million hectares of tropical forest, by 1989 this was down to only *one million.* Japanese firms are also involved in logging in Indonesia and Malaysia, with the TNCs Mitsubishi, Mitsui, C.Itoh and Sumitomo active in the trade. The Philippines now has one of the most severe deforestation problems of any developing country.

In Africa there are large-scale European interests in Cameroon, the Central African Republic, Congo, Gabon, Ivory Coast, Liberia and Zaire, with French companies particularly active. France's Rougier group of companies have interests in Cameroon, such as the *Société Forestière et Industrielle de la Doume* (SFID); in Gabon, through Rougier-Gabon and the *Société des Bois Deroules-Gabon,* as well as subsidiaries such as SADER and Ets Rayer, involved in peeling and plywood manufacture; and in Central Africa through the *Société Centrafricaine de Deroulage.*[23]

While no British companies are involved in logging tropical timber, UK companies are involved in transporting and importing timber. In late 1991 it was reported that Britain's largest timber firm had been importing wood from the Philippines, which banned log exports in 1989. Illegal exports still take place and, as Britain has not imposed an import ban, these find their way into Britain via the TNC Meyer International. The company was reported to be selling Philippines mahogany, lauan, in some of its 200 builders merchants shops.[24]

The NGO, Friends of the Earth (FOE–UK), has documented how British, German and Dutch companies tricked one of Africa's poorest countries, Ghana, out of £30 million revenue from its forests. A report issued in March 1992

revealed widespread fraud, corruption and other illegal practices by TNCs operating in Ghana which plundered 250
square kilometres of its rainforest. The Ghanaian authorities
found that the TNCs used a number of methods to export
timber illicitly at less than its value, and effectively pocket the
difference.

Some 'corrupt agents' were used, alleges the FOE report,
to make false declarations about the value of the timber
being shipped. The agents would submit prices to a government bureau that were lower than the prices the timber
would fetch on world markets. Timber exported was sometimes of a higher grade than that declared to the Ghanaian
authorities, the report alleges. In both cases, the exporting
firms would then get the higher price, the government the
lower price. The report also alleges that companies imported
machinery and professional services and invoiced the government for more than these had cost. By these and other
methods, says the report, Ghana was cheated out of the real
value of its timber exports, losing around £30 million. In the
late 1980s the government granted an amnesty for companies to return money; by the end of 1990, 106 firms and
individuals had voluntarily paid back a total of £6.6 million,
just over a fifth of the money lost.[25] In the meantime,
Ghana's forest was being plundered.

If trees being felled were replaced by new ones, then the
international trade in logs might not cause such harm to the
environment. But this is hardly the case. 'Perhaps the most
damning indictment of Europe's involvement in tropical forestry is that, as far as can be established', say Nectoux and
Dudley in a study for FOE, 'none of these operations . . . are
managed on a sustainable basis'.[26] Basic ecological considerations are not taken into account.

There is evidence that the need to earn more foreign exchange is encouraging governments to consider schemes to
log forests in an unsustainable manner. In late 1991, for
example, the government of Honduras considered entering
into a contract with a US pulp and paper manufacturer, the
Stone Container Corporation, which would have given the
company control of up to 1.6 million hectares of tropical
forest – one seventh of the country's land area. It was appar-
ently intended that timber should be chipped and exported
for conversion into paper products all over the world. 'Ab-
sent from the agreement are any requirements for Stone to

produce environmental impact studies or reforest logged-over areas', reports Oliver Tickell[27].

The agreement could have brought an extra $20 million a year in foreign exchange to Honduras, but the environmental cost, in terms of a huge degraded land area, could have been higher. Such costs were publicized by environmentalists and, after sustained domestic protest, the government pulled out of the deal, fearing that its popularity was at stake; elections were beginning to loom. The case was an example of how, in a democratic society, local protest can thwart the power of TNCs.

## Discrediting critics

TNCs have their critics; they also have carefully thought-out strategies about how to deal with them. Public health specialist, Andrew Chetley, recalls how in the early 1970s the United Nations set up a Committee of Eminent Persons to enquire into the high profits of the pharmaceutical and chemical companies:

'A small subcommittee of at least six Swiss companies (including Ciba-Geigy, Sandoz and Roche) was established to weaken the impact of the enquiry and avoid the introduction of an international code of conduct for TNCs. During one meeting the companies outlined a five-point strategy for dealing with critics:

1. The critic is identified as an opponent of the system and thus discredited as a discussion partner.
2. Dubious motives are attributed to the critic: ideological or nationalistic prejudices, envy, stupidity, ignorance and lack of experience.
3. When criticism is global or circumstantial: the contrary is 'proved' by means of isolated instances (e.g. description of an individual project).
4. When criticism is indisputable (e.g. in the case of ITT in Chile): emphasis is put on the fact that it is an individual case, moreover it is still under investigation.
5. In any case, it should be said in public that defending free enterprise was in everybody's interest. Therefore, it should be shown, especially in the mass media, that criticism of multinationals was basically criticism of free enterprise and that behind it were the enemies of the free world, whose view of life was based on Marxism'.[28]

TNCs are considered 'good' by some, 'bad' by others. A wider consensus might be that they are powerful, secretive and unaccountable, and that their size often dwarfs the countries where they operate. At least for some economic functions, the corporations are considered by Third World governments to be necessary. The question is, what are these functions and are they beneficial to development? Sometimes the answer could be 'yes', that the expertise of TNCs is preferable to alternatives, such as parastatal involvement, but only providing that the companies involved are not exploiting the country. To stay in business, TNCs have to perform trading activities profitably, but to benefit the country they must be willing to perform them responsibly. In other cases, the answer is 'no'; TNCs have introduced much of the inappropriate technology that is now all too widespread in the developing world. By the early 1990s the corporations were increasingly being seen as key agents for transferring technology to developing countries.

It is their claim, frequently unchallenged, to have the technology the Third World needs that is one of the most disturbing aspects of their work. TNCs are experts in the kind of technology that works in Western countries, but it is all too often totally inappropriate for the needs of the developing world. Alternative ways of transferring technology from North to South – through intermediate technology development institutes, for example – therefore emerges as vital if real needs in the South are to be met. If a developing country wants to run a high-tech activity, it may then need TNCs, and will have to grapple with how to control them or risk losing out.

To exercise more control over TNC activities and encourage them to be more responsible, Third World governments should consider employing a small number of people who have recently worked for TNCs and who know the tricks of their trade. TNCs are often experts at getting around rules and regulations they are supposed to keep to; only insiders know the game well enough to match them. There may be a role for *responsible* TNCs, but there is an urgent need for their activities to be more open, democratic and accountable to people in developing countries as well as to shareholders in the North. Greater openness and accountability would mean that the worst aspects of their operations would at least be open to the possibility of change. The United Nations system does not have the power to enforce such improvements. Control of TNC activity is ultimately up to governments, who are more likely to exercise effective control and win the battle to make the corporations more accountable if they act together. South–South co-operation on the issue would help to bring these powerful agents of world trade to account.

# 7 Transnationals: agents of death?

Many of the goods and services that countries of the South buy from the North have the potential to assist in economic and social development efforts. Oil, agricultural equipment, and banking services for example, can help towards the smoother running of economies. But some exports from the North are controversial to the point of death. Overwhelmingly they are exported by TNCs; chief among them are pesticides, drugs, breast milk substitutes, and dirty products and industries.[1]

## Pesticides

Chemical pesticides have a 'double connection' with international trade. Firstly, many are exported by Western-based TNCs although some are produced in factories in the Third World by subsidiaries of TNCs, set up by means of foreign investment. Secondly, pesticides are purchased largely to apply to crops that are grown in the Third World for export. Farmers hope that by using pesticides they will keep pests at bay and achieve the best possible harvest. But pests often become resistant to pesticides, and farmers may react by spraying higher quantities, eating into farm profits without necessarily controlling the pests, and perhaps poisoning and even killing themselves; the World Health Organization (WHO) estimates that three million people a year suffer acute pesticide poisoning.[2] Around 25 million agricultural workers in developing countries suffer from occupational pesticide poisoning each year.[3]

Information about the hazards of pesticides is often unavailable to the people who apply them and who are most at risk. In practice, they are mostly women; in Malaysia, for example, 95 per cent of the pesticide appliers on plantations are women who are often less protected and less well trained than men.

Pesticides are often a great deal more difficult to handle in Third World countries than in the West. Labels on cans may not be understood, soap and water may not be available to wash chemicals off the skin after an accidental spillage, protective clothing may be too expensive or too warm to wear. Ironically, the chemical pesticides that are sprayed on crops can encourage rather than kill pests, as they may kill the beneficial insects, ladybirds for instance, that eat the destructive insects, thus affecting nature's way of control. Pesticides also cause damage to the environment, by running off into rivers and reservoirs, contaminating drinking water and fish.

As subsidies to farmers in Western nations are being lowered, so sales of pesticides in the West are falling; in Britain they fell by 4.5 per cent in 1990.[4] TNC pesticide manufacturers have increasingly looked to the Third World as an outlet for their products. A WorldWatch paper, published in 1987, showed that between 1972 and 1985 imports of pesticide into Asia increased by 261 per cent, into Africa by 95 per cent, and into Latin America by 48 per cent.[5]

In 1981, two American writers, David Weir and Mark Schapiro, documented what they described as a

'scandal of global proportions – the export of banned pesticides from the industrial countries to the Third World. Massive advertising campaigns by multinational pesticide corporations – Dow, Shell, Chevron – have turned the Third World into not only a booming growth market for pesticides, but also a dumping ground. Dozens of pesticides too dangerous for use in the United States are shipped to underdeveloped countries. There, lack of regulation, illiteracy and repressive working conditions can turn even a 'safe' pesticide into a deadly weapon'.[6]

Their book, together with an Oxfam publication the following year, set in motion one of the most successful NGO campaigns of the 1980s – to end the export or donation to the Third World of pesticides which had been banned in the West.[7]

Voluntary groups from 16 countries who were concerned about pesticides formed the Pesticides Action Network (PAN), and in 1985 launched a campaign to ban the manufacture, sale, use or trade of the so-called 'Dirty Dozen' – considered to be the world's most dangerous pesticides – camphechlor, chlordane heptachlor, chlordimeform, DBCP, DDT, the drins (aldrin, dieldrin and endrin), EDB, HCH/

lindane, ethyl parathion, paraquat, pentachlorophenol, and 2,4,5-T. These were selected for their toxicity and the health problems they posed. In 1985 most of them were either banned or severely restricted in Western countries but were being exported to the Third World by agrochemical companies. As the chemicals were used mostly on export crops, some of them eventually returned as residues in foods; a 'circle of poison' was therefore drawn.

Mounting concern about dangerous pesticides led the UN Food and Agriculture Organization (FAO) to develop the Code for Safe Pesticide Use in the Third World, which was adopted in 1985. PAN successfully campaigned for a Prior Informed Consent clause to be included in the Code, whereby importing countries would be notified of intended exports of hazardous products and have the right to refuse them. This clause was included in the Code in 1989. The Code is voluntary, 'although all the major agrochemical companies subscribe, and would be acutely embarrassed if they were found to be exporting products which governments had rejected'.[8]

The onus is therefore on Third World governments to prevent pesticides which they consider dangerous from coming into their country. Indonesia was one of the first countries to take action against imports, banning a total of 57 pesticides in 1987. Violations of the Code of conduct do, however, occur. In May 1991, for example, the Swiss chemical company, Ciba-Geigy, was reported to have admitted selling a pesticide containing DDT to Tanzania in violation of the Code. A Ciba-Geigy spokesperson said that the company 'made a mistake' in delivering 450000 litres of a product, called Ultracide combi, to Tanzania's cotton-marketing board.[9]

Around a quarter of all pesticides are applied to cotton. Cotton pests have shown great ingenuity in becoming resistant to chemicals, with the result that farmers, in desperation, have sprayed increasing amounts. But the spraying often has little effect, other than to increase farmers' costs and reduce their profits, and many cotton farmers have turned to integrated pest management. This uses a combination of traditional practices such as biological control, making herbicides from plant extracts, composting and inter-cropping, alongside chemicals, to keep pests at bay.

While the export of dangerous pesticide products from the West to the Third World appeared to have slowed in the early 1990s compared with the start of the 1980s, Barbara Dinham warns that transnational chemical companies are trying to overcome this by building factories in developing countries enabling them make locally the chemicals that they are no longer allowed to export. 'In Asia, foreign corporations have co-operated with local companies to establish joint ventures. But the initial rush into South America has cooled, and some corporations are pulling out', she says; nonetheless 'investment in chemical plants in the South is likely to continue increasing.'[10] She notes that 33 developing countries have facilities for formulating pesticides and that at least 11 produce their active ingredients.

Pesticides, either imported or made in a local factory that may have been built with foreign investment, seem likely to go on causing deaths and illness in the developing world. Clearing up the mess of international trade – and also aid – in pesticides is causing a further problem, especially in Africa. Pesticide donations to sub-Saharan Africa comprise perhaps 80 per cent of all pesticide imports, according to Janice King Jensen of the US Environmental Protection Agency; obsolete and out-of-date pesticides have now accumulated to huge proportions in sub-Saharan Africa, with thousands of tonnes of unused and deteriorating pesticide left lying around. Frequently in the open and exposed to the hot sun, the pesticides are liable to leak from their rusting containers and cause damage both to health and to ground water. Over 6500 tonnes of such products have been identified in 20 African countries. Morocco and Algeria have the largest stocks with 1862 and 937 tonnes respectively.[11]

Many of the stocks include lindane, dieldrin and DDT, which are now widely banned, and some of which have been donated under aid programmes. Jensen points out that 'a serious disposal crisis' now exists over these obsolete products. African countries rarely have disposal facilities, and the FAO has started a programme for the disposal of existing stocks. The London-based Pesticides Trust suggests that a 'return-to-sender' policy be incorporated in future pesticide sales.[12]

## Drugs

Essential drugs are in short supply in many developing countries, and a large proportion of meagre health resources is often spent on importing drugs.[13] The EC exports about

$2.5 billion worth of drugs each year to the developing world; some of these are banned or have been withdrawn in at least one EC country because they are considered unsafe – but they are still allowed to be exported. In the Third World they may be labelled 'safe' and people will buy them in the hope that their pain will be removed and their health restored. In reality, the drugs might kill them.

A list of products banned or withdrawn in EC countries is not readily available to the public. But a list was compiled by the Dutch-based organization WEMOS with the help of the UN list of products whose consumption and/or sale has been banned, withdrawn, severely restricted or not approved by governments. In a unique survey, WEMOS says that a 'large proportion of the products sold by European pharmaceutical companies are not essential drugs according to WHO definitions . . . at least 60 product categories are banned or withdrawn in one or more EC countries . . . at least 75 brand name pharmaceuticals – representing 13 product categories – are on the market in Third World countries that are banned or withdrawn in one or more EC countries'. Banned products are those that have been withdrawn from sale, 'having regard to its safety in relation to its use'.[14]

Painkillers (analgesics) are among the world's most widely used drugs. According to information in national guides with prescription information, 57 analgesics were on the market in the Third World in 1988 that are banned or withdrawn in one or more EC country, 39 of them containing metamizole sodium. For example, dipyrone, largely manufactured by the German company, Hoechst, was found in a survey of prescribing guides in 1987 to be the second most frequently used painkiller after paracetamol. But dipyrone is banned or restricted in many industrialized countries, and most of its sales are in the Third World where it can often be obtained over the counter without a prescription.

In the early 1970s, dipyrone became associated with agranulocytosis – because of improved monitoring for adverse effects – and with a potentially fatal allergic reaction called anaphylactic shock. It was withdrawn in Denmark, Greece and Ireland and restricted for use in Belgium, Germany and Italy. It seems there are about 7000 cases of agranulocytosis a year worldwide, of which about one in every five is fatal.

'The fast effective way to relieve pain', reads an

advertisement for Glifanan, which contains glafenine. Made by Roussel (which is 49 per cent French state owned), the product was withdrawn in Germany in 1983, and later in Belgium in 1990 after causing the deaths of two people and also several serious adverse reactions. The Netherlands and Spain have now banned it, while France, Italy and Portugal have stopped its sale. Roussel continues to market the product in Africa, the Caribbean, the Middle East and Asia; Glifanan is among the top selling drugs in francophone Africa. 'These products should not be exported', says the WEMOS survey; 'marketing which suggests that glafenine is a safe analgesic is completely indefensible'.

When products are withdrawn from European markets and manufacturers accept they should stop making them, it would seem that the Third World is a useful place to unload any surpluses and so reduce losses. The anti-diarrhoea drug, clioquinol, for example, was withdrawn from Western markets in the 1970s and early 1980s after it became associated with SMON, a crippling and sometimes fatal disease of the nervous system which leads to blindness and lower limb paralysis. Until February 1989 there were, however, two products containing clioquinol produced by an EC-based company on sale in Indonesia for the treatment of diarrhoea.[15] This was five years after they had been withdrawn in Europe.

A four-point programme to control the export of drugs is needed, believes WEMOS. There should be full disclosure of information on all drugs banned, withdrawn or severely restricted inside the EC, and more insight into the criteria for the registration of drugs. Drugs that are banned, withdrawn or not licensed in an EC country because of concerns about safety, or unproven efficacy, should only be exported after Prior Informed Consent has been given by the importing country. Finally, registration of drugs in Europe should be to the highest possible standards. 'The basic premise of export control', says WEMOS, 'is that the same standards should be applied for the domestic market as for the export of pharmaceuticals'. This premise could apply to the export of any product, certainly to pesticides, a sister-case to the export of drugs.

## Breast milk substitutes

Feeding a baby with breast milk is universally recognized to be superior to bottle-feeding; it gives the right blend of nutrients, antibodies and white blood cells which protect against disease. Recent research also suggests that breast-fed babies have higher intelligence.[16] In Western countries where there are clean and ample supplies of water to mix with the powder, and sterilizer to wash and clean bottles, breast milk substitutes are considered by some mothers to be convenient. But when they are exported, usually via TNCs, to the very different conditions of the Third World, breast milk substitutes become controversial and deadly.

In poorer countries there is often no clean and ample supply of water and sterilizer. Mothers do their best, but the formula mixture they feed their babies may be contaminated by dirty water and cause health problems such as diarrhoea and worse, death. While the full extent of the damage caused by breast milk substitutes is unknown, the 1991 UNICEF report *The State of the World's Children* says that reversing the decline in breast-feeding in the developing world could save the lives of an estimated 1.5 million infants every year.[17] UNICEF points out that bottle-fed babies are '25 times more likely to die in childhood than infants who are exclusively breast-fed for the first six months of life'.[18]

Exports of breast milk substitutes from North to South began in the late nineteenth century and the trade has grown steadily. The market leader in the late twentieth century is the Swiss food group, Nestlé. Other prominent companies include Cow & Gate, Wyeth, Carnation, Boots, Ross-Abbott and Mead Johnson. Especially during the past 40 years, powerful advertising has persuaded millions of mothers to foresake breast-feeding and use powder instead.

Until 1973 the public in the Western world knew little or nothing about the effects that the powder was having on the health of Third World babies. In that year *New International-ist* magazine published an article by two paediatricians, David Morley and Ralph Hendrikse.[19] Drawing on their long experience of Africa, they explained the problem in concise, readable language. The following year, War on Want published a booklet *The Baby Killer*, with a telling cover showing a sick baby inside a feeding bottle.[20] The report was a bestseller and led to television films and translations which gave the matter wide publicity.

When translated into German by the Third World Action Group in Berne, Switzerland, the report was given the title *Nestlé Totet Babys* which means 'Nestlé Kills Babies'. Nestlé filed a libel suit against the group, which they eventually won. The judge, imposing only modest fines, said in his summing up that Nestlé's advertising in developing countries went considerably further than in industrialized countries. There was a need, he said, for Nestlé to 'fundamentally re-think its advertising practices in developing countries . . . for its advertising practice up to now can transform a life-saving product into one that is dangerous and life-destroying'. If Nestlé wanted to be spared the accusation of immoral and unethical conduct, he went on, they will have to change advertising practices.[21]

In 1975 there was another lawsuit on the matter, but this time in reverse – a company was sued. A group of Catholic nuns, the Sisters of the Precious Blood, filed a suit against the American company, Bristol Myers, charging them with 'making mis-statements in its proxy statements'. 'In other words, lying', says Gabrielle Palmer of the UK-based Baby Milk Action Coalition, 'when the nuns as shareholders had challenged the company to provide detailed information about its promotional practices abroad, they were informed there was no promotion where chronic poverty or ignorance could lead to product misuse'.[22] Yet Bristol Myers market their product in countries such as Guatemala where only about half the population have access to safe drinking water. The nuns collected evidence from 18 countries and the company settled out of court.

But the industry was not moved. 'In spite of all the publicity and the lawsuits, the companies, including Nestlé, continued their widespread promotion', says Palmer.[23] Churches and concerned groups in the United States began a consumer boycott of Nestlé products which soon spread to Canada, Europe and New Zealand. As the boycott grew under the co-ordination of the newly-formed worldwide NGO coalition, the International Baby Food Action Network (IBFAN), Nestlé stepped up its spending on public relations in an attempt to counter the threat to business. Palmer notes that the company paid a $1 million fee to the PR firm Hill & Knowlton who sent 300 000 glossy booklets to clergy and religious bodies.

WHO and UNICEF both became convinced that a Code of Conduct was needed for the marketing of breast milk substitutes. This was approved by governments at the World Health Assembly in Geneva in May 1981 by 118 votes to one with three abstentions. The sole vote against was cast by the United States. The Code's first four provisions call for 'no advertising of breast milk substitutes, no free samples to mothers, no promotion of products through health care facilities, no company mothercraft nurses to advise mothers'.[24] The idea behind the code was that each country should put the provisions into effect in either a legally binding or a voluntary way.

After the Code was adopted each company wrote its own version, 'none of which came near to the WHO basics', says Palmer.[25] But by 1984, Nestlé had said it would keep to the WHO code in developing countries, even in the absence of national laws; in response, the consumer boycott was lifted. Much of Nestlé's large-scale advertising of breast milk substitutes stopped. But other marketing practices continued. In 1986 an investigation in the Philippines revealed that 37 per cent of babies were fed in hospital on free supplies from Nestlé. The provision of such supplies is in direct contravention of the code. Palmer says that virtually all 21 hospitals, clinics and maternity units that were visited in Pakistan in February 1988 used free milk supplies donated by a number of different companies.[26] In Singapore and Malaysia, there was also evidence of companies breaking the WHO code. The consumer boycott of the market leader, Nestlé, was re-imposed.

As public pressure for change was intensified, UNICEF's Executive Board called in 1991 on 'manufacturers and distributors of breast milk substitutes to end free and low-cost supplies of infant formulae to maternity wards and hospitals by December 1992'.[27] In other words, it asked the companies to keep to a code that has been agreed 10 years earlier. If UNICEF estimates are correct, and 1.5 million children die each year as a result of bottle- rather than breast-feeding, then the lives of 15 million children had been lost 'to the bottle' in these 10 years.

The companies see events rather differently. A letter sent to clergy in Britain in July 1991 by Nestlé's Managing Director, Peter Blackburn, claimed that 'Nestlé support and promote breast-feeding everywhere. In all developing countries, Nestlé has been in the forefront of supporting and monitoring ethical marketing practices in strict accordance with the WHO code . . . '.[28]

After the infant formulae companies had agreed to support UNICEF's new call in 1991, church groups in the United

States claimed that things were not all they seemed. Nestlé's commitment (to end free and low-cost supplies of infant formulae to maternity wards and hospitals by December 1992) 'falls seriously short on several points', said Timothy Smith, executive-director of the New York-based Interfaith Center on Corporate Responsibility, in response to Mr Blackburn's letter. The centre co-ordinates the corporate responsibility programmes of Protestant and Roman Catholic churches in the United States, and was involved in negotiations that led to the 1981 WHO Code of Conduct.

Mr Smith said that Nestlé only agreed to end free supplies 'when governments acted to require action by industry rather than *also* ending supplies unilaterally as encouraged to do so by WHO and UNICEF. From our point of view this makes a mockery out of Nestlé's supposed commitment to a 1992 end free supplies deadline'. He claimed that Nestlé 'has not made an unequivocal commitment to end free supplies but rather stated a general direction that could take a decade to implement', and added that Nestlé's free supplies 'continue in many countries around the world as a normal part of doing business . . . it is inaccurate and quite misleading for Nestlé to state that it is compliance with the Code'.

In 1984 Mr Smith says that he advocated an end to a boycott of Nestlé and subsequently found the company 'very willing to move forward on points like clarifying what gifts would not be permitted to doctors. However, when we turned to the issue of supplies, Nestlé representatives reneged on their agreement explaining it would be "commercial suicide" if they unilaterally ended free supplies and other companies continued this practice. From our point of view it seemed that Nestlé had decided that market pressures were more pressing than the moral commitments they had made to end supplies'.

A IBFAN report, published in September 1991, which investigated the most recent practices of baby milk companies, found that 'no company demonstrates full compliance with the International Code. Nestlé, the market leader . . . is found to violate the Code more often than any of its competitors, but scant regard for the Code is shown by most other companies, including Hipp, Mead-Johnson, Meji, Milupa, Nutrica/Cow & Gate, Snow Brand and Wyeth'.[29]

'Market pressures – more pressing than the moral commitments' sums up why seemingly respectable companies are involved in trade of a highly dubious nature, which only account for a small fraction of their profits. But as such trade only serves to undermine their good name, it puts their own long-term interests – and profits – in jeopardy. Engaging in trade such as promoting breast milk substitutes in violation of an internationally accepted code seems not only morally dubious but also commercially questionable in anything other than the short term.

## Dirty products and industries

The export of dirty products and industries from North to South arises chiefly because Northern countries want to dump the waste of some of their products in other countries, rather than handling them at home. They also need certain products that can only be produced by polluting the environment, and would prefer such activity not to take place in their own countries. As public awareness in the North about the dangers of toxic wastes and dirty industries has grown, so has the desire to export both products and industries and, as the South is keen to diversify, there has been a transfer of such dirty products and industrial activities to the South, despite the fact that the North is more able to afford the technology to treat the waste.

Although the international transfer of waste, on a large scale, is relatively new, Greenpeace says that it has documented over 1000 attempts to export waste all over the globe. Over 160 million tonnes of waste has probably been shipped, Greenpeace says, ranging from sewage sludge to medical waste, from radioactive waste to industrial incinerator waste. Waste deals have resulted in thousands of tonnes of toxic waste being exported 'to almost every country in the world', says the NGO.[30] The international waste trade is increasingly targeting South America, Central America and the Caribbean.

Waste traders almost invariably present their proposals as 'development' plans that will bring prosperity, generating employment and economic and social benefits. The deals offered are sometimes highly lucrative. International waste traders offered Guinea Bissau, in West Africa, four times the country's GNP if it would take 15 million tonnes of foreign industrial wastes over a five-year period. 'Realizing the inherent environmental and health dangers involved in the deal,' says Greenpeace, 'government officials chose not to accept the deal'. This exemplifies the position in which developing countries find themselves 'that of having to make the seeming choice between poison and poverty'.[31]

The dumping of dirty products can involve deception and secrecy. In October 1987, for example, the Haitian department of commerce issued an import permit to the *Khian Sea* ship for the import of fertilizer. However, the ship's cargo was not fertilizer but 13476 tonnes of toxic municipal incinerator ash from Philadelphia in the United States, which was dumped on a beach in Haiti. When the Haitian government discovered this deception it ordered the *Khian Sea* to remove the ash. But only some was removed; anything between 2000 to 4500 tonnes was left behind, a classic case of the waste that is needed to fuel and maintain the wealth of an industrialized nation being dumped in a fraudulent way on a poorer nation.

Since the mid-1980s, developing countries have moved swiftly to ban the import of wastes. While only three developing countries banned such imports in 1986, by 1991 the number was 83. At the Bamako Convention in 1990, African states banned the import of toxic waste into their countries. But Western countries producing the waste have taken only limited steps to ban their exports. Some regional deals have been struck; since 1989, the Lomé Convention bans all radioactive and hazardous waste exports from the European Community to the African, Caribbean and Pacific group of countries. But waste still goes from Europe to non-Lomé South American countries; Germany, which has the toughest domestic environmental laws, is the biggest European exporter of waste products.[32]

There is evidence that public pressure has persuaded companies to change their policies. The US-based Cyanamid chemical company decided, in April 1991, to discontinue shipments of mercury waste to South Africa because of escalating public protest. Greenpeace says that the company's waste exports helped to contaminate a South African river 'with some of the worst mercury poisoning ever recorded'.[33] But there are differing opinions over how waste should be defined. The waste industry has maintained that waste imported from the West to the Third World for recycling is not waste, as the final product has a useful purpose.[34]

With the export of dirty products likely to become more controversial and difficult in the 1990s, Western countries may become more interested in exporting at least some of the industry that churns out dirty products, for example, pesticides. They appear to have useful allies in the world's largest multilateral aid agency, the World Bank.

In an internal World Bank memo, leaked to a British weekly magazine in February 1992, Lawrence Summers, chief economist and vice-president of the bank, wrote about why the rich should pollute the poor:

'Just between you and me, shouldn't the World Bank be encouraging more migration of the dirty industries to the LDCs (least developed countries)? I can think of three reasons:

1. The measurement of the costs of health-impairing pollution depends on the for-gone earnings from increased morbidity and mortality. From this point of view a given amount of health-impairing pollution should be done in the country with the lowest cost, which will be the country with the lowest wages. I think the economic logic behind dumping a load of toxic waste in the lowest-wage country is impeccable and we should face up to that.
2. The costs of pollution are likely to be non-linear as the initial increments of pollution probably have very low cost. I've always thought that under-populated countries in Africa are vastly under-polluted; their air quality is probably vastly inefficiently low compared to Los Angeles or Mexico City. Only the lamentable facts that so much pollution is generated by non-tradable industries (transport, electrical generation) and that the unit transport costs of solid waste are so high, preventing world-welfare-enhancing trade in air pollution and waste.
3. The demand for a clean environment for aesthetic and health reasons is likely to have very high income-elasticity. The concern over an agent that causes a one-in-a-million change in the odds of prostate cancer is obviously going to be much higher in a country where people survive to get prostate cancer than in a country where under-five mortality is 200 to 1 000. Also, much of the concern over industrial atmospheric discharge is about visibility-impairing particulates. These discharges may have very little direct health impact. Clearly trade in goods that embody aesthetic pollution concerns could be welfare-enhancing. While production is mobile the consumption of pretty air is non-tradable.'[35]

The memo, with its view of the world which rests solely on the most narrow economics, prompted calls for Mr Summers' resignation. The World Bank responded by saying that it was meant ironically and should not be taken literally. But the sentiments of the memo are believed to be held by many in the World Bank who take the view that raising the GNPs of developing countries, via the transfer of dirty industries, is more important than environmental and health matters. Short-term gains are thus elevated over long-term considerations. Mr Summers survived calls for his resignation and is closely involved with the Global Environmental Facility, which the World Bank and other agencies set up in 1991 to fund environmental projects. The World Bank is funded by Western countries out of aid budgets. The peoples of donor countries have not been asked whether they think that aid should be used to smooth the export of dirty products and industries.

If dirty exports include products that damage the health of people in the importing country, then *tobacco* could be included. The export of tobacco products and the facilities to make cigarettes is widespread. With smoking declining in Western nations by 0.5 per cent a year, so the big tobacco companies have tried to persuade people in the Third World to buy more of their products. Non-smoking women are one of their chief targets. To some extent they are succeeding; in 1988, tobacco products worth $1934 million were exported from industrialized to developing countries. In 1989 this rose to $2213 million; by 1990 the trade reached $2646 million – a 36 per cent increase in two years.[36]

In most developing countries there are none of the restrictions on tobacco advertising and the warnings on cigarette packets that are common in Western countries. The world's large tobacco firms – American Brands, BAT, the Imperial Group, Philip Morris, R.J. Reynolds and Rothmans – have set up subsidiaries across developing countries, and also continue to export to them. At least some of these products have been found to have a higher tar and nicotine content than brands sold in Western countries. 'In Pakistan, for example, two of the most popular brands, Capstan and Morven, each have a yield of 29 mg tar per cigarette. Tar concentrations for a range of popular cigarettes sold in the United Kingdom and in Australia in 1981 never exceeded 19 mg per cigarette'.[37]

This trade can damage health in more ways than one. People who start smoking have to use money that they might have spent on food or health care to buy cigarettes. According to Dr D. Fami-Pearse of the University of Lagos, people in Bangladesh on low incomes who have been persuaded to smoke five cigarettes a day have had to cut food purchases by 15 per cent, which reduces their daily calorific intake by 300 from an already low 2000.[38]

Exports of pesticides, drugs, breast-milk substitutes and dirty industries and products from the West to the Third World have several things in common. Sales, or demand for them, are often falling in Western countries and Third World markets are pumped as a way out. Double standards operate, and the products can cause death. The trade involves not just the export of products but also the export of funds to build factories and the means to produce deadly products. As the agents of most of these exchanges, TNCs might reasonably be accountable to the global community for their actions. No such accountability exists.

# 8 Finance, debt and trade

Unless it is conducted on a straight exchange basis, international trade has to be financed. Third World importers need money; not just money of their own country, but foreign money in the form of dollars, pounds, yen, and so on – the so-called 'hard' currencies. They are 'hard' because the people who accept them in payment for goods and services traded internationally know that, in turn, they will be accepted by others in payment for goods and services. There is worldwide confidence that the currencies of the Western world will be acceptable. By contrast, Third World currencies are considered 'soft'. Ghana, for example, cannot buy equipment from Japan and pay in its currency, the cedi, because Japan may lack confidence that other countries will accept cedis in return.

Developing countries that wish to import goods like oil and machinery must therefore possess hard currencies. Most of them earn such currencies by exporting primary commodities and, to a lesser extent, manufactured goods and services. Such exports are considered vital, especially by countries that have no oil. Without exports, there is no money to buy oil, no vehicular transport or energy to drive machinery. As previous chapters have shown, the way the international trading system operates means that developing countries are not earning enough foreign currency to buy all they need.

Some developing countries import more than they export, financing the balance with grants from donor countries, or by borrowing on the money markets. But when such grants and borrowing are insufficient, balance of payments deficits can arise. To help them overcome their deficits, developing countries have sought advice from the Washington-based organizations, the International Monetary Fund (IMF) and the World Bank. Set up in negotiations at the US town of Bretton Woods in 1945, the IMF's purpose is 'to promote international monetary co-operation and expansion of world trade; . . . to assist . . . in the elimination of foreign exchange restrictions which hamper world trade.'[1] The bank, by contrast, funds development projects. In practice, as John Maynard Keynes is reputed to have pointed out, the fund is a bank and the bank is a fund.

The IMF helps countries with balance of payments problems by suggesting measures that reduce government expenditure, switch resources into exporting to earn foreign exchange, and develop a more market-orientated economy. Typically, the IMF will suggest that a government should devalue its currency – making its exports cheaper and hopefully more attractive to foreign buyers; and cut its spending on sectors such as health and education, and eliminate food subsidies. The country will be asked to remove barriers that stand in the way of imports, and may be urged to privatize government-run activities such as commodity marketing boards, and generally to remove restrictions that hinder the operation of the free market. Unless a country takes the IMF medicine it will find that international banks will not lend it any money, and even that its development aid is under pressure. The World Bank, the IMF's sister, makes structural adjustment loans, again on condition that countries change their economies in a way the bank thinks is best.

Such 'conditionality' is one of the most controversial aspects of development, especially in view of the debt crisis facing many developing countries. In the 1980s conditionality was central to 'structural adjustment' plans that heavily indebted countries were required to make. They were asked to adjust the structure of their economies before they qualified for either debt relief or further international loans. There is now considerable evidence that such adjustment programmes have worked badly, generally not succeeding in helping a country to increase its exports or the pace of economic development, and hitting hardest at the poorest sectors of populations. Zimbabwe's 'Economic Structural Adjustment Programme' (ESAP) has been called by the country's poor the 'Extended Suffering for African People's Programme'.

Much of the structural adjustment medicine has been taken by Africa. Between 1980 and 1988, 33 countries on the African continent had borrowed money with conditions from the IMF, and 15 had structural adjustment loans with the World Bank. The medicine was not only nasty, it did not usually cure. 'There appears to have been a neglect of Africa's long-term needs in formulating the policies', says Frances Stewart, a University of Oxford researcher; 'it seems that in some respects the policies are moving Africa *away* from a satisfactory medium-term development path'[2].

This is clearly illustrated in the area of agricultural commodities. A typical structural adjustment programme will encourage a government to pay higher prices to the producers of such commodities. But this only serves to *increase* production at a time when, as Chapter 3 has shown, there is a very real need for *less* to be produced. As structural adjustment policies are being adopted simultaneously by a large number of countries, the results for producers are disastrous. Such policies are 'in part responsible for the worsening terms of trade in the 1980s and *will lead to a continued deterioration if the same policies are followed in the 1990s*', says Stewart.[3]

IMF/World Bank structural adjustment policies are leading to lower prices for agricultural commodities, and also hitting hard at other economic sectors. Stewart points out that cuts in public expenditure 'almost invariably affect items which are essential for long-term development', notably expenditure on health, education and training. 'The stagnation and even reversal of the achievements in education is particularly harmful'.[4] Cuts in public investment which usually accompany a structural adjustment programme also reduce growth potential, while trade liberalization allows in more imports and puts local industry under pressure, discouraging the regional trade which is an important hope for many Third World economies. Adjustment packages have also failed in the short term. Stewart concludes that they have failed to restore economies to a viable short-term path and to eliminate imbalances. The wisdom of continuing with such failed policies must therefore seriously be called into question.

Countries in the other developing continents have also 'taken the medicine'. In Latin America, for example, 28 of the region's 32 countries adjusted along IMF lines; economic stagnation, rising unemployment and a decline in per capita income of seven per cent were some of the results.[5] Asia has been less affected, although the Philippines needs to allocate 37 per cent of its national income to pay off debts; by contrast, the country spends only 17 per cent on health and education put together, less than half what is spent on servicing debts (see below).

# Debt

By 1991 the level of foreign indebtedness had drastically altered the role that many developing countries play in the world trading system. Imports had been severely cut back and there was evidence of a scramble to export additional products, such as timber, at heavy cost to the environment. Debt had emerged as the biggest single obstacle to development, with about 50 developing countries carrying a severe debt burden, over half of them in Africa. In his report on Africa in August 1991 (see Chapter 3) the then United Nations Secretary-General, Mr Javier Perez de Cuellar pointed out that whereas, in 1986, sub-Saharan Africa's foreign debt was 54 per cent of national output, in 1990 it was 112 per cent. It now costs Africa $23 billion a year to service its debt, about the same as it receives in development aid. 'It is simply not possible for Africa to develop under such a debt burden', he said.[6]

At the end of 1990, developing countries owed $1280 billion to Western countries, international aid agencies, the IMF, and banks.[7] Their yearly earnings from international trade were under $1000 billion; the overall debt of developing countries was therefore more than the value of their exports. To 'service' that debt – to pay interest and repay part of the capital – cost developing countries $143.5 billion in 1990.[8] They received $85 billion in aid and investment from abroad, thus paying richer countries nearly $60 billion *more* than they received.[9] New aid and investment was wiped out by past debt. In 1991, according to OECD figures, the severely indebted low-income countries paid a higher proportion of their export revenue on debt service than at any time during the 1980s – 31.3 per cent of such revenues, compared with 23.8 per cent in the 1980s.[10]

Foreign debt has turned from a problem to a crisis for many developing countries, for a number of reasons. In the early 1980s world interest rates soared due to the restrictive monetary policies being pursued by incoming, right-wing governments in the United States, West Germany and Britain. This meant that countries which had taken out loans had to repay at much higher rates, sometimes more than double that applied when they borrowed. Interest rates – typically below 10 per cent in the 1970s – had shot up to around 20 per cent by the early 1980s. While they were paying more in interest, their earnings from commodities such as coffee, tea, sugar and copper, on which they depend, slumped dramatically. They were paying out more, but receiving much less. At the same time grandiose so-called development schemes, 'cathedrals in the desert', were going ahead, often encouraged by Western interests, which frequently came to nothing. But repayments had to be made. African countries, with weaker economies and being more dependent on export crops for foreign earnings, were most vulnerable, but all the developing continents took the strain.

In Asia one of the most seriously indebted countries is the Philippines. Under the regime of Ferdinand Marcos, massive loans were taken out for projects which rarely benefited either the population or the economy. In 1991, the country owed nearly $35 billion and had to pay about $7 billion a year to service the debt. To do that it had to switch money from essential services such as health and education. To raise money to pay off debts, deforestation is continuing, with whole mountainsides torn apart for their trees and minerals. The flash floods in central Philippines in November 1991, which caused over 2000 deaths, appear to have been caused by deforestation which upset the ecological balance.

In Africa one of the most seriously indebted countries is the new democracy, Zambia, where IMF conditions have obliged the government to substantially increase the price of maize-meal, the food of the poor. Paul Vallely, a journalist, tells of a family he met who, because of the price rise, were considering eating just on *alternate* days so that shoes could be bought for one of their children to go to school.[11]

In Latin America, the effects of the debt burden on the people of Peru shocked the global community in 1991 but little remedial action was taken. Government services have been cut back drastically to try to repay foreign debt and this has led to stark consequences. In early 1991, a severe outbreak of cholera was reported from Peru at a time when cholera as a major disease was in retreat. Cholera is a disease of poverty, and recent WHO figures show that nearly three-quarters of all the world's cholera is in this one country of some 20 million people. Priests in Peru have spoken of the deterioration of people's health in recent years. Cholera has been the culmination.

Since the debt crisis began 10 years ago, according to UNICEF figures, Africans have seen their standard of living fall by 20 per cent, Latin Americans by 10 per cent. Without debt relief, both Third World peoples and economies will continue to suffer, and the West will also be affected. Heavily indebted countries with tropical forests, for example, will be more likely to axe their forests to earn foreign exchange to pay off the debts. Between 1981 and 1990, the pace of deforestation in the developing world increased by nearly 50 per cent – from 12 million to 17 million hectares a year – but, in the heavily indebted countries, deforestation more than doubled in the debt decade. Without debt relief this trend is set to go on and most of the world's remaining tropical forests, the global lung, will be felled.

Several plans have emerged to tackle debt. The Baker Plan of 1985 was designed to restore growth in the developing world; it called on Western banks to provide $20 billion in new loans over the next three years to heavily indebted countries, mainly in Latin America. The banks ignored the plan. Only $4 billion worth of new loans were made. At the 1988 G7 summit in Toronto (a meeting of the world's largest seven industrialized nations), creditor countries offered write-offs of a third of developing country debt. The UN Secretary-General refers to this as a 'marked advance in the debt strategy, in that for the first time creditor governments recognized the need for concessional debt relief'.[12] By August 1991, 19 countries had benefited under the Toronto terms, 17 of them African. But the savings were small – amounting to little over $50 million, less than two per cent of the debt service payments of the countries involved.

Because of Toronto's limitations a number of other proposals were put forward, specifically the Brady Plan of 1989, and also the Trinidad terms which emerged at a meeting of Commonwealth Finance Ministers in September 1990. The Brady Plan was significant in that it acknowledged there is no alternative to debt reduction; it was designed to lower the amount of commercial debt while ensuring a new mix of official and private funding. But the plan has proved of limited value; by mid-1990 only one African country, Morocco, had benefited from the initiative.

The Trinidad terms are an improvement on the Toronto terms in that they would write off two-thirds of eligible debt, and reschedule the remainder over 14 to 24 years. Indebted countries only qualify for relief, however, if they have in place a structural adjustment programme that has been agreed with the IMF (see above). So a country can obtain debt relief but only if it changes the structure of its economy, and tries to increase the volume of its commodity exports. As already mentioned, with many countries embarking on similar policies, a higher global volume of exports will most likely result in lower world prices and lower overall earnings. So, to earn debt relief, countries are expected to pursue policies which worsen their terms of trade.

Some rescheduling of debt has taken place through the 'Paris Club', an *ad hoc* forum for industrialized countries to consider applications from debtors for rescheduling – it met, for example, in December 1991 to consider how to implement the Trinidad terms. Debt rescheduling is increasing fast; between January and September 1991, $64.8 billion of debt was rescheduled, compared with $16.9 billion in 1990 and an average of $8.8 billion from 1982 to 1986.[13] But debt 'forgiveness' is tiny; in 1990, only $6.6 billion of debt was actually cancelled – about 0.5 per cent of total Third World debt.[14]

Debt relief has also been granted by Western governments for political reasons, rather than to help those who are most in need. Poland was forgiven large debts in the late 1980s because it was the first East European country to turn its back on communism. Egypt had its debt cut in half for the support it gave the West in the Gulf War. Other African countries, with even more pressing problems, have not been as fortunate. Two-thirds of Africa's debt is owed to official creditors, so the scope for government action is considerable. In August 1991, the UN Secretary-General called for the cancellation of all Africa's official bilateral debt, and also for the cancellation of semi-official debts, such as export credits. He urged that ways be found to substantially reduce multilateral debt and that commercial debt, already heavily discounted on the financial markets, should be written down still further. This would mean that banks would accept a lower amount in repayment.[15]

Many commercial banks have discounted Third World debt in their balance sheets, without actually writing it off. Britain's 'Big Four' banks, Barclays, National Westminster, Lloyds and Midland, for example, are owed £9000 million by Third World debtor countries. They have made a provision in their books to lose a substantial part of this money – varying from 40 to 80 per cent – and have received over

£1000 million in tax relief as a result. But this is of no help to Third World debtors who are still expected to repay in full. The pressure group, the World Development Movement, launched a campaign in 1991 that urged the banks to cancel the debt owed to them by the developing world.

Commercial banks were eager to lend to the developing world in the 1970s, and even more so in the early years of the 1980s, when higher interest rates offered the prospect of higher profits. In the period 1979/81, commercial banks made as many new loans as they did in the 1973/9 period.[16] But their ardour had cooled markedly by the 1980s when they feared they would not get their money back. The 1991 World Debt Tables confirm a quite dramatic shift in bank policy and in the structure of new lending. Whereas, in 1981, commercial bank lending accounted for 40 per cent of all new lending to the developing world, in 1991 the figure was down to only 5 per cent. Official grants and loans accounted for around two-thirds of new flows, and foreign direct investment for nearly 30 per cent. Commercial banks have therefore become much less important as new lenders but are still important because of their attitude to past loans.[17]

The World Bank estimates that a two-thirds reduction in official debt would give many indebted countries a realistic prospect of putting their debt servicing on a sustainable basis. But this depends to a considerable extent on commodity prices which, as noted above, IMF/World Bank adjustment policies are driving downwards. Inevitably the worsening debt position of many developing countries has led to late payments, and raised the spectre of complete default. In 1991 the severely indebted low-income countries were able to make only half their scheduled debt repayments. The burden of trying to repay was a burden on people and a serious obstacle to development efforts.

One oddity of the international financial system is the way that developing countries are asked to pay much higher rates of interest on money they borrow from lending countries than the rates that apply in those countries. In the early 1980s, for example, interest rates in six major industrialized countries averaged around four per cent. But between 1982 and 1985 the average rate of interest paid by six major Third World borrowers was 16.8 per cent. Developing countries were asked and expected to pay higher rates of interest, presumably because banks considered them a higher risk of default. 'It is a sad commentary on the workings of the international financial markets that poor countries and their people have to pay interest rates four times those in rich countries'.[18]

## Countertrade

As lack of foreign exchange has caused such problems for developing countries, the question arises as to whether they could trade without it. Money serves as a medium of exchange but is not always necessary for exchange to take place. If countries can agree on a straight exchange of goods or services between one another, then money is not needed. Around 10–15 per cent of North–South trade is done in this 'counter' manner (also called 'barter' and 'swap' trade), around 10 per cent of South-South trade, and about 60 per cent of trade between developing countries and Eastern Europe.[19]

Countertrade has the considerable advantage that it bypasses the international financial system, and allows a country to trade without foreign exchange. In the early 1990s this was a major consideration for many developing countries. Countertrade has the advantage of being 'balanced trade' – it does not give one of the participating countries a trade surplus and another a trade deficit. 'In whatever form it takes, countertrade gives Third World countries new ways of financing imports, enables resource-starved countries to conserve foreign exchange . . . and also maintain market shares and vital imports of essential goods and services', says Chaldeans Mensah of the University of Alberta, Canada.[20]

The 1980s witnessed a considerable upsurge in countertrade, as governments of developing countries looked for ways of bypassing an international financial and economic system that was causing a drain on their foreign exchange and leading to debt problems. One study has shown that 1350 countertrade transactions involving developing countries took place between 1980 and 1987.[21] These included agreements between Uganda and Cuba under which the countries exchanged cotton, beans and hides for sugar, pharmaceuticals and paper; Ghana and Egypt bartered wooden logs for cotton threads; Colombia bartered meat for fish with Peru. Some countertrade deals are not 'pure' barter. Money is sometimes involved when the exchange is not considered exact. Indonesia, India, China, Brazil and Iran have emerged as the South's largest countertraders. Brazil, one of the most heavily indebted countries, stepped up countertrade in the early 1980s as its debt burden became more intense.

'Initially the exchange goods offered by developing countries were almost exclusively raw materials, but their product range has now widened considerably to include not only semi-finished and finished products but also increasingly services', say Halbach and Osterkamp of the Ifo Institute, Munich.[22] Countertrade is, however, no panacea. Arranging a countertrade deal can involve greater effort and cost than under an exchange with money. As money, 'the means of exchange', is missing, an alternative is needed. This involves reaching agreement on the exact amount of goods and services to be exchanged. There can be a hidden cost in countertrade in that a country may be able to obtain lower-cost goods in a monetary transaction than it can by bartering its goods. With countertrade it may, in effect, be exchanging more of its own goods than it would otherwise do, if it had the money to buy from the cheapest source. Some developing countries that have been heavily involved in this trade are now trying to reduce their reliance on it, while other countries are embracing it.[23]

The GATT, the IMF and the World Bank all oppose countertrade as they appear to see it as a violation of free trade principles. But as long as the international market is working badly for developing countries, then their countertrade is likely to grow, especially between themselves (see also Chapter 11).

## Financial reform

IMF/World Bank policies appear to be failing the developing world and the majority of humanity; this failure points to the urgent need to reform the international monetary system. Reform is vital if developing countries are to secure a better deal from the international trading and monetary system, and even higher export revenues. The IMF and the World Bank's 'structural adjustment' policies have a poor record; if the two organizations will not change their policies, and if indebted countries continue to suffer short-term hardship with little prospect of future improvement, then there is a case for both to be abolished and replaced by bodies that are responsive to real needs. One step to reform, and one that could be taken in the 1990s and help towards wider reform, is the allocation of Special Drawings Rights to developing countries.

Developing countries are short of foreign exchange and have not been able to increase their earnings for a great many reasons. One result is that they cannot buy as much as they would like to from other countries. This has not only affected their own development; it has also hit the countries of the North. Cutbacks in imports by developing countries are estimated to have cost Europe, North America and Australasia about 6 million jobs in the 1980s.[24] If both developing and industrialized countries would gain if the former had more foreign exchange, then why not create it? In 1969 the IMF created a new international monetary currency, Special Drawings Rights (SDRs). These are basically 'book entries' and were initially allocated to countries in accordance with their volume of world trade; they are an addition to a country's gold reserves and were intended to act as a kind of 'paper gold' to back up the existing reserves of physical gold.

Gold has traditionally given confidence to the world trading system.[25] If Country A has gold stocks, it has something in reserve that Country B can lay claim to should Country A effectively go bankrupt. In the late 1960s it became clear that most of the world's gold, outside South Africa and the USSR, had been mined. With the volume of world trade increasing, the IMF wanted to increase gold stocks to support the trade. As that was not possible, paper gold in the form of SDRs was the next best thing. There was speculation that SDRs might eventually replace gold as the chief reserve asset of the world monetary system.

During the 1972 UN Conference on Trade and Development (UNCTAD III) the government of India suggested that additional SDRs be allocated to developing countries. But although such allocations would help the countries of both North and South, and would not be difficult to administer, the North would not agree and issue has since been neglected. Larger trading countries such as the USA, West Germany and Britain appeared to consider that intervention to help the market work better was a distortion of pure economic forces. Fears that SDR allocations would be inflationary are misplaced; SDRs would help to put resources back to work, in both North and South; they would help economies to function more efficiently. Far from being inflationary, they would help to increase trade and development and real wealth.

Although SDRs almost disappeared from the international agenda in the 1980s, the 1990 South Commission Report, *The Challenge to the South* revived the idea, saying 'there is a strong case for giving a modest amount of SDRs on a regular basis exclusively to developing countries so as to ensure a more balanced international distribution of liquidity'.[26] It went on to say that the long-term objective should remain that of making SDRs 'the main reserve asset of the international monetary system'. The report sees this as a central aspect of reform of the world monetary system. If SDR allocations could be used to help countries out of balance of payments and debt problems, they would help to increase their trade and real wealth, and also help to bring greater stability.

A more central role for the SDR could also make it the forerunner of a single world currency. In the Bretton Woods negotiations of 1945, the British economist, John Maynard Keynes put forward the idea of a single world currency, to be called the 'Bancor'. Had nations grasped that idea immediately, a single world currency would have been far easier to put into practice in the 1940s than the 1990s, owing to the widening of the gap between countries in different hemispheres. The slowness with which the 12 EC nations are moving to a single currency highlights the difficulties that would arise if the 150-plus trading nations of the world decided to pursue any such idea on a global scale. Additional allocations of SDRs are a more immediate need, but the eventual extension of the SDR into a global currency remains a powerful idea.

# 9 International trade organizations

## The General Agreement on Tariffs and Trade (GATT)

GATT is an international contract that lays down practical rules for world trade; it came into force in 1948. The GATT organization, based in Geneva, is the chief international body concerned with negotiating the reduction of trade barriers. GATT is a code of rules and also a forum in which countries can discuss and try to overcome their trade problems. Its intention is to provide 'a secure and predictable international trading environment in which industrial and commercial entities have the confidence to invest, to create jobs and to trade'.[1]

GATT's task is to regulate international trade, most of which is between countries in the North. The organization has done little to help the South increase its trade, nor has it succeeded in curbing protectionism and trade barriers imposed by the North which hurt the South. The 23 countries that originally signed the GATT in 1948 were at the time engaged in drawing up the charter for a proposed International Trade Organization (ITO) which would have been a United Nations specialized agency. GATT is based largely on parts of the draft ITO charter relating to trade policies, and was concluded in order to get trade liberalization under way quickly. It was expected that responsibility for the agreement would soon be assumed by the ITO. However, plans for the ITO had to be abandoned when it became clear that its charter would not be ratified; GATT was left as the only international instrument laying down rules for most of the world's trade – but it did not cover agriculture and services.

Although it contains 38 articles, the agreement is based on a small number of 'fundamental principles'. The first is embodied in Article 1, paragraph 1 of GATT, the 'most favoured-nation' (MFN) clause; this states that trade must be conducted on the basis of non-discrimination. All contracting parties are bound to grant, to each other, 'treatment as favourable as they give to any country in the application and administration of import and export duties and charges. Thus no country is to give special trading advantages to another or to discriminate against it: all are on an equal basis and all share the benefits of any moves towards lower trade barriers'.[2] Exceptions to this basic rule are supposed to be allowed only in certain special circumstances. The MFN clause might be more accurately called the 'equal treatment' clause. Whatever its name, the clause has frequently been ignored by Western countries in their dealings with developing countries.

The second basic principle has also been flouted; it states that where protection is given to domestic industry, it should be extended through tariffs, not through other commercial measures. Among other things, the aim of this rule is to make clear the extent of protection. But, in 1990, nearly a quarter of protectionist measures were in the form of non-tariff measures (see Chapter 4). Although the prohibition of quantitative restrictions is a further basic provision of GATT, it has been pushed aside in sensitive product areas, such as textiles. Quantitative restrictions are only supposed to be used by countries with balance-of-payments difficulties; even then, restrictions must not be applied beyond the extent necessary to protect the balance of payments and must be progressively reduced and eliminated as soon as they are no longer required. GATT recognizes that developing countries may need to impose import quotas to prevent an excessive drain on their foreign exchange reserves caused by the demand for imports generated by development, or because they are establishing or extending domestic production.

GATT has 'waiver' procedures whereby a country may, when its economic or trade circumstances so warrant, divert from particular GATT obligations. It is recognized that, on occasion, governments feel they have no choice but to offer domestic industries temporary protection from imports. The 'safeguards' rule of GATT permits a member country to impose import restrictions, in some circumstances, or to suspend tariff concessions on products which are being imported in such increased quantities and under such conditions that they cause or are likely to cause serious injury to competing domestic producers. In recent years, however, some governments have used discriminatory bilateral arrangements, often called 'voluntary' export restraints. GATT also has an 'Anti-Dumping Code' to stop countries selling goods abroad at less than the cost in the country where they are made. The code lays down the conditions under which anti-dumping duties may be imposed as a defence against dumped products. But it has not prevented dumping.

Between 1948 and 1979, seven rounds of GATT were held to try to liberalize trade – at Geneva in 1947; Annecy, France, 1949; Torquay, England, 1951; Geneva, 1956; Geneva, 1960/61 (the Dillon Round); Geneva 1964/7 (the Kennedy Round), and Geneva 1973/79 (the Tokyo Round). The Tokyo Round reduced worldwide tariffs by a third, to an average of around five per cent; it also concluded agreements on non-tariff measures, and on trade in dairy products, bovine meat and civil aircraft.

While these rounds have led to a lowering of international trade barriers, GATT has been seen by the South as of limited relevance to them – although membership had grown to 107 countries by 1992, which suggests that most governments of the South did not wish to be excluded from its deliberations. On sensitive issues, such as textiles, governments of the North have blatantly snubbed GATT rules and been strong enough to get away with it. The Multifibre Arrangement is in direct contravention of GATT rules but has existed since 1974 (see Chapter 4).

The problem is that the GATT has no mandate to enforce its regulations. It can only rely on the goodwill of member-countries and, in practice, its regulations run a poor second behind considerations of national sovereignty. While tariffs have come down in the past 50 years, non-tariff barriers have increased. In an attempt to reduce both tariff and non-tariff barriers, to tackle domestic policies which affect trade, and also to consider bringing agriculture and services under GATT rules, the eighth session of GATT talks, the Uruguay Round, was launched at the Argentine resort of Punta del Este in 1986.

## Uruguay Round

The Uruguay Round was by far the most ambitious attempt to liberalize world trade. In 1986, negotiating governments set themselves a four-year time frame and decided to cover

14 areas relating to trade – tariffs, non-tariff measures, tropical products, natural resource-based products, textiles and clothing, agriculture, GATT articles, safeguards, multilateral trade negotiation agreements and arrangements, subsidies and countervailing measures, dispute settlement, trade-related aspects of intellectual property rights including trade in counterfeit goods, trade-related investment measures and finally the functioning of the GATT system. Negotiations therefore covered matters such as trade in textiles and clothing over which GATT rules had been ignored for over 30 years. On tariffs, the Round aimed to cut existing tariffs by not less than 30 per cent, bringing them down to a world average of around 3.5 per cent.

Agreement had to be reached in all 14 areas, decided negotiators, if agreement in any one area was to be ratified. It was a brave attempt at 'all or nothing'. After four years of negotiations and progress in most of the areas, governments met for 'a final meeting' in Brussels in December 1990 to try to resolve outstanding issues and to finalize the round. But differences, especially over agriculture, caused the talks to break up without agreement.

The agriculture problem concerned a festering dispute over agriculture between the United States and the European Community. The US originally argued for the scrapping of all domestic farm supports and export subsidies. By December 1990 it had scaled this down and was seeking cuts of 75 per cent in domestic supports, and 90 per cent cuts in export subsidies by the year 2000. The US was supported in this call by the so-called Cairns Group of developing and industrial countries – Argentina, Australia, Brazil, Canada, Chile, Colombia, Hungary, Indonesia, Fiji, Malaysia, New Zealand, the Philippines and Thailand – all exporters of food who are looking for access to markets at present denied them.

Because of its Common Agricultural Policy and powerful farming lobby, the EC offered to reduce farm subsidies by only 30 per cent over the period 1986–96, half of which reduction had already been made by 1990. On export subsidies, it offered only a vague commitment to reduce the amount of farm produce that attracts the subsidies. The December 1990 'final talks' were turned into a private dispute between the US and the EC on agriculture, with matters that affect the developing countries coming in for little debate, and with negotiators from the other GATT member countries left hanging around.

Negotiations on the Uruguay Round dragged on inconclusively throughout 1991; in December the GATT Director-General, Mr Arthur Dunkel, put a 436-page draft 'final act' before negotiators and set Easter 1992 as another deadline.[3] As Easter came with no agreement, the deadline was extended to the end of June 1992, but this date also passed with no agreement. Even if agreement is reached in 1992 it will be towards the end of 1993 or even 1994 before the decisions come into effect.

The 'Dunkel draft' indicates what a successful outcome to the Uruguay Round will mean for the developing world. On agriculture, it is clear that successful lobbying by governments of developing countries, and also by NGOs, secured a number of important changes for developing countries. The draft says that 'all domestic support in favour of agricultural producers . . . shall be reduced, from the year 1993 to 1999, by 20 per cent'. This would include inputs such as low-cost seed, and services such as credit. It means that governments who are paying, for example, subsidies to their farmers to produce food, would have to reduce them by 20 per cent. Developing countries will, however, have 'the flexibility to apply lower rates of reduction . . . provided (they) are no less than two-thirds of that specified', says the draft. They will also be able to implement the reduction over a period of 10 years, rather than six years. Most developing countries will therefore have to reduce agricultural support by 13.33 per cent, over a 10-year period. The least developed countries (47 in number) 'shall be exempt from reduction commitments'.

Fears had been expressed that efforts by developing country governments to achieve self-sufficiency in food would be affected if they had to reduce support to farmers by significant amounts. When the United States initially argued for the abolition of all farm support, it was not clear whether developing countries would get special treatment – at one time it even seemed possible that they would have to end farm support virtually overnight.

While Third World farm supports are modest by Western standards, they are playing a role in helping food-deficit countries to increase food output and become self-sufficient. The government of Zimbabwe, for example, increased the farm-gate price of maize by 80 per cent between 1979 and 1981, and production tripled in the following five years. A World Bank report says that 'the Zimbabwean experience shows that if . . . supportive agricultural services are available, smallholders will respond with increased production'.[4]

The reductions that governments of developing countries would have to make in domestic support are modest – 1.3 per cent a year over 10 years – and would not apply in the 47 poorest countries. Countries would be required to cut export subsidies to farmers by 36 per cent. The 'two-thirds' proviso would apply to most developing countries, meaning they have to reduce export subsidies by 24 per cent, with the least developed countries exempt. Countries would also have to cut the volume of subsidized food they export by 24 per cent, and, with the same provisos applying, this would mean a reduction of 16 per cent in most developing countries, with the least developed exempt. The Dunkel draft would oblige countries to reduce the tariffs they presently apply against imported foodstuffs by an average of 36 per cent over a six-year period. Developing countries would again benefit from the 'two-thirds' and 10-year provisos and would therefore reduce tariffs on imported foodstuffs by 24 per cent. The 47 least developed countries would again be exempt.

Michael Davenport, a research associate of the Overseas Development Institute (ODI), calculates that the changes envisaged in the Dunkel draft would mean a five per cent rise in world prices of traded foodstuffs.[5] This is good for the Cairns Group, which should be able to increase export earnings. For most developing countries, however, it could be damaging. A rise in world prices of cereals would mean food-importing countries facing higher import bills. Most of the least developed countries are food importers and they would not be shielded from higher import bills. While a rise of five per cent in the prices of imported cereal seems modest, it adds to the economic burdens of the poorest countries.

Higher world cereal prices would, however, mean that Third World farmers did not face as much competition from abroad, and this could help to increase domestic food output. Low grain prices have led to farmers in some parts of Africa, in Nigeria for example, being undercut by cheap imports, and this has caused lower domestic output of staple foods. There may still, however, be a certain amount of low-cost food available for export from the West to the developing world, meaning that Third World farmers could still be undercut by imports.

On commodities like sugar, which are produced in both Western and developing countries, the scaling down of farmer support and export subsidies in surplus countries, in the EC for example, should mean that less sugar is exported, and this could help to lift prices, and benefit Third World sugar-exporting countries. With tariffs on manufactured goods due to be lowered, countries that could step up their output of such products would gain. But the gains would be modest. An ODI report concluded that, overall, developing countries will increase their exports by three per cent if there is a successful outcome to the Uruguay Round. All the gains, however, come from the ending of restrictions to trade in textiles and clothing. The benefits go chiefly to Asia and secondly to Latin America – high- and middle-income developing countries gain more from trade liberalization, says the report. Africa gains least and a number of African countries could be worse off overall.[6]

Under GATT rules, countries can apply for 'derogations', which mean they are exempt from its regulations for certain goods. Japan may seek a 'derogation' to enable it to maintain its present ban on the import of rice. The US is seeking exemptions on services.

## Services, Trips and Trims

Having urged that services be included in the Uruguay Round, the United States insisted in 1991 that liberalization of services should not be applied to the US (see Chapter 5). In particular, it sought exemptions for financial services, maritime transport, air transport and basic telecommunications; these sectors make up about three-quarters of world trade in services. The reason for the abrupt change of policy was that powerful lobbies in the US told their government of how they could be affected by free trade in services. In banking, for example, liberalization could allow banks from Asia and Latin America to set up in the US and be a threat to long-standing American banks. The powerful American maritime transport industry pressed for total exclusion from the Uruguay Round liberalization agreement.

A further contentious area concerns trade-related aspects of intellectual property rights ('Trips'). International rules concerning the protection of intellectual property are largely embodied in the Paris Convention on patents, trademarks and other forms of industrial property, and the Berne Convention on copyright. Both are administered by a UN body, the Geneva-based World Intellectual Property Organization, and lay down certain minimum standards of protection but leave much to the discretion of national governments.

Since the early 1980s the protection of intellectual property rights has become a source of tension in bilateral trade relations. One of the chief 'rights' issues concerns counterfeit goods. Westerners who travel in the developing world are sometimes amazed to find well-known brand goods on sale at a small fraction of what they cost in the West. Tennis shirts bearing the logo of a leading French manufacturer, for example, are freely on sale in Thailand, for less than one-tenth of the cost in French shops. One of the Uruguay Round's aims was to negotiate an international agreement to combat such practices. Owners of patents want payments to be made to them by users of their products.

The extension of patenting laws to the Third World means that companies can control and market crop varieties in countries which may have donated the genetic material used to breed those varieties. Most of the raw materials for the high-yielding seed that is developed in the laboratories of Western companies comes from Third World fields. The irony is that farmers who have received no reward for parting with the raw material that makes manipulation of genes possible may be asked to pay royalties.

Trade-related investment measures ('Trims') are seen by developing countries as an important and natural part of their development policies. Such measures help them to regulate the activities of TNCs, laying down, for example, a requirement that foreign investors use local materials and technology. Trims were brought into the Uruguay Round of negotiations because some governments believe that certain measures applied to investors and investment could restrict or distort trade. The new regulations liberalize Trims, weakening the ability of countries to lay down regulatory measures. TNCs are under no obligation to use local technology or raw materials in a country where they operate; a hotel chain, for example, is now free to bring in all hotel food from outside the country; 'laws requiring foreign enterprises to purchase inputs from local sources will have to be revoked'.[7]

The liberalization of Trims means that if a developing country agrees that a TNC can pursue a particular activity, the country has no choice but to accept the technology that the company brings in. This could mean that countries are landed with higher-tech rather than intermediate technology. 'The Indian government has pointed out, for instance, that the withdrawal of controls on capital goods and technology imported by TNC affiliates is likely to lead to the use of capital-intensive labour-saving technologies'.[8] Developing countries are free 'to deviate temporarily' from the Trims provision and might be expected to take advantage of this. But the uncertainty over how long 'temporary' can reasonably be taken to mean can only create tension which is hardly conducive to a settled climate for development.[9] By limiting, in the long-run, a developing country's choice of materials and technology, the liberalization of Trims could seriously weaken links between trade and development, having a negative effect on development efforts and weakening a country's control over TNCs at a time when there is an urgent need for tighter controls (see Chapter 4).

On non-tariff measures, the Uruguay Round proposes 'tarification'. The idea is that quantity restrictions be replaced by an equivalent tariff, which will then decline by at least 30 per cent from 1993 to 1999. But in April 1992 the EC refused to 'tarify' the quantity restriction it applies against bananas from Central America and Colombia (see Chapter 2).

A new Multilateral Trade Organization is due to be set up in the aftermath of the Uruguay Round to implement the agreement; it will consist of the existing GATT plus other departments, services for example, which are necessary because of the Round's agreement. Countries that violate the Uruguay Round agreement would be brought before a disputes panel and may be liable to pay compensation to countries that have lost markets because of the violation.

## GATT and the environment

When GATT began work in 1948, few people gave any thought to the impact of trade, and trade barriers, on the environment. When the Uruguay Round began in 1986, there was considerable debate about global environmental issues. But such issues were not being connected with international trade, and failed to find their way onto the Uruguay Round agenda. By 1992, the connection was being made, and the Round came in for criticism for omitting the environmental dimension.[10]

In March 1992, GATT produced a study, *Trade and the Environment* (see Chapter 2), but this has not satisfied environmentalists. Its view that increased trade leads to higher incomes and the *opportunity* to spend more on the environment may be true, but increased trade can, in some situations, damage the environment and mean that more *needs* to be spent. The study says that one 'especially unconvincing case for restraints on environmental grounds involves tropical timber'. A ban on log exports would 'simply encourage logs to be sawn and perhaps processed into panels before being exported from developing countries'.[11] But this situation is rather more complex. The study omits to mention that a ban on log exports, if enforced, sends signals to investors that they can no longer hope to come into a tropical country and mine its forests. A ban therefore makes a contribution to scaling down the rate of deforestation. The position is also complicated in that while some tropical countries, for example the Philippines, impose a ban on log exports, even if it is not strictly enforced, others such as Malaysia want to export logs to earn foreign exchange and would resent any global environmental regulations which prohibited such exports.

Following the Uruguay Round, the problem is that a country that bans the export of logs has to apply similar treatment to its own domestic industry. Non-discrimination must apply; if trees cannot be axed for export, they cannot be axed for use by local industry. From a development viewpoint, this is one of the most worrying aspects of the GATT, one that goes beyond purely environmental issues. It would seek to remove a country's right to do what it wants with its own resources; a country is expected to subject itself to the free play of international economic forces. This could lead to considerable conflict between countries.

The GATT study is on firmer ground when it argues that the liberalization of trade and less protectionism are likely to mean that food in high-income countries would be produced with fewer chemicals 'which in turn would reduce chemical residues in food and in the natural environment'.[12] This would also appear to be true in developing countries; a study of rice production in several Asian countries in the late 1970s found that fertilizer and pesticide use were 'highly correlated with the domestic producer price of rice'.[13] Reducing the level of domestic farm support could therefore help the environment in both developed and developing countries.

When there is conflict between free trade and environmental issues, GATT is firmly in the free trade camp, even appearing insensitive to environmental considerations. In August 1991, for example, a GATT panel ruled against United States legislation which banned imports of tuna from Mexico. The ban was in force because fleet drift-nets killed too many dolphins. GATT's ruling against the US legislation could be seen as the organization's way of stating that free trade should have priority over environment considerations. But it is by no means clear that governments and people are willing to accept that free trade should take place if it causes environmental damage.

There is also uncertainty about where GATT stands on the Montreal protocol (an agreement reached by representatives from most of the world's governments who gathered in Canada in 1987 to review the problem of the destruction of the ozone layer and the role of CFCs), which envisages trade sanctions against countries that fail to reduce their use of CFCs. A GATT official admitted, 'we don't know what would happen if someone took this kind of action'.[14] While there is no environmental clause in the Uruguay Round agreement, pressure is likely to grow for international trade to be scrutinized for its environmental impact. A United States senator, Max Baucus, has called for a global 'green round' in the wake of the Uruguay Round.[15] The Uruguay Round will almost certainly be the last of the big trade rounds which do not take environmental factors into account. Quite minor changes in GATT's articles would help – it could incorporate the concept of sustainable development, for example, and recognize the need to protect areas of environmental importance.

Some of the changes made under the Uruguay Round will benefit the developing world, especially improved access to Western markets. But GATT's weakness is that its philosophy depends on the pure economics of free trade, with extending trade throughout the world and ensuring that production takes place in the cheapest country; the market is supreme. So GATT is inevitably political; its member nations are expected to follow free trade principles and let the market decide; government intervention in the market on social or environmental grounds can be challenged and compensation may have to be paid. The irony of GATT is that a body pledged to the free play of market forces lays down rules which interfere in the development efforts of poorer nations. The organization needs reform; there are higher human goals and aspirations than free trade. Especially if the needs of the poorest are to be met, free trade will often have to be offset by social considerations.[16]

## The United Nations Conference on Trade and Development (UNCTAD)

The countries of the South who gained their independence in the 1940s and 1950s were soon to discover the limited nature of that independence. Although they were politically free, little if anything had changed economically. They continued to produce primary goods for their former colonial masters, and by the early 1960s it had become clear that these goods were earning less – the terms of trade were moving against them. When they tried to diversify into manufactured goods, the new developing countries found that the West erected barriers against all but very small quantities.

Existing international organizations were of little help. GATT was chiefly concerned with trade between Western countries and had nothing to offer about how to increase the prices of minerals and agricultural commodities. There was no secretariat of the South to which developing countries could turn. A new kind of organization was needed, they believed, if trade was to help their development.

At the 1961 General Assembly of the United Nations a resolution was passed expressing concern at the deteriorating terms of trade of developing countries. UNCTAD was born out of that resolution; under the auspices of the Economic and Social Committee of the UN, a conference on trade and development was called for 1964, and took place in Geneva that year. 'At that time it was simply a one-off conference', say Morton and Tulloch, 'Western countries, which had opposed the convening of the conference, were also against the creation of a standing body which would cut across and perhaps usurp the functions of GATT'.[17] With support from East European countries, developing countries won the argument that a new UN body should be created. The UN Conference on Trade and Development became a permanent organ of the UN General Assembly in December 1964. The hostility of many Western countries to an organization they did not want or welcome has lingered over its activities for some 30 years.

While the 1964 conference achieved little, the personal dynamism of UNCTAD's first Secretary-General, Argentinian economist Don Raul Prebisch, gave the new organization an initial high profile. Under Prebisch's leadership the Secretariat developed imaginative schemes for developing countries to earn more from their commodities and enjoy improved access to Western markets for their manufactured goods. But the pace of discussion proved excruciatingly slow. It was agreed that a major UNCTAD session be held every four years. When UNCTAD II met in New Delhi in 1968, all it achieved was a draft agreement on commodity arrangements that meant very little in practice. UNTCAD III in Santiago, four years later, continued talking about commodities but added monetary issues to the agenda, with a proposal from India that IMF Special Drawings Rights be issued to developing countries, with a specific link to development purposes (see Chapter 8).

The first three UNCTAD sessions achieved virtually nothing because developing countries had no power to persuade Western countries to agree to changes in the international trading system. Between 1972 and UNCTAD IV in Nairobi in 1976, there were, however, some sizeable shocks to the international economy. Oil-exporting countries forgot their differences and came together to raise the price of oil fourfold. Industry in the West staggered under the higher prices and began to wonder whether the producers of other raw materials, such as copper and tin, could do the same. The call for a new international economic order had come in May 1974 at a special session of the UN General Assembly (see Chapter 1) and relationships between rich and poor countries seemed to be about to change. For millions of the world's poor, it was perhaps the most hopeful period of the twentieth century. It seemed that at last they had a chance of getting realistic prices for the goods they traded on world markets.

Producers of raw commodities in the South began to realize that, as suppliers of materials to the North, they had considerable potential power. The oil-exporting countries promised support to other commodity producers. If those producers withdrew their supplies, then the economies of Western countries could be plunged into chaos. 'If we fail to get an acceptable new international system of trade between rich and poor worlds', said a leader in the *Observer* on UNCTAD IV, 'we risk a new type of economic warfare – on the model of the oil crisis – which could be as costly in resources as the wars of the past'.[18]

Having supported the call for a new international economic order in 1974, governments of Western countries had the opportunity at UNCTAD IV to agree to changes in international trade that were acceptable to the developing world. The omens had seemed good; the UNCTAD Secretariat had put forward proposals for 'an integrated programme for commodities' with four chief elements: that commodity agreements be negotiated for 18 of the world's largest traded commodities, with prices 'remunerative and just to producers and equitable to consumers'; that a $6 billion common fund be set up to finance those agreements; that developing and industrialized countries negotiate more multilateral trade agreements – with a certain volume of goods changing hands at an agreed price; and that developing countries be enabled to process more of their commodities. Countries would contribute to the common fund in accordance with their role in world trade, with the large trading countries of the Western world paying more than the smaller countries.

If the requests seemed reasonable, the response from Western governments was similar to their response at the first three UNCTAD sessions. Again there was a reluctance to concede anything, and for weeks the talks dragged on inconclusively. Agreement was eventually reached to put some elements of an integrated programme for commodities into place, although, on the common fund, the conference ended merely by saying that 'steps will be taken . . . towards the negotiation of a common fund'.[19] The 18 commodity agreements were supposed to be negotiated by the end of 1978, but there was virtually no progress. The long drawn-out negotiations that followed on the common fund coincided with the growing realization that non-oil commodity producers were in a much weaker bargaining position than the oil-producing countries. The West conceded nothing of importance because it still held power over the trading system; the prospect of a new international economic order ended in Nairobi.

It is worth recording that UNCTAD IV dealt with debt issues – some five years before debt was widely seen as a major issue. By 1976 it was already clear that debt was a smouldering timebomb. The resolution passed on debt in Nairobi speaks of the 'mounting debt burden' of many developing countries, and welcomes the fact that governments of developed countries had pledged themselves at the conference 'to respond in a multilateral framework by quick and constructive consideration of individual requests with a view to taking prompt action to relieve developing countries suffering from debt-service difficulties'.[20] If such prompt action had been taken in the years following UNCTAD IV then developing countries would have been in a stronger position to cope with the new shocks that hit them in the early 1980s, especially rising interest rates. But Western countries did not take the Nairobi resolution seriously. The severe debt crisis that faces the developing world can partly be traced to the unwillingness of richer nations to help developing countries get on top of the debt problems in the later years of the 1970s.

UNCTAD V in Manila was brought ahead to 1979, in order that it was not held in the same year as presidential elections in the United States. At the Nairobi UNCTAD, it had seemed to developing countries as if the US was unwilling to make any initiatives for fear of what electors might think back home if generous concessions were made in an election year. Bringing the conference forward, however, achieved little. Raul Prebisch told delegates in Manila that 'for the first time in history, technology offers the possibility of solving problems of human well-being but the possibility is being spoiled by governments'.[21]

Resolutions were adopted by the gathering asking the Secretariat to carry out studies on the marketing, distribution and processing of commodities – work that it was doing anyway. It was becoming apparent that these four-yearly sessions were of very little benefit to the countries of the South, who were struggling to earn foreign exchange from commodities and manufactured goods. Governments of Western countries showed their unwillingness to negotiate any serious changes in the world trading system by sending quite low-level delegations to UNCTAD sessions, usually at best a junior minister.

By the early 1980s, UNCTAD's integrated programme was in tatters, defeated by the unwillingness of Western countries to take it seriously. Although a common fund had been agreed in principle, it was allocated only $750 million rather than $6 billion, and was clearly going to be of limited benefit. UNCTAD VI at Belgrade in 1983 and UNCTAD VII in Geneva in 1987 again achieved little worthwhile.

In 1992 (five years after the previous conference, a return to a US presidential year, and an indication of the lower expectations of UNCTAD), the eighth session was held in Cartagena de Indias, Colombia. Its aims were modest, one of them being how to restructure itself to ensure survival. It was agreed that UNCTAD should continue to be the focal point in the UN for dealing with matters of trade, finance, investment, services and technology. But as the organization has little power, and lacks the whole-hearted support of Western nations, its role will be limited. It will publish useful statistics which will show how the world is; it will act as watchdog, but without teeth.

The story of UNCTAD between 1964 and 1992 has been captioned in its initials. UNCTAD's initials also stand for 'until the next conference try and delay' or 'under no circumstances take any decisions'. Both sum up this trade and development organization sadly, but brilliantly. It has become a victim of the West's unwillingness to make concessions, to take decisions that would improve the lot of developing countries in world trade. Although the work of the UNCTAD Secretariat in drawing attention to the importance of the issues, and in keeping comprehensive statistics about developing country trade is valuable, the organization in 1992 was a shadow of what it could have been. Western countries were continuing to strangle the organization they never wanted to see.[22]

# 10 Alternative trade

Sahara Khatoon is one of a 17-member group in Bangladesh which makes sikas – jute supports for hanging baskets – for a co-operative marketing organization which sells on the international market. Her day is a long one; she gets up at 5.00 a.m., milks her cows, cleans the stable and cooks a meal. At around 10.00 a.m. she makes sikas for two hours before turning to other household jobs. In the evening Sahara Khatoon tries to spend three or four hours making the sikas until she drops into bed exhausted around midnight. Her work making sikas will have earned her the equivalent of about 50 UK pence. While this is low, Sahara says that she is much better off now than in 1981 when the group started. Before the group began, she was 'very poor and didn't have enough to eat'; now she says that all the group members eat properly and can afford to send their children to school, which was previously out of the question.

Before Sahara Khatoon joined the group, she was illiterate and not even able to count. Now she has learned from the co-operative marketing organization, the Jute Works, how to keep accounts. Like other group members, Sahara has learnt how to budget for her family and this has given her a bigger say in family affairs, which is hardly common in Bangladesh. Her group is one of several hundred throughout the country that are producing for the Jute Works – in all, some 7000 women are involved in making products for the firm. These are then sold on world markets, many of them through alternative trading organizations (ATOs). One of their customers is the northern England-based ATO, Traidcraft.[1]

As conventional North–South trade is surrounded by obstacles and has so far yielded few benefits for most people in developing countries, so interest has grown in 'alternative trade'. This activity has already brought results and offers hope of a better deal from international trade for many millions in the developing world.

Alternative trade basically consists of the NGOs and businesses in the North buying goods from producer groups in the South and then selling them through shops, mail order catalogues, churches, and so on, sometimes at slightly higher prices than would normally apply. Some ATOs specialize in making information available about alternative products. As the Northern ATO deals directly with producer groups, or with co-operatives like the Jute Works, the trade eliminates the intermediary, so giving producers a better chance of a decent return. This kind of trade therefore offers a different and potentially more profitable route for Third World manufactured and primary products.

Interest in alternative trade began in the mid-1960s; Britain's largest aid agency, Oxfam, started an alternative trading organization, Oxfam Trading, in 1965. There are now several hundred ATOs in the countries of the North – 130 in the United States alone – all of whom are working along broadly similar lines. The combined annual turnover of these organizations is around £250 million. While this represents only a tiny fraction of current Third World merchandise exports of $738 billion, there is a considerable potential for growth.

Although some Northern ATOs are an off-shoot of aid and development agencies, all normally operate as independent businesses, trying to survive in a competitive commercial world. As ATO prices are sometimes higher, this means that the products have to be of good quality. The products they buy and sell typically include crafts, both decorative and utilitarian; furnishings and household goods; clothing; and foodstuffs, particularly coffee and tea. Some ATOs extend their ranges by selling non-Third World goods such as recycled paper. Sales channels also vary; shops, mail order and local groups account for the bulk of the sales; some ATOs act as wholesalers to commercial outlets.

The Dutch-based International Federation for Alternative Trade (IFAT) helps ATOs to co-ordinate their activities; comprising some 40 organizations, it helps to establish aims and trading practices. While its member-ATOs are mostly Northern-based, the federation includes a small number of alternative trading organizations from the developing world – for example, the prophetically named 'Last Hope International' of Nigeria (see Appendix 3 for complete list). Third

World ATOs are usually exporters of products that are seeking alternative trade routes.

IFAT says that ATOs differ from the more usual commercial trade channels in a number of ways:

1. They give priority to small producers which find it difficult to undertake export trade without a sympathetic marketing partner.
2. They are especially interested in the organizational structure of producer groups; they prefer groups in which members have a say in the way they are run and which provide other benefits such as education or welfare schemes.
3. They pay fair prices which allow the producer a reasonable return and will often give advance payments on orders.
4. They build their range around products made by the producers they want to support.
5. They promote their suppliers among their customers, giving information about the project, the locality and the difficulties faced by small producers.
6. They aim to provide information on overseas marketing requirements and assist with matters such as design, technology, packaging, labelling and sales promotion.[2]

While there is a huge diversity, 'there are broadly two kinds of ATO. One sort takes the producers as its starting point and will try to sell whatever they produce. This sounds good in principle but it means you can end up with some rather unusual or unsuitable products – and it may not help in the process of awareness raising', says Graham Young of Traidcraft.[3] Other ATOs, says Young, are orientated towards the Western market, keeping a clear eye on the selling potential. These organizations will work with producers to meet a particular market niche. The drawback here is that the desires of the producer can get lost in the process. The best lies somewhere in between, believes Young, 'and a lot of ATOs occupy this middle territory . . . sticking with producers during hard times, social unrest, adverse weather conditions and even dishonesty . . . trying to operate fair business practice in your home operation, and doing justice, but more than that – going further than might justly be expected.'[4]

Since the mid-1960s, ATOs have developed in most Western countries. ATOs in Australia include CAA Trading which buys handicrafts, clothing, jewellery, household goods, tea and coffee from around 15 developing countries, and also from Aboriginal groups; the Sydney-based World Development Tea Co-operative, which imports a range of 'Ceylon' tea from Sri Lanka; and a church-allied organization, Trading Partners, based in Victoria, again buying handicrafts, jewellery and household items. New Zealand has Trade Aid, established in 1973, which is innovative in that it pre-pays many of its craft producers, some by as much as 12 months in advance, so that they can buy raw materials for production. Among ATOs in Japan are Refugees International Japan which buys only handicrafts made by refugees.

United States-based ATOs include Friends of the Third World, Fort Wayne, which buys foodstuffs, handicrafts and clothing from 30 countries; Pueblo to People in Houston; and Equal Exchange of Massachusetts. In Canada, the chief ATO is Oxfam-Canada's Bridgehead, buying and distributing a wide range of Third World products. In Germany one of the chief ATOs is GEPA: Aktion Dritte Welt Handel, which turns over more than £10 million worth of handicrafts and foodstuffs a year. The Netherlands has SOS Wereldhandel, buying and selling similar products, and other organizations. There are also thriving ATOs in the Scandinavian countries.

The ATOs based in Britain provide a good example of the growth and thinking of alternative trading and also some of the problems.

## Oxfam Trading

Oxfam Trading was the first and is the largest alternative trading organization in Britain. With retail sales in 1991 of over £16 million, Oxfam Trading sells Third World products in its 840 shops in Britain, and also through mail order catalogues. Handicrafts make up over half its range, in the form of decorative items, baskets and utilitarian products; floor coverings and furnishings account for around 25 per cent; clothing, furniture and jewellery 13 per cent; and foodstuffs such as coffee, cocoa, tea, nuts, honey and spices the remaining seven per cent. All products are purchased direct from producer groups in the developing world for a fair price; consumers in Britain may sometimes pay more for them because they know that producers are directly benefiting the poor. Oxfam says that it targets its orders to people with particular needs, such as minority groups and refugees.

According to Ben Whittaker, author of a book on Oxfam's first 40 years, the idea of Oxfam Trading began after the agency's workers, 'visiting the scene of disasters abroad, were shown goods people had made and wanted to sell to regain their self-respect, and suggested that these could be tried in Oxfam shops'.[5] 'Oxfam saw that by providing a fair market for Third World products, paying prices judged to be fair in the local economy, and buying through organizations which ensured that the bulk of the price reached the actual producers, it could begin to attack one root cause of poverty: the dependence of small-scale producers on local traders, who pay them low prices', says Oxfam worker, Belinda Coote.[6]

Oxfam Trading sales built up slowly to reach £2.1 million in 1979; the 1980s witnessed quite rapid growth but then levelled out during Britain's economic recession. Its director, Martin Honeywell, describes prospects for the 1990s as 'very exciting; the market for ethnic handicraft and giftware is growing rapidly, market research shows that more and more consumers are looking for ethnically traded products, those that fairly reward producers for their time and skill. New handicraft and giftware products, and dry food goods will allow consumers to exercise their ethical preferences in wider markets'.[7]

## Traidcraft

Traidcraft, the second largest ATO in Britain, was set up in 1979 and became a public limited company in 1984. It initially took over, by agreement, part of the business of Tearcraft, an ATO that was part of the church aid agency Tearfund. With a turnover in 1991 of £5.5 million, Traidcraft operates on a Christian basis. 'We use the phrase – acting in love and justice', says Traidcraft worker, Graham Young; 'this reflects our Christian roots but it is also a useful way of describing the general concept'.[8] The organization says it is a 'response to God's call to "bring good news to the poor, to proclaim liberty to the captives, to set the downtrodden free". It is committed to showing that there is an alternative way to trade, that rejects self-interest and promotes justice'.[9]

151

Handicrafts account for just over a third of Traidcraft's turnover; textiles and clothing, furnishing, tea, coffee and wholefoods from developing countries also figure prominently in its range. In addition, recycled paper products are sold. Most of Traidcraft's sales are made by way of mail order, and through around 2000 local representatives who are often drawn from churches. While a sizeable proportion of sales are made to church members, the local representatives also exhibit Traidcraft's goods outside churches. Goods are again purchased from Third World groups that are organized for the benefit of their members. An associate organization, Traidcraft Exchange, is engaged on education work in Britain; it also provides an extensive business advisory service for small-scale Third World enterprises producing goods for export.

Traidcraft stresses that it is a public company, not an aid organization. Its 1991 Financial Statement says that the company 'aims to maximize the benefits to the overseas producers from whom the company buys'.[10] Not all ATOs in Northern countries take the view that their organizations should try to maximize their profits. Some ATOs see their work as a purely symbolic witness to a fairer trading system. Traidcraft's External Affairs director, Richard Evans, says that his organization's work is a witness but also far more. He points to the economic benefits that the sales of its products bring to the poor, and the evidence that the goods it buys and sells are making a difference to people who produce them.[11]

## Twin Trading

The Third World Information Network (TWIN) is a London-based organization with a trading associate, TWIN Trading Ltd. Its central concept is 'networking between First and Third Worlds'.[12] TWIN publishes a quarterly newsletter, *The Network* which it says is 'for the equal exchange of information on trade and technology'. The TWIN groups help associations of small-scale producers to overcome the obstacles that make it difficult for them to trade on world markets; they offer producers a consultancy service, provide technical support, try to ensure that producers retain more of the benefits of their output, and also help them to implement social and economic development programmes from the extra income they earn.

TWIN has worked with organizations in Latin America to develop the market for coffee and honey, including the *Coalicion de Ejidos de Costa Grande* in Guerrero, southern Mexico. This involves over 2000 small-scale coffee producers who are faced with the struggle of maintaining their livelihoods in face of declining world coffee prices. Members of the *Coalicion* visited Britain in 1990 to learn more about the UK coffee market, and to establish their own trading agency in Britain. TWIN has also provided credit to nut producers in Brazil to help them establish an alternative market for their trade which meant they did not have to deal with intermediaries who paid them only low prices.

These activities are all inter-dependent, says TWIN's 1991 Annual Report; 'trade development projects require up-to-date and relevant information, networking, i.e. the exchange of contacts and the co-ordination of projects helps to create "space" for small-scale producers and their products in international markets, consultancy is a way of sharing the experience and knowledge gained through practical trading initiatives'. Michael Barrett Brown, the chair of TWIN, says that its aim is to move alternative products away from limited markets, such as wholefood shops, and into more mainstream markets.[13]

## Joint efforts

In a joint activity to promote alternative trading, four British ATOs, Oxfam Trading, Traidcraft, TWIN Trading and Equal Exchange, came together in 1991 to market a high quality arabica coffee, Cafedirect. This is grown by over 20 000 coffee producers in Mexico and Costa Rica. Working on small, family farms they have combined in associations and co-operatives to improve their own conditions and to make direct export possible.

The collapse of the International Coffee Agreement (see Chapter 3) has led to depressed coffee prices and considerable difficulties for small-scale coffee producers. Selling at a higher price to the Cafedirect project provides direct income to the Latin American producers with no agents or other intermediaries to pay. This collaboration means the producers get a bigger order, they are paid above market prices for more of their produce, and economies of scale in shipping, roasting, packaging and distribution make the coffee available to British consumers at a reasonable price. Higher incomes enable the producers to improve transport, provide scholarship funds, purchase agricultural equipment and make other community and social improvements.

'Ethical issues are very much on the agenda for all the large supermarket chains. With an eye on the still increasing momentum of the ecological movement, there is an awareness that consumers believe Third World producers deserve a better deal,' says a representative of the ATOs. In addition to sales through their normal channels, the ATOs are hoping to persuade the large supermarket chains to handle the coffee. 'Cafedirect is the first opportunity the consumer has had to make his or her feelings known in an area that large suppliers will no longer be able to ignore'.[14]

Pressure for an extension of alternative trading in coffee is also coming from developing countries. In March 1992, small-scale coffee growers from 15 countries launched a Small Farmers' Co-operative Society to help them widen the market for their crops. The society covers some 250 000 growers in Africa, Latin America and the Caribbean; low world coffee prices have stimulated this producer action.

One of the most significant joint activities of British ATOs is the proposed launch, in October 1992, of a Fairtrade Mark. In an initiative that builds on the Dutch 'Max Havelaar' scheme, it is intended that the mark will be attached to shop products in Britain that have been traded on fair terms. The Max Havelaar Quality Mark is attached to coffee in the Netherlands that has been traded fairly. 'By mid-1991 more than 300 000 coffee farmers were selling through the Max Havelaar scheme, and it is making a real difference to their lives', says Belinda Coote.[15] Max Havelaar coffee succeeded in capturing a £25 million share of the Dutch coffee market within two years, and is now available in over 6000 supermarkets in the Netherlands. Research indicates that nearly three-quarters of Dutch people know of the Fairtrade Mark idea.

## The Body Shop

Although it is not an ATO in the traditional sense, the Body Shop has operated a fair trading scheme with developing countries since 1987. Through a 'Trade not Aid' scheme, The Body Shop says that in an 'unpatronizing and nonexploitative manner', it encourages local communities in developing countries to make products for the company. It stresses that projects have to be commercially viable 'for both parties'.

One of its projects is sited in Nepal, where the Body Shop has commissioned a range of hand-made paper products from a village near Kathmandu. This is helping to revive a craft that dates back to the eleventh century, but which had declined because of restrictions on the use of a particular shrub which was the main source of fibre. Under the project, alternative plants were identified for use. Products on sale in the Body Shop include notebooks, gift bags, drawer liners and writing paper. A scheme in Brazil has been developed with the Kayapo Indians in the eastern Amazon Basin, to enable them to produce nut oil using nuts harvested from the forests. This makes a contribution to forest preservation, as it enables trees to yield a profit while standing, rather than cut down. Brazil Nut Oil Conditioner has been on sale in the Body Shop since 1991. Honey and beeswax from Tanzania are among other ingredients from developing countries on sale in its shops.[16]

*New Consumer*

Set up in 1989, New Consumer is a 'not-for-profit' organization that publishes books and a monthly magazine in Britain to provide consumers with the information they need to use their purchasing power 'to improve their environment and society'.[17] In 1991 it published *The Global Consumer: Best buys to help the Third World*.[18] The book gives detailed information on brand goods that can directly benefit the Third World; it also lists others which – diplomatically – it recommends should be avoided. On footwear, for example, it says 'it is difficult to see Brazilian shoes as a good deal; better to go for the Asian suppliers'.[19] New Consumer is establishing a foundation to help the Fairtrade Mark off the ground in Britain.

A number of ATOs in Britain have educational teams which seek to raise awareness about conditions for people in the Third World. Products from ATO shops and sources will often have labels or come with small leaflets which explain that the product has been traded in a different way. The label on Cafedirect, for example, says 'Cafedirect's promise is high quality coffee for the consumer, and a higher income for the small farm producer. This coffee comes direct to you from the producers, and the price includes a premium for them'.

Alternative trade has led to better returns for producers and shows that international trade can be conducted on a fair basis and help people out of poverty. But inevitably there are problems; for some producer groups, notably women's groups, there are examples of where the prevailing norms of society hinder the progress the groups should receive. Rachel Sylvester quotes a former Oxfam worker who 'describes her dismay' after visiting a Bangladeshi women's co-operative making jute hanging baskets. 'We'd been buying from them for a long time, but hardly anything had changed for the women there. If the women's group got an order, men would get involved and the women only had power over a small part of the process.'[20]

One of the biggest problems for many of the Third World peoples who produce for alternative trade is that changes in customer tastes in the West can make for instability. Products that are much in demand this year may be completely out of fashion next year. The tastes of people in Western countries are fickle, liable to rapid change. But a sudden change in consumer tastes can mean considerable problems for producers. Sahara Khatoon, mentioned above, fared well from making sikas in the 1980s. But by 1992, the demand for hanging baskets had declined, causing uncertainty for Sahara and her group. During the 1980s there was a buoyant demand in British shops for ducks of all shapes, sizes and materials. By the early 1990s, however, ducks were little in demand. 'The market for handicrafts is perpetually changing', said a development worker closely involved with alternative trade, 'but handicraft producers cannot change quickly enough'.

Some ATOs could be criticized for placing too much emphasis on handicrafts. It is not necessarily a good thing for people in developing countries to be too dependent on handicrafts; there are other products that can be made. But Richard Evans of Traidcraft says that although the organization is now putting more emphasis on functional products, such as clothing, handicrafts often provide the first opportunity for people in developing countries to earn a cash income.[21]

The way to increase alternative trade would seem to lie in getting products with the Fairtrade Mark into the large supermarkets and chain stores. Some ATOs are now active in trying to persuade mainstream shops to stock alternative products. With ethical issues 'on the agenda' for large stores, a sizeable expansion of this fairer trade is a real possibility. Provided this widening out of alternative trade can be achieved, it is just possible that the 1990s could see something of a trade revolution with a growing number of producers getting the fair deal denied to them under the 'normal' routes of the international trading system. And if the Fairtrade Mark can be seen in a wide range of shops, it will also help to raise trade issues in shoppers' minds. Alternative trade is already raising consciousness about the issues, and leading to better returns and a decent livelihood for many producers; it could be an important part of international trade in the future.

# 11 South–South trade and producer co-operation

A member of a trade delegation from Cameroon, on a visit to nearby Zaire, found that Zaire was importing, from outside the region, large quantities of salt, sugar, detergent, metal containers and other products that could have been bought much more cheaply from Cameroon. Importers in Zaire were put in touch with exporters in Cameroon.

In the duty free shop at Gaborone international airport in Botswana, passengers can purchase South African wine, but not Zimbabwean wine. Yet Botswana and Zimbabwe are both members of a regional group which is trying to increase co-operation among its member states.

In view of the difficulties that countries of the South have in trading with the North, it is not surprising that they are interested in increasing trade with each other. South–South trade makes abundant sense. The South possesses enormously varied resources which can be deployed for exchanging goods within the Southern hemisphere. If countries of the South trade more with each other, they can reduce their dependence on the North and have a more diversified trading base. They will have the opportunity to break away, at least to some extent, from the exploitative pattern of North–South trade, and to develop a more fair and just pattern of international trade. They may be able to buy the goods at cheaper prices, as in the above case of Cameroon and Zaire. But countries of the South have often shown a slowness to promote each other's goods, as passengers at Gaborone airport discover.

While South–South trade shows promising growth, a number of factors hold it back:

○ History. Most countries in the South have little tradition of trading with each other.

○ Many developing countries are producing similar types of commodities. There is little scope, for example, for Uganda to trade coffee with next-door Kenya.

○ Poor 'connections'. While telecommunications are improving, road, rail and air links between developing countries (especially in Africa) are often poor. Transporting goods is often difficult; the driving licence held by a driver of one country, for example, may not be valid in a neighbouring country. Countries may have different widths of railway tracks, meaning that trains cannot run across borders.

○ The South does not have a bank to promote South-South trade. It lacks financial institutions to finance exports. Developing countries will usually not accept each other's currencies for trading transactions; this means that a currency of the North is often needed to facilitate South–South trade – but such foreign exchange is usually scarce.

○ The national development programmes of countries in the South have often inhibited rather than encouraged trade with other developing countries. This may be changing.

○ Developing countries have little money to develop the institutions, banks, transport links to foster South–South trade.

○ Political differences between countries holds back co-operation.

○ Freight charges are often higher for South–South than they are for South–North trade (see Chapter 5).

○ The South lacks a secretariat, such as an equivalent of the North's Organization for Economic Co-operation and Development (OEDC).

These factors have combined together to put a brake on South–South trade. Despite the constraints, however, there has been growth. In 1970, developing countries traded just under 20 per cent of their merchandise with each other, $11.2 billion out of total merchandise trade of $55.9 billion. By 1990 they were trading 25.2 per cent of their goods with each other, $186.7 billion out of $740 billion. Just over $21 billion of exports was traded with developing countries in other continents, while about $165 billion – nearly 89 per cent – was done between countries in the same region.[1]

Regional groupings – developed to promote economic co-operation between countries of a region – have not, however,

been successful in facilitating any major growth of trade between members. Between 1970 and 1990 only modest increases have occurred. Almost two-thirds of South—South
trade in 1990 involved south and south-east Asian countries;
they traded 20 per cent of their goods with each other in
1970 and by 1990 this had risen to 23 per cent. West Asian
countries traded 11 per cent of their goods with each other in
1970; by 1990 this had fallen to 10.2 per cent. African countries traded 5.6 per cent of their goods with each other in
1970, 7.4 per cent in 1990. In Latin America regional trade
fell from 17.3 per cent in 1970 to 14 per cent in 1990.[2]

While the scope for lifting the 25 per cent of trade that
developing countries do with each other is considerable, the
problem for the countries of the South lies in breaking out of
the colonial pattern with only limited financial resources. In
colonial times it was common for the economy of a country
in the South to be developed purely along lines of serving the
'master's' economy. A plantation would be developed, say
160 kilometres (100 miles) from a country's coastline, and a
rail link would be built between plantation and seaport, for
transporting to the North. Africa has many such rails to the
sea. There was then no point in laying down track that
crossed African borders. 'The French built only what they
needed to find and export Gabon's raw materials . . . (the)
Colonials' habit of building only those roads and ports and
power plants that served their purposes, while ignoring the
rest of the country, still stifles Third World economies'.[3]

This pattern is changing, but only slowly. There are now
roads across the borders of most African countries, for example, but there can still be lengthy delays and 'red tape' at
customs posts. Encouraging efforts have been made by the
countries of southern Africa to develop transport links. But
with nearly 80 per cent of their trade with countries of the
North, it is understandable that the South has been more
concerned with maintaining such trade, and has given less
priority to developing the potential of trade with countries in
a similar position.

One of the most pressing needs of the South is for its own
bank to promote South–South trade. *The Challenge of the
South* (see below) speaks of the setting up of a Southern bank
as a 'compelling necessity'.[4] Such a bank would help to
smooth trade between developing countries; it would help
provide the credit that is needed to facilitate exports, pro-

mote joint ventures and possibly balance of payments financing and commodity price stabilization schemes. There is a particular need for export credit. Exports can frequently only take place if customers in the importing country are able to buy them on credit terms. The capacity of developing countries to grant export credit is 'extremely limited'; in practice, a high rate is charged by existing banks for these credits. The report is hopeful that a bank of the South could offer export credit at lower rates, and thereby 'provide vital support for South–South trade'.[5]

Developing countries have not yet reached agreement over the bank; investment funds would be needed to get it off the ground, which again are in short supply. While the collapse of the Bank of Credit and Commerce International (BCCI) – a major bank based in the South – chilled the climate for a new Southern bank, the need for it remains.

The benefits of South–South trade, including a bank, have been extolled since the early 1960s at many meetings of the Group of 77 and summits of the non-aligned countries, but little actual progress has been made. During the late 1980s, however, there was a step that could mark the beginning of more concerted South–South co-operation. In July 1987 the South Commission was established, following a non-aligned summit the previous year. Consisting of 28 prominent individuals, the Commission was given the task of analysing 'national development experience with a view to elaborating an integrated perspective and vision for the future'. In 1990, it published a 325-page report, *The Challenge to the South*, which shows how developing countries would gain strength and bargaining power through mutual co-operation. The report contains an agenda for the South and could prove an important landmark. With the publication of the report, the Commission finished its work and was followed by the setting up of the South Centre, which has the task of promoting the implementation of the Commission's recommendations.

But the South Centre has insufficient resources to become an OECD of the South. Whereas the Paris-based OECD employs over a thousand professional staff, the South Centre has two full-time professionals in Tanzania and one in Geneva. Neither has certain funding for even this limited operation and the centre may have to close.

During the late 1980s, there were several new initiatives to develop South–South co-operation. In April 1988, at a meet-

161

ing in Belgrade, the South established its own 'Global System of Trade Preferences', with 48 countries agreeing to offer one another trade concessions, such as lower import tariffs, on some 1300 products. The agreement should help encourage additional South–South trade, even in a modest way. According to UNCTAD, annual imports of the items included in the preferences come to around $10 billion.[6]

Also in 1988, the Group of 77 decided to set up a trade information network among developing countries. Three focal points are being established, in Duoala, Cameroon; Karachi, Pakistan; and Bogotá, Colombia – each within the office of the national Chamber of Commerce. If a company in Nigeria has, for example, been importing leather goods from Europe, but would prefer to buy them in Africa, it contacts the Duoala office and a search is made on a database. This would then yield information about the categories of leather goods that are produced in Africa, specifying which countries.

At the non-aligned summit in 1989 a decision was taken to establish a 15-member summit level group of developing countries, comprising Algeria, Argentina, Brazil, Egypt, India, Indonesia, Jamaica, Malaysia, Mexico, Nigeria, Peru, Senegal, Venezuela, Yugoslavia and Zimbabwe. The group – called G15 – was set up 'in the belief that there is considerable potential for greater and mutually beneficial co-operation among developing countries with a view to enhancing collective self-reliance in an increasingly interdependent world.'[7]

The summit agreed that greater South–South co-operation will 'complement and reinforce domestic programmes for national development and social and economic progress'. It is also believed that 'such co-operation would provide greater cohesion and credibility to all developing countries in their pursuit of a more positive and productive North–South dialogue'.[8] The summit group hopes to serve as an 'action-oriented forum for regular consultations among developing countries with a view to fostering the co-ordination of policies and actions of South countries at the global level and to assist in the formulation and implementation of programmes of co-operation among them.'[9] The Group of 15 is likely to establish a small secretariat.

An important potential route for developing countries to increase South–South trade is through countertrade which dispenses with money (see Chapter 8). This has been called 'a useful mechanism for overcoming difficulties of payments, export credit and foreign exchange which might otherwise be serious obstacles to the expansion of South–South trade'.[10] So far, however, most countertrade between developing countries has been conducted through intermediaries in the North – who have reaped many of the benefits. Provided that developing countries can organize for countertrade without Northern middlemen, this could be a considerable growth area.

## Regional trade

Regional economic co-operation between countries of the South has been tried and tested and has gone through numerous difficulties in the past 30 years. Regional groups have been troubled with disagreements about the pace and style of co-operation, and these have inevitably held up progress. Many countries have been unwilling to forgo national sovereignty for the good of the region as a whole. Extra trade within regions could be generated by the right kind of regional trade organization, especially through the development of free trade areas, or common markets. But, as the following details show, the groupings have not, so far, led to any significant increase in trade within most regions of the South.

### Africa

In view of Africa's economic difficulties, and its generally low returns from international trade, increased intra-African trade could be an important alternative. According to an International Labour Office (ILO) study, 'without a regional market, sub-Saharan Africa will not be organized on a sufficient scale to become an area of economic growth. Without political co-ordination in all areas . . . it will remain too weak in the face of the large groupings which are being established everywhere in the world.'[11]

The study estimates that roughly $25 billion of the $71 billion worth of manufactured goods that Africa imports every year could be saved through subregional and regional trade. This is equivalent to the creation of an additional five million jobs within the region, applying an incremental capital/labour ratio of $5000 prevailing in 1988. There is also considerable scope for savings in food imports. 'If the current food import bill of about $10 billion from outside the region could be cut by, say, 50 per cent and substituted with regional products, an additional one million jobs could be created,' notes the study.[12]

When African leaders met in Nigeria for the Organization of African Unity summit in 1980, they drew up the Lagos 'Plan of Action' which included a commitment to an all-African common market by the year 2000. But with attempts at regional markets in Africa making only slow progress, there seems little chance of achieving such an aim.

Africa's first regional economic grouping was established in 1967 when Kenya, Tanzania and Uganda formed the **East African Community.** The EAC was a free trade area, although the weaker members, Tanzania and Uganda, had the right to apply certain tariff duties against the economically stronger Kenya. An airline was set up, and a bank which aimed to invest three-quarters of its funds in Tanzania and Uganda. But despite its intention to help the weaker members, Kenya appeared to make more economic ground, especially with lucrative tourism. This led to tensions and, in February 1977, Tanzania closed its borders with Kenya to stop tourists coming across. This was effectively the end of the EAC. Political differences between the three countries, verging at times on war, did not create the right atmosphere for economic co-operation.

The 16-member **Economic Community of West African States** was formed in 1975 and consists of the 11 francophone and five anglophone countries in West Africa. ECOWAS has made limited progress towards the goal of reducing trade barriers between member countries. Trade between members increased from 3.1 per cent of their trade in 1976 to 6.1 per cent in 1990.[13] Improved communications helped facilitate the increase. Some member countries, including Burkina Faso, Mali and Niger, are trading considerably more with each other. ECOWAS is aiming to eliminate all tariffs and trade barriers by 1994. Conflict over labour has marred the community's progress; it is supposed to allow the free movement of nationals to work in other member countries, but Nigeria expelled workers from Ghana in the mid-1980s, when tensions flared between the two countries.

The 10-nation **Southern African Development Co-ordination Conference** (SADCC), comprising Angola,

Botswana, Lesotho, Malawi, Mozambique, Namibia, Swaziland, Tanzania, Zambia and Zimbabwe, was formed in 1980 to reduce the economic dependence of member states on South Africa. The 10 countries are home to 77 million people. Although only a loose association of countries, SADCC has been the most active and successful of Africa's regional groups in co-operating on joint projects. The incentive for this activity has been to escape from the shadow of apartheid. Member countries have especially co-operated on schemes to improve ports, roads and other transport links and communications between them – to build improved access to ports, for example, in order not to send goods through South Africa. Around $8 billion has been spent on this activity, about 80 per cent of which has come from the funds of SADCC member countries, the remaining 20 per cent from donor countries.

By 1990, SADCC could point to over 600 projects in the pipeline, at various stages of implementation or seeking funds. The Maputo-based Southern African Transport and Communications Commission (SATCC), one of the few organs of SADCC to have legal status, has co-ordinated quite complex projects. While 10 years ago a telephone call from Gaborone to Maputo was typically routed via Johannesburg, Capetown, London and Lisbon, calls now go directly.

Yet SADCC's success has been limited and is still fragile. Some schemes have failed to get off the ground because of lack of funds. Trade between member states grew little between 1980 and 1990 when it was only around 4.5 per cent of their total trade – and Zimbabwe accounts of around 80 per cent of this. Serious transportation weaknesses were highlighted over food supplies in 1990. The SADCC region then had an overall food surplus of 1.35 million tonnes, chiefly because of good harvests in Zimbabwe, Zambia and Tanzania. Yet in Angola and Mozambique, tens of thousands were short of food to the point of starvation. But there was little trade between the food-deficit and food-surplus countries; trade and transport mechanisms for food distribution were inadequate. Although there are now exceptions, roads between SADCC countries are still generally poor, making movement of the food difficult.[14]

If post-apartheid South Africa eventually becomes a member, SADCC will be a regional grouping with enormous potential. Such a grouping would control a large amount of the world's minerals, putting it in a powerful bargaining position with the outside world and giving the hope of higher export earnings. As a materially wealthier country, South Africa could help stimulate the economics of its neighbours, through trade and joint ventures. A wider southern African common market could be an important stimulus to encourage the formation of an all-African common market.[15]

The **Preferential Trade Area for Eastern and Southern Africa** (PTA) was set up in 1984 with 14 countries in the region as members. Its goal is to steadily reduce tariffs between countries in the area, with an eye to their complete elimination. Originally 1992 was the target date for a full common market but this is unlikely to be met. The PTA has also turned its attention to transport; in early 1992 a plan was finalized to build rail links between three capital cities – Khartoum, Addis Ababa and Nairobi.

A **Central African Customs and Economic Union** was formed in 1966, comprising Cameroon, Central African Republic, Chad, Congo, Gabon and Equatorial Guinea.

*Asia*

Set up in 1967, the **Association of South-East Asian Nations** (ASEAN), comprises Brunei, Indonesia, Malaysia, the Philippines, Singapore and Thailand. Its original aims were modest. The ASEAN countries, with a joint population of 320 million, did not aim at a free trade area but at a gradual relaxation of trade barriers between member countries, joint negotiations with other trading blocs, such as the European Community, and co-operation on industrial projects. Members have made steady progress in economic co-operation. Whereas, in 1970, 14.7 per cent of ASEAN trade was within the region, in 1989 this had risen to 17.7 per cent.[16] Twenty-four years after ASEAN was created, its economic ministers met in October 1991 and agreed plans to establish a free trade area over the next 15 years. These plans were endorsed, in January 1992, by leaders of the six countries. Fears of rising protectionism, and the possible growth of trade blocs in the North if the Uruguay Round collapsed, appeared to quicken the desire to set up the Asean Free Trade Area.

It was decided that tariffs in the area would be lowered from January 1993 on 15 products, including cement, electrical items, pharmaceuticals, rubber products and vegetable oils. By 2008 it is planned that tariffs on all products will be in the range of 0–5 per cent. However, non-tariff barriers and services are excluded. This means that ASEAN countries can still use trade restrictions other than tariffs, if they wish. It is therefore uncertain whether the creation of Afta will lead to any substantial increase in regional trade.

Malaysia has proposed the setting up of a wider regional free trade arrangement, the East Asia Economic Grouping, comprising the ASEAN countries, and also North Korea, South Korea, Japan, Taiwan, Hong Kong, Vietnam, China, Australia and New Zealand. The existing **Asia Pacific Economic Co-operation Group** (APEC), which was set up in 1989, comprises China, Hong Kong, Taiwan, Japan, South Korea, the United States and Canada, Australia, New Zealand and the six ASEAN countries. The proposed new Asia groupings would therefore include North Korea and Vietnam, and exclude the United States and Canada. APEC's aim is to promote multilateralism in a rather general manner, but Malaysia appears to take the view that APEC has failed in this.[17]

## Latin America and the Caribbean

Formed in 1969, the **Andean Pact** comprises Bolivia, Colombia, Ecuador, Peru and Venezula. Chile was a founder member but withdrew in 1976. The pact's original aim was for free trade between members by 1981, but by 1992 this aim had still not been achieved. Tariffs imposed by members on each other's exports have been reduced to between five and 20 per cent, and 1995 has been set as the date for the achievement of an Andean free trade zone. Trade between members – which is not made easier by the chain of mountains that run through the middle of the region – has varied widely between three and 15 per cent of their total trade, and there is little evidence that the underlying trend is upwards. Brazil and Argentina are working on plans to start a common market by 1994 that could embrace Chile, Paraguay and Uruguay.

Costa Rica, El Salvador, Guatemala, Honduras and Nicaragua set up the **Central American Common Market** in 1960; this collapsed in 1969 following a dispute between El Salvador and Honduras. While regional trade continued, it stagnated in the 1980s amid political tensions between the countries. In June 1990, Central American presidents announced that they intended to form an Economic Community of the Central American Isthmus. One of its aims would be to reduce trade barriers, another to jointly promote the region's exports and its potential for tourism.

Set up in 1973, the **Caribbean Community** (CARICOM) comprises Antigua, the Bahamas, Barbados, Belize, Dominica, Dominican Republic, Grenada, Haiti, Guyana, Jamaica, Montserrat, St Kitts-Nevis-Anquilla, St Lucia, St Vincent, and Trinidad and Tobago. CARICOM has made the fastest progress of any regional grouping in the South towards a common market, although without immediately stimulating intra-regional trade. In 1988, members dismantled all barriers to trade within the community, apart from a small number of goods. By the beginning of 1991 they hoped to have been able to apply a common external tariff against goods from outside the region, but the aim had to be put back, owing to nervousness in some countries about the likely impact of it on their economies. They are aiming at a full common market by 1993 and monetary union by 1994. Trade between CARICOM members accounted for 6.7 per cent of their total trade in 1976. In 1989, this had declined to 4.5 per cent.[18]

With only a few exceptions, regional groupings in the South have not led to any sizeable increase in trade among members; in some cases, such trade has fallen over the last 20 years. But this does not necessarily mean that such groupings will not ultimately lead to an increase. The progress of common markets is universally slow; if it continues on course, it will have taken the European Community 37 years, after its establishment in 1956, to set up a single market in 1993. There are huge problems with the surrender of sovereignty that regional co-operation involves. The 1990s will be the testing time for the South's regional groups.

South–South trade retains promise, even though it has many hurdles to jump. While it is a promising route for developing countries, the trade will not replace South–North trade. Most of the world's wealth is concentrated at present in the North. If the South wants to tap some of that wealth, it has to trade with the North, although on better terms than now exist. If countries of the South only trade with each other, they will miss out on a wealthy market.

Should the North help the South to develop its South–South trade? Should donor countries provide some of the necessary funding? The ILO Jobs and Skills Programme for Africa study said that while the achievement of collective self-reliance was the responsibility of the African States, 'the international community can greatly assist in the process. There is an urgent need for both the multilateral financial institutions to accord much higher priority to the financing of subregional, regional and multinational projects. Bilateral (aid) donors also need to give higher priority to regional projects.'[19] The establishment of the trade information network mentioned above was assisted by funding from the United Nations Development Programme (UNDP).

The North has more to gain from an increase in South–South trade than at first seems apparent. A poverty-stricken South is hardly in the interests of the North; increased South–South trade will help the South to develop its resources and tackle poverty. If the North does not help the countries of the South to expand their markets with each other in the 1990s, then the markets of the North will come under great pressure to take more of the South's goods and services – including labour. A South that gets poorer will increasingly want to get into the richer Northern markets. There is a role for the North – and it is in their interest – to help developing countries develop their trade with each other. However, there are other ways in which countries of the South can work together to get more benefit from the international trading system.

## Producer co-operation

In July 1975 a severe frost in the coffee-growing Paraná district of Brazil killed 550 million coffee trees and damaged a further 1440 million. When news of the frost reached London and the major commodity markets, the price of coffee doubled virtually overnight. Buyers took the view that supplies would be short and that it was wise to buy coffee without delay. Brazil's frost was followed by other disasters in coffee-producing countries. Floods in Colombia destroyed several million coffee trees, while in El Salvador the crop suffered because of very dry weather. An earthquake in Guatemala destroyed crops and disrupted transport; coffee-rust disease spread through Nicaragua causing heavy losses; war in Angola, and a dispute between Kenya and Uganda, cut supplies.

These setbacks to coffee production caused world output of the crop to fall by 12 per cent in the 1975/6 season, and by around 25 per cent in 1976/7. What happened to prices? From July 1975 to March 1977 the coffee price soared from under £500 a tonne to just over £4000 a tonne, more than eight times higher than 20 months before. A 25 per cent cut in production had led to an eightfold increase in price.

Coffee-growing countries were exporting less, on average 75 per cent of previous levels, but they were earning a great deal more revenue from the lower output. Instead of exporting, say, 10 000 tonnes at £500 a tonne, and receiving revenue of £5 million, a coffee-producing country might export 7500 tonnes at as much as £4000 a tonne – making revenue of £30 million. Few would have sold all their coffee at the top of the market, but if it brought £2000 a tonne, revenue for the country in this example would still have been £15 million; that is, three times more money from the lower output. Ultimately, it is not the volume of a crop a country exports that funds development projects, but the *money* that is in the till.[20] World coffee prices did not stay over the £4000 mark for long; between mid-1977 and mid-1989, until the collapse of the International Coffee Agreement, they fluctuated mostly between £3000 and £1000 a tonne (see also Chapter 3).

The producers of all commodities could learn the lesson of what happened to coffee in the 1975/7 period – that lower output leads to higher prices and the possibility of higher returns. For many years, coffee producers had agreed on export quotas and while these were useful they were not enough. In the 1990s and beyond, producers need to agree on output quotas. In the case of coffee, the 1975 cut in output was unplanned. A *planned* cut, through output quotas, would also be likely to raise prices, giving producers the chance of earning more revenue from less output. A further benefit from this type of policy is that fewer resources are needed to grow coffee – around a quarter of the land now under coffee could theoretically be released for other purposes, including food production to meet local needs. On all commodities, this 'sell less, earn more' policy requires producers to co-operate. Co-operation may be difficult but the alternative, the present system, is leading developing countries into bankruptcy and economic decline, pushing them even further away from being able to meet the most basic needs of their peoples.

Another option for commodity producers is to make use

of export taxes. A report to the Commonwealth Secretariat, *Export Taxes on Primary Products*, suggests that countries exporting primary raw materials could gain substantially by jointly agreeing to impose export taxes on their products.[21] It shows how developing countries can obtain higher revenues from their exports of primary commodities, and that it is feasible for producing countries to act in concert, put taxes on their exports and increase their overall revenue. Seventeen commodities were examined, many of which are produced almost exclusively in developing countries.

The report looked at what might happen if countries imposed a 10 per cent, 20 per cent or 25 per cent export tax. In the consuming country, the price would rise, and this would mean that less was purchased – but not much less, the report asserts, for most products. On eight of the world's largest trade commodities – coffee, cocoa, tea, bananas, bauxite, copper, tin and tropical timber – fall in demand would be modest, and producers would gain overall, no matter which of the three rates they applied.

With a 10 per cent tax, the additional revenue from the eight products is estimated to be around $4 billion a year while a 25 per cent tax could bring in $10.5 billion. If sugar-producing countries could agree to impose a 25 per cent export tax, the increase in export revenue is calculated to be around 23 per cent; for cocoa, coffee, and copper producers 13 per cent, and for tea-producing countries nine per cent. The report suggests that for coffee, cocoa and tea, the most advantageous export tax for producing countries to levy would be over 100 per cent.

For six primary products – palm oil, phosphate rock, iron ore, zinc, nickel and manganese ore – there might, however, be no gains for producers from an export tax. Even if a 10 per cent rate were imposed, the resulting falls in amounts purchased would leave producers worse off. But the producers of most products would stand to gain, and the report expressed the belief that export taxes would be administratively simple to operate and would not mean that countries had to export only a quota of a product, as some have done under an international commodity agreement. Negotiation between primary producing and consuming countries would be unnecessary, so export taxes have the advantage that they bypass North–South negotiations, although they do call for substantial South–South co-operation.

The Commonwealth Secretariat report shows what producing countries can achieve if they have the determination to do it. Perishable commodities may not be suitable, however. In 1974 several Latin American banana-producing countries agreed to impose a $1 tax on every case of bananas exported. Producers acted to impose taxes because banana prices had not increased for some 20 years. But three large fruit companies who purchased the bananas from growers – United Brands, Castle and Cooke, and Del Monte – refused to pay the tax, and these companies controlled over 90 per cent of the market. In the ensuing conflict, bananas were left to rot, growers' incomes were affected and the countries gave in, settling for taxes in the 25–35 US cents range.[22]

Managing the supply of commodities that come on to the world market 'can be effective only if it is undertaken by producers accounting for the bulk of world exports', said the 1990 South Commission Report; 'producer countries which have a significant share of the world market should be persuaded to join such management schemes'.[23] The larger the number of producing countries, the greater the difficulty there is likely to be in reaching agreement. But the more the price of a commodity falls, the greater the incentive for producing countries to come together and surmount the obstacles. Producer co-operation stands as one vital way in which developing countries can secure a fairer deal from international trade.

## Conclusion

'The current attitudes of the rich will not bring effective development measures out of the present structures of trade and finance. There is not the will to do so. The poor need to increase their efforts to co-operate with each other in the struggle against the rich'.[24]

These words were written in 1972 at the end of the UNCTAD III gathering in Chile. They are still true today. While it is in the long-term interests of Western countries to help developing countries to earn more from trade and help them out of poverty, the poor cannot rely on the goodwill of the rich. While co-operating with the West, the developing world has to develop its own power that will improve its bargaining position and make it a force to be reckoned with. Producer countries are not without power if they can organize.

172

International trade, as it is now practised, means low returns for materially poor countries and peoples. It is like a game in which the poor have some powerful pieces yet the rich have been clever enough to seize the rulebook. If the poor can organize their pieces they can change the way the game is played; if they put themselves in a stronger bargaining position they can change the game around. Organizing together to get a better deal from commodities, to increase trade with each other, to step up alternative trade, exercise more control over TNCs – all need to be key elements in a developing country strategy to change the international trading system for the good of the majority of humanity.

The developing world could earn considerably more from trade. The end of the Multifibre Arrangement and other restrictions on market access could yield the developing world around $50 million a year and be the economically most useful outcome of the Uruguay Round. But developing countries wanting to improve their trading position would be unwise to rely too much on the free trade philosophy of GATT or on concessions from the West. The *Human Development Report 1992* estimates that barriers on the movement of labour from developing countries cost them at least $250 billion a year (see Chapter 5), but most industrialized countries seem unlikely to relax immigration controls to allow free movement of labour to take place. While extolling the virtue of the free movement of goods, industrialized nations are shown to have different standards when it comes to people. It would be an illusion to believe that the $250 billion a year potential from labour will be realized unless there is a rethink of these double standards that apply on goods and labour.

It is increased co-operation among themselves that stands to yield developing countries the highest benefits. There is a strong case for them to trade *lower volumes* of goods and services, especially primary commodities and tourism, while at the same time aiming at *higher returns*. It would not be unreasonable for developing countries to think in terms of a doubling of returns from primary commodities if they can organize it – that is, an additional $300 billion a year, a 30 per cent increase in their overall trade earnings. In 1990, the developing world's imports of goods and services exceeded exports by about $30 billion; this small balance of payments deficit could be turned into a healthy surplus if commodity-producing countries organize to maximize their export earnings.[25]

Developing countries could earn more from international trade while, ironically, devoting fewer resources to it – as in the above example of coffee. Devoting too many scarce resources to trade can be detrimental to development; trade should be one part of development policy rather than the dominant part. Overexposure to an international system which is difficult for them to control has clear dangers for developing countries; the ideal is to use resources more effectively both on international trade and on internal development, and to achieve a healthy balance.

The Brandt Report was based on the vision that growth in industrial countries would 'pull up' poorer countries, but this has not happened. During the 1950s economists such as Arthur Lewis and Raul Prebisch stressed the dangers of developing countries relying too much on international trade as 'an engine of growth'. Samir Amin's argument, noted in Chapter 1, is powerful – that developing countries should submit 'external trading relations to the logic of domestic development priorities', concentrating more on national and regional development.[26] This would help to keep international trade in proportion.

A reformed international trading system is only likely to make a contribution to overcoming poverty if a country has internal economic and political structures in which people are able to receive economic benefits and have a say in the way their country is run. This would include having a say over the nature and extent of trade. Millions of people are engaged in world trade who have never been consulted about whether *they* believe it is a good thing for their families and communities. The genuine participation of people in matters which affect the use and direction of resources – in particular over whether to produce for local use or the international market – is vital if trade is ever to make a contribution to local economies. Trade could offer a way out of poverty, but only if it democratized.

With the growth of participation and democracy in the developing world, it is just possible to see a well-organized developing world that is getting a good deal from international trade and where people such as growers and miners are participating and receiving some of the benefits. Translating that vision into reality is one of the chief tasks of the

1990s. The South today needs a new development stimulus. Producer co-operation, more South–South trade and alternative trade, against a background of genuine participation, could be a powerful combination that helps countries, battered by an unjust international trading system, to take the initiative in developing a more just system that helps to provide that new stimulus.

# Appendix 1: selected statistics

(With acknowledgements to UNCTAD for Tables 1, 2 and 3, and to the World Bank for Tables 4, 5 and 6.)[1]

## Table 1 Value of exports of developing countries and territories by economic grouping

Millions of dollars (f.o.b.)

| Economic grouping | 1950 | 1960 | 1970 | 1980 | 1989 | 1990 | 1991* |
|---|---|---|---|---|---|---|---|
| DEVELOPING COUNTRIES AND TERRITORIES | 18900 | 28300 | 57900 | 573500 | 651500 | 738000 | 781400 |
| *By major category* | | | | | | | |
| Major petroleum exporters | 3846 | 8822 | 19773 | 327668 | 160743 | 206342 | 196590 |
| Other developing countries and territories | 15050 | 19521 | 38164 | 245850 | 490716 | 531631 | 584834 |
| *of which:* | | | | | | | |
| Major exporters of manufactures | 3789 | 4620 | 12060 | 122615 | 316970 | 339387 | 379497 |
| Remaining countries | 11261 | 14901 | 26104 | 123235 | 173746 | 192244 | 205337 |
| *of which* | | | | | | | |
| America | 4332 | 5072 | 9465 | 47764 | 48496 | 52708 | 55053 |
| Africa | 2450 | 4154 | 7579 | 27137 | 27322 | 29072 | 30028 |
| West Asia | 426 | 604 | 1066 | 5688 | 14975 | 16311 | 15450 |
| South and South-East Asia | 3981 | 4876 | 7480 | 39790 | 78751 | 89867 | 100462 |
| Least developed countries | 1729 | 2964 | 4992 | 12725 | 12492 | 11411 | 12001 |
| Heavily indebted countries | 6590 | 9611 | 18258 | 129548 | 139606 | 157937 | 158912 |
| *By income group (per capita GDP in 1985)* | | | | | | | |
| High income | 4751 | 9496 | 22464 | 326731 | 304211 | 353708 | 375318 |
| Middle income | 10302 | 13349 | 26590 | 219833 | 311751 | 346277 | 367626 |
| Low income | 3843 | 5498 | 8883 | 26954 | 35497 | 37988 | 38480 |

## Table 2 Value of imports of developing countries and territories by economic grouping

Millions of dollars (c.i.f.)

| Economic grouping | 1950 | 1960 | 1970 | 1980 | 1989 | 1990 | 1991* |
|---|---|---|---|---|---|---|---|
| DEVELOPING COUNTRIES AND TERRITORIES | 17300 | 30800 | 58700 | 471300 | 626800 | 723500 | 780300 |
| *By major category* | | | | | | | |
| Major petroleum exporters | 2734 | 6465 | 11360 | 144942 | 114582 | 125381 | 129610 |
| Other developing countries and territories | 14570 | 24292 | 47309 | 326638 | 512231 | 598074 | 650729 |
| *of which:* | | | | | | | |
| Major exporters of manufactures | 3841 | 6474 | 16921 | 150683 | 292259 | 336897 | 381037 |
| Remaining countries | 10729 | 17818 | 30388 | 175685 | 219972 | 261177 | 269692 |
| *of which* | | | | | | | |
| America | 4060 | 5745 | 10410 | 60448 | 49752 | 53611 | 54793 |
| Africa | 2654 | 4367 | 7706 | 39337 | 43729 | 52003 | 48928 |
| West Asia | 594 | 1234 | 2112 | 17452 | 24830 | 32499 | 30460 |
| South and South-East Asia | 3273 | 6165 | 9037 | 53840 | 95143 | 115724 | 128155 |
| Least developed countries | 1498 | 2936 | 5237 | 20564 | 22079 | 24109 | 23122 |
| Heavily indebted countries | 5855 | 9700 | 18714 | 134558 | 110969 | 131327 | 136706 |
| *By income group (per capita GDP in 1985)* | | | | | | | |
| High income | 4119 | 7347 | 16449 | 185554 | 269469 | 296808 | 329970 |
| Middle income | 9622 | 16489 | 32343 | 239914 | 303202 | 366441 | 391576 |
| Low income | 3563 | 6921 | 9877 | 45842 | 54115 | 60206 | 58793 |

Notes:   The totals have been adjusted to include estimates for countries and territories for which data for all years are not available.

* Provisional figures.

177

**Table 3 Region-to-region exports** Millions of dollars (f.o.b.)

| Origin / Destination | Year | World | Africa | West Asia | South and South-East Asia |
|---|---|---|---|---|---|
| Developing Africa | 1970 | 12 021 | 672 | 117 | 259 |
| | 1980 | 94 942 | 2978 | 1801 | 1144 |
| | 1987 | 51 967 | 3030 | 1259 | 1215 |
| | 1988 | 55 302 | 3661 | 1985 | 2006 |
| | 1989 | 56 136 | 3875 | 1751 | 1455 |
| | 1990 | 62 464 | 4108 | 1845 | 1504 |
| Developing West Asia | 1970 | 10 543 | 260 | 781 | 837 |
| | 1980 | 210 976 | 3524 | 11 120 | 25 729 |
| | 1987 | 84 902 | 3058 | 11 939 | 13 922 |
| | 1988 | 86 976 | 3438 | 11 780 | 14 304 |
| | 1989 | 100 234 | 3176 | 12 233 | 16 748 |
| | 1990 | 106 272 | 2955 | 10 190 | 14 792 |
| Developing South and South-East Asia | 1970 | 14 278 | 485 | 374 | 2904 |
| | 1980 | 141 561 | 4229 | 7461 | 30 197 |
| | 1987 | 252 836 | 4202 | 8374 | 47 626 |
| | 1988 | 311 538 | 5248 | 9538 | 64 773 |
| | 1989 | 348 967 | 5998 | 9601 | 76 186 |
| | 1990 | 384 521 | 6925 | 10 887 | 89 384 |

## Table 4 Exports of goods, 1990 Merchandise exports, US $ millions; average annual growth rate 1980–90 (%); merchandise exports share of GDP (%)

| Low-income | Exports | Growth | Share | Lower middle-income | Exports | Growth | Share |
|---|---|---|---|---|---|---|---|
| Afghanistan | – | – | – | Albania | – | – | – |
| Bangladesh | 1674 | 7.6 | 7.3 | Algeria | 12817 | 5.3 | 25.0 |
| Benin | 93 | – | 6.4 | Angola | 3000 | – | 35.0 |
| Bhutan | – | – | – | Argentina | 12353 | 1.4 | 11.7 |
| Burkina Faso | 160 | 10.1 | 5.0 | Bolivia | 923 | 1.4 | 20.6 |
| Burundi | 75 | –1.9 | 6.8 | Botswana | – | – | – |
| Cambodia | – | – | – | Bulgaria | – | – | – |
| Central African Rep. | 130 | –1.3 | 10.0 | Cameroon | 1200 | –1.3 | 10.8 |
| Chad | 200 | – | 18.1 | Chile | 8579 | 4.8 | 30.9 |
| China | 62091 | 11.0 | 17.0 | Colombia | 6766 | 10.6 | 16.5 |
| Egypt, Arab Rep. | 2985 | 2.1 | 8.5 | Congo | 1130 | 5.9 | 39.4 |
| Ethiopia | 297 | –0.3 | 4.9 | Costa Rica | 1457 | 3.1 | 25.6 |
| Ghana | 739 | 3.8 | 11.8 | Côte d'Ivoire | 2600 | 2.7 | 26.2 |
| Guinea | – | – | – | Dominican Rep. | 734 | 1.3 | 10.0 |
| Haiti | 138 | –12.4 | 5.0 | Ecuador | 2714 | 4.3 | 25.0 |
| Honduras | 916 | 2.4 | 33.5 | El Salvador | 550 | –0.8 | 10.2 |
| India | 17967 | 6.5 | 6.3 | Guatemala | 1211 | –1.7 | 15.9 |
| Indonesia | 25553 | 2.8 | 23.8 | Iran, Islamic Rep. | 15000 | 21.1 | 12.6 |
| Kenya | 1033 | 1.0 | 11.8 | Jamaica | 1347 | 0.6 | 34.0 |
| Lao PDR | – | – | – | Jordan | 1146 | 10.3 | 29.3 |
| Lesotho | – | – | – | Lebanon | – | – | – |
| Liberia | 500 | –2.7 | – | Malaysia | 29409 | 10.3 | 69.4 |
| Madagascar | 335 | –1.5 | 10.8 | Mauritius | 1182 | 9.6 | 47.6 |
| Malawi | 412 | 4.3 | 22.1 | Mongolia | – | – | – |
| Mali | 347 | 9.9 | 14.2 | Morocco | 4210 | 5.4 | 16.7 |
| Mauritania | 468 | 3.8 | 44.5 | Namibia | – | – | – |
| Mozambique | – | – | – | Nicaragua | 379 | –5.3 | – |
| Myanmar | 322 | –10.1 | 1.4 | Panama | 321 | –0.3 | 6.8 |
| Nepal | 162 | – | 5.2 | Papua New Guinea | 1140 | 6.2 | 34.7 |
| Niger | 435 | 4.3 | 17.2 | Paraguay | 959 | 10.7 | 18.2 |
| Nigeria | 13671 | –1.6 | 38.6 | Peru | 3277 | 0.3 | 9.0 |
| Pakistan | 5590 | 9.0 | 13.9 | Philippines | 8681 | 2.5 | 19.8 |
| Rwanda | 112 | 0.1 | 5.2 | Poland | 13627 | 3.0 | 21.4 |
| Sierra Leone | 138 | –1.4 | 15.4 | Romania | – | – | – |
| Somalia | 130 | –3.3 | 13.9 | Senegal | 783 | 5.6 | 13.4 |
| Sri Lanka | 1984 | 6.8 | 24.4 | Syrian Arab Rep. | 4173 | 8.7 | 28.3 |
| Sudan | 400 | –0.9 | 4.7 | Thailand | 23002 | 13.2 | 28.7 |
| Tanzania | 300 | –7.4 | 12.5 | Tunisia | 3517 | 4.9 | 28.1 |
| Togo | 300 | 2.4 | 18.5 | Turkey | 12959 | 9.1 | 11.9 |
| Uganda | 151 | –1.9 | 5.0 | Yemen Rep. | – | – | – |
| Vietnam | – | – | – | Zimbabwe | – | – | – |
| Zaire | 999 | –11.2 | 13.3 | | | | |
| Zambia | – | – | – | | | | |

| Upper middle-income | Exports | Growth | Share | High-income | Exports | Growth | Share |
|---|---|---|---|---|---|---|---|
| Brazil | 31243 | 4.0 | 6.6 | Australia | 35973 | 3.9 | 11.4 |
| Czechoslovakia | 17950 | – | 40.4 | Austria | 41876 | 6.2 | 25.7 |
| Gabon | 2471 | 1.4 | 52.4 | Belgium | 118002 | 4.7 | 75.6 |
| Greece | 8053 | 3.8 | 12.0 | Canada | 125058 | 5.9 | 20.9 |
| Hungary | 9588 | 5.5 | 29.1 | Denmark | 34801 | 5.1 | 26.4 |
| Iraq | 16809 | – | – | Finland | 26718 | 3.0 | 20.1 |
| Korea | 64837 | 12.8 | 27.4 | France | 209491 | 3.4 | 18.0 |
| Libya | 14285 | 1.8 | 41.4 | Germany | 397912 | 4.2 | 28.6 |
| Mexico | 26714 | 3.4 | 11.2 | Hong Kong | 29002 | 6.2 | 41.4 |
| Oman | 458 | – | – | Ireland | 23796 | 7.3 | 61.0 |
| Portugal | 16416 | 11.7 | 28.9 | Israel | 12047 | 7.5 | 22.6 |
| Saudi Arabia | 31065 | –9.7 | 34.3 | Italy | 168523 | 3.5 | 16.2 |
| South Africa | 23612 | 1.7 | 23.3 | Japan | 286768 | 4.2 | 9.6 |
| Trinidad & Tobago | 2080 | –3.7 | 40.8 | Kuwait | 8300 | –11.1 | 4.5 |
| Uruguay | 1696 | 3.2 | 20.6 | Netherlands | 131479 | 4.4 | 48.2 |
| Venezuela | 17220 | 1.8 | 35.7 | New Zealand | 9045 | 3.4 | 20.6 |
| Yugoslavia | 14365 | 0.1 | 16.3 | Norway | 34072 | 7.2 | 30.0 |
| | | | | Singapore | 52627 | 8.6 | 152.1 |
| | | | | Spain | 55607 | 7.4 | 11.7 |
| | | | | Sweden | 57326 | 4.4 | 27.1 |
| | | | | Switzerland | 63699 | 3.5 | 29.0 |
| | | | | United Arab Emirates | – | – | – |
| | | | | United Kingdom | 185891 | 2.7 | 18.3 |
| | | | | United States | 371465 | 3.3 | 8.8 |

# Table 5 Imports of goods, 1990 Merchandise imports, US $ millions; average annual growth rate 1980–90 (%)

| Low-income | Imports | Growth | Lower middle-income | Imports | Growth |
|---|---|---|---|---|---|
| Afghanistan | – | – | Albania | – | – |
| Bangladesh | 3646 | 8.0 | Algeria | 9605 | –4.6 |
| Benin | 483 | – | Angola | 1200 | – |
| Bhutan | – | – | Argentina | 4077 | –8.4 |
| Burkina Faso | 480 | 1.0 | Bolivia | 716 | –2.4 |
| Burundi | 235 | 5.0 | Botswana | – | – |
| Cambodia | – | – | Bulgaria | – | – |
| Central African Rep. | 170 | 6.1 | Cameroon | 1300 | –3.3 |
| Chad | 450 | – | Chile | 7023 | 0.6 |
| China | 53345 | 9.8 | Colombia | 5590 | –2.3 |
| Egypt, Arab Rep. | 10340 | –1.7 | Congo | 570 | –3.1 |
| Ethiopia | 1081 | 4.2 | Costa Rica | 2026 | 2.5 |
| Ghana | 1199 | –0.1 | Côte d'Ivoire | 2100 | –1.2 |
| Guinea | – | – | Dominican Rep. | 2057 | 3.5 |
| Haiti | 272 | –6.2 | Ecuador | 1862 | –3.2 |
| Honduras | 1028 | –0.7 | El Salvador | 1200 | –0.5 |
| India | 23692 | 4.2 | Guatemala | 1626 | –1.4 |
| Indonesia | 21837 | 1.4 | Iran, Islamic Rep. | 13000 | 8.0 |
| Kenya | 2124 | 1.6 | Jamaica | 1685 | 1.1 |
| Lao PDR | – | – | Jordan | 2663 | –0.5 |
| Lesotho | – | – | Lebanon | – | – |
| Liberia | 450 | –2.2 | Malaysia | 29251 | 5.6 |
| Madagascar | 480 | –0.4 | Mauritius | 1616 | 11.2 |
| Malawi | 576 | 0.7 | Mongolia | – | – |
| Mali | 640 | 6.7 | Morocco | 6908 | 4.6 |
| Mauritania | 248 | –5.1 | Namibia | – | – |
| Mozambique | – | – | Nicaragua | 750 | –2.8 |
| Myanmar | 270 | –14.5 | Panama | 1539 | –3.0 |
| Nepal | 543 | – | Papua New Guinea | 1288 | 2.6 |
| Niger | 230 | –8.8 | Paraguay | 1113 | 1.5 |
| Nigeria | 5688 | –15.1 | Peru | 3230 | –4.0 |
| Pakistan | 7377 | 4.0 | Philippines | 13080 | 2.3 |
| Rwanda | 279 | 11.4 | Poland | 9781 | 1.2 |
| Sierra Leone | 146 | –2.3 | Romania | – | – |
| Somalia | 360 | –4.3 | Senegal | 1620 | 4.6 |
| Sri Lanka | 2689 | 2.1 | Syrian Arab Rep. | 2400 | –8.3 |
| Sudan | 600 | –8.3 | Thailand | 33129 | 10.2 |
| Tanzania | 935 | –0.5 | Tunisia | 5524 | 3.5 |
| Togo | 700 | 1.4 | Turkey | 22300 | 7.0 |
| Uganda | 458 | 3.2 | Yemen Rep. | – | – |
| Vietnam | – | – | Zimbabwe | 1851 | – |
| Zaire | 888 | –4.0 | | | |
| Zambia | – | – | | | |

| Upper middle-income | Imports | Growth | High-income | Imports | Growth |
|---|---|---|---|---|---|
| Brazil | 22459 | –0.3 | Australia | 39740 | 4.7 |
| Czechoslovakia | 19862 | – | Austria | 49960 | 5.2 |
| Gabon | 760 | –1.8 | Belgium | 119725 | 3.1 |
| Greece | 19701 | 4.3 | Canada | 115882 | 8.4 |
| Hungary | 8646 | 1.3 | Denmark | 31562 | 4.2 |
| Iraq | 4314 | – | Finland | 27098 | 4.7 |
| Korea | 69585 | 10.8 | France | 232525 | 3.2 |
| Libya | 3976 | –10.4 | Germany | 341248 | 3.9 |
| Mexico | 28063 | –1.1 | Hong Kong | 82495 | 11.0 |
| Oman | 2608 | – | Ireland | 20716 | 3.8 |
| Portugal | 25333 | 8.2 | Israel | 15197 | 4.7 |
| Saudi Arabia | 24069 | –10.0 | Italy | 176153 | 4.2 |
| South Africa | 18258 | –3.7 | Japan | 231223 | 5.6 |
| Trinidad & Tobago | 1262 | –12.8 | Kuwait | 4800 | –5.7 |
| Uruguay | 1415 | –1.1 | Netherlands | 125909 | 3.5 |
| Venezuela | 6364 | –4.6 | New Zealand | 9466 | 3.6 |
| Yugoslavia | 18911 | 0.6 | Norway | 26889 | 2.5 |
| | | | Singapore | 60647 | 6.7 |
| | | | Spain | 87487 | 9.0 |
| | | | Sweden | 54536 | 3.5 |
| | | | Switzerland | 69427 | 3.8 |
| | | | United Arab Emirates | – | – |
| | | | United Kingdom | 224914 | 4.9 |
| | | | United States | 515635 | 7.6 |

# Table 6  Terms of trade, 1990 Barter terms of trade index, 1987=100; ratio of terms of trade effect to GNY in constant 1987 prices (%)

| Low-income | Index | Ratio | Lower middle-income | Index | Ratio |
|---|---|---|---|---|---|
| Afghanistan | – | – | Albania | – | – |
| Bangladesh | 95 | –0.3 | Algeria | 99 | –0.2 |
| Benin | – | – | Angola | – | – |
| Bhutan | – | – | Argentina | 112 | 1.5 |
| Burkina Faso | 100 | 0.0 | Bolivia | 97 | –0.5 |
| Burundi | 70 | –2.1 | Botswana | – | – |
| Cambodia | – | – | Bulgaria | – | – |
| Central African Rep. | 109 | 0.8 | Cameroon | 91 | –0.8 |
| Chad | – | – | Chile | 131 | 7.6 |
| China | 111 | 1.4 | Colombia | 92 | –1.5 |
| Egypt, Arab Rep. | 76 | –1.7 | Congo | 99 | –0.6 |
| Ethiopia | 84 | –0.9 | Costa Rica | 114 | 3.3 |
| Ghana | 75 | –3.8 | Côte d'Ivoire | 80 | –6.8 |
| Guinea | – | – | Dominican Rep. | 98 | –0.2 |
| Haiti | 97 | –0.2 | Ecuador | 109 | 1.8 |
| Honduras | 104 | 0.7 | El Salvador | 114 | 1.2 |
| India | 96 | –0.2 | Guatemala | 102 | 0.3 |
| Indonesia | 111 | 2.5 | Iran, Islamic Rep. | 72 | –3.9 |
| Kenya | 103 | 0.3 | Jamaica | 88 | –5.2 |
| Lao PDR | – | – | Jordan | 112 | 2.3 |
| Lesotho | – | – | Lebanon | – | – |
| Liberia | 111 | – | Malaysia | 94 | –4.1 |
| Madagascar | 102 | 0.3 | Mauritius | 114 | 5.6 |
| Malawi | 93 | –1.9 | Mongolia | – | – |
| Mali | 97 | –0.4 | Morocco | 86 | –2.7 |
| Mauritania | 107 | 3.1 | Namibia | – | – |
| Mozambique | – | – | Nicaragua | 110 | 1.1 |
| Myanmar | 127 | 0.6 | Panama | 138 | 2.3 |
| Nepal | – | – | Papua New Guinea | 75 | –12.5 |
| Niger | 77 | –4.9 | Paraguay | 110 | 1.5 |
| Nigeria | 100 | 0.1 | Peru | 78 | –2.9 |
| Pakistan | 95 | –0.8 | Philippines | 93 | –1.5 |
| Rwanda | 98 | –0.1 | Poland | 103 | 0.9 |
| Sierra Leone | 80 | –7.1 | Romania | – | – |
| Somalia | 111 | 1.8 | Senegal | 106 | 0.7 |
| Sri Lanka | 90 | –2.3 | Syrian Arab Rep. | 87 | –3.5 |
| Sudan | 100 | 0.0 | Thailand | 99 | –0.4 |
| Tanzania | 108 | 0.7 | Tunisia | 99 | –0.3 |
| Togo | 114 | 2.5 | Turkey | 98 | –0.3 |
| Uganda | 88 | –0.8 | Yemen Rep. | – | – |
| Vietnam | – | – | Zimbabwe | – | – |
| Zaire | 163 | 5.1 | | | |
| Zambia | – | – | | | |

| Upper middle-income | Index | Ratio |
|---|---|---|
| Brazil | 123 | 1.9 |
| Czechoslovakia | – | – |
| Gabon | 96 | –1.9 |
| Greece | 105 | 0.6 |
| Hungary | 87 | –6.9 |
| Iraq | – | – |
| Korea | 108 | 2.4 |
| Libya | 97 | –3.6 |
| Mexico | 110 | 1.4 |
| Oman | – | – |
| Portugal | 105 | 1.5 |
| Saudi Arabia | 95 | –2.4 |
| South Africa | 93 | –2.2 |
| Trinidad & Tobago | 110 | 4.2 |
| Uruguay | 104 | 0.8 |
| Venezuela | 164 | 14.8 |
| Yugoslavia | 121 | 3.6 |

# Appendix 2: Armaments

Developing countries began to import substantial amounts of armaments in the 1970s; before then their purchases rarely exceeded $2 billion a year. But the Third World rapidly became 'the world's leading market for conventional weapons', accounting for as much as three-quarters of international trade in military systems.[1] Between 1978 and 1985, the least developed countries ordered an estimated $258 billion worth of arms and ammunition from foreign suppliers. Included in these transactions were 13 960 tanks and self-propelled cannon, 27 605 armoured personnel carriers and 34 948 surface-to-air missiles.[2]

While these imports fell in the 1980s, largely as a result of economic factors, they still remained high compared with the spending of developing countries on other sectors of their economies. By the beginning of the 1990s, with peace and disarmament beginning to break out across the world and with Western nations trying to check their own military spending, manufacturers of armaments in the West did all they could to increase sales to developing countries. But with economic recession affecting most countries, the salespeople were finding few customers.

In 1990 the United States and the former Soviet Union continued to be the dominant armaments exporters, accounting between them for around two-thirds of the total trade. Britain and France accounted for a major share of European Community arms exports. Some 60 per cent of export sales were made to governments of Third World countries. Although many had reduced their arms imports, some were substantially increasing them. India, for example, increased its purchases of arms from abroad from $1016 million in 1984 to $3378 million in 1989, while Iran's arms imports shot up from $268 million to $656 million in this period. Other countries imported less; Egypt and Syria, for example, and by 1990 the considerable efforts of the arms salespeople to export more of their wares ran into difficulties. Worldwide armament imports declined from $34 billion in 1984 to $21 billion in 1990.[3] Most of these exports are from a Western company to a Third World government. Collaboration between arms companies across national boundaries is beginning but is still in its infancy.

While the countries of the Middle East are among the largest importers, with Saudi Arabia topping the import league, the direction of armament exports is tending to move towards south and east Asia. The US State Department's Arms Control and Disarmament Agency has pointed out that Asia's share of the world arms market almost quadrupled in a decade, jumping from six per cent in 1977 to 23 per cent in 1988.[4]

The trade in armaments means that money which could have been available for development purposes, such as agriculture, health, education and transport, is spent instead on military equipment. While still United States President, General Dwight Eisenhower admitted: 'every gun that is made, every warship launched, every rocket fired, signifies in the final sense a theft from those who hunger and are not fed, from those who are cold and not clothed'.[5] Armament imports further exacerbate the debt problem facing many countries; according to the Stockholm International Peace Research Institute, arms purchases account for a fifth of Third World debt.[6] The imports help to lend 'legitimacy' to authoritarian governments, giving them the approval of the exporting country. They also provide the tools to repress people who are fighting for improved human rights such as greater democracy. British armoured personnel carriers have been used in Indonesia, for example, to break up demonstrations.

Armament sales also fuel wars either external or internal; most of the wars since 1945 have been fought in the Third World, with devastating consequences for local people. Nearly all the famine-afflicted countries in Africa – notably Ethiopia, Sudan, Somalia and Mozambique – suffered from warfare in the 1980s which shattered economies and left millions destitute.

The morality of Western countries selling armaments to countries where they can undermine development, encourage human rights abuses and fuel wars is highly questionable.

Few countries have embraced the sales of arms to the Third World with more fervour than Britain, especially during the 1980s. In 1980, Britain's Prime Minister, Margaret Thatcher, called arms export revenue 'a handy sum but not enough'. Between 1980 and 1986, Britain's armament exports tripled to become one of the country's most reliable earners of foreign exchange. Over three-quarters of Britain's arms exports go to Third World countries. When Prime Minister, Mrs Thatcher acted as Britain's foremost armaments salesperson, personally negotiating deals for British firms, including a multi-billion pound deal with Saudi Arabia in 1985 and a contract to sell jet fighter aircraft to Malaysia.

Britain's arms trade is more usually conducted by the companies themselves and also by people employed by the government's Defence Export Services Organization. Some of its 250 employees ply the Third World for business for British firms, sometimes pushing older-style military equipment that is no longer required by the Ministry of Defence. The Ministry organizes regular defence equipment exhibitions, inviting people from across the developing world.

British arms salesperson also take full advantage of exhibitions in Third World countries. In 1989, 13 British firms attended the arms exhibition in the Iraqi capital Baghdad, including British Aerospace, displaying Hawk fighter jets. The sales of these jets to Iraq was subsequently halted following public protests but, according to the London-based Campaign Against Arms Trade (CAAT), British sales – plus more substantial sales by France and the former Soviet Union – helped Iraq to build up its war machine and give Saddam Hussein the power he needed to pursue an eight-year war with Iran, and later to invade Kuwait.[7]

While exporting governments claim to exercise some control over which countries receive their armaments, in practice that control is lax. British arms exporters are supposed to need licences to sell abroad, but there is no open, public record of those licensed to trade. Countries which are subject to arms trade bans can usually find their way around controls that exporting governments are not, in any case, over-keen to observe. The debacle over the export by British firms of a 'supergun' to Iraq illustrated the clear breaking of an arms embargo; the deal slipped through the net of government controls. Former arms dealer, Said K. Aburish, says 'UK policy is not clear at all – in fact it's very murky and muddy indeed'.[8]

Illicit arms transactions take two forms, says Michael T. Klare, Professor of Peace and World Security Studies at the University of Massachusetts. *Black-market* sales generally entail illegal sales of military hardware stolen or misappropriated from government stockpiles, and then via devious and clandestine routes to other destinations. *Grey-market* sales generally entail the transfer of 'dual-use' systems (helicopters, communications systems, computers and other products that can be used for both military and civilian purposes) to military users through legitimate export channels, usually on the pretext that they are intended for civilian rather than military use. He points out that black-market sales of $5–10 billion a year, 'coupled with a substantial trade in arms-making technology' could eliminate much of the statistical decline in Third World military imports observed since 1983.[9]

But debt, shortage of foreign exchange, and the end of the superpower conflict meant that, by the start of the 1990s, the North–South armament business was under pressure. At the same time, a number of developing countries were stepping up their own output of armaments and looking to export markets – including Brazil, China, Egypt and North Korea. To control this trade in death, the CAAT proposed an international register of arms production and exports, coordinated by the United Nations; this was set up in December 1991. They also want all applications for arms export licences from UK companies to be published in advance and be subject to public and parliamentary scrutiny; a ban on arms exports to countries at war and those with poor human rights records; and also that such exports take into account the impact on development. The West's interest in embracing such proposals seemed limited to stopping the proliferation of nuclear, missile and chemical arms, however.

The Gulf War in 1991 may have encouraged Western exporting governments to consider the wisdom of selling armaments to countries which might eventually turn their guns around and point them *at the seller*. Vague guidelines have been agreed to control armament exports, but there is little action to retrain people who work in arms factories in other skills, or to convert factories for other uses.

# Appendix 3: ATOs

Afristar Ltd
Kaivokatu 10 C/ 5th Floor
00100 Helsinki
Finland

Alternative Handel
Linnegatan 13-21
5-413 04 Goteborg
Sweden

Alternative Handel
P.O. Box 2802 Toyen
0608 Oslo 6
Norway

Bridgehead Inc.
20 James Street
Ottawa, Ontario K2P 0T6
Canada

Butik Salam
Brandts Passage 34
5000 Odense C
Denmark

CAA Trading
P.O. Box 184
Kilkenny SA 5009
Australia

Caritas Fairness Shop
Zentralstr. 18
6003 Luzern
Switzerland

CTM
Via Concciapelli 43
39100 Bolzano
Italy

DWL/Team
Rawiestrasse 5
D-4500 Osnabruck
Germany

Equal Exchange Ltd
29 Nicholson Square
Edinburgh EH8 9BX
Scotland, UK

Equal Exchange
101 Tosca Drive
Stoughton
MA 02072, USA

EZA
Lengfelden 169
A-501 Bergheim
Austria

Fair Trade Foundation
132 Highland Avenue
Middletown
CT C06457, USA

Friends of the Third World
611 West Wayne Street
Fort Wayne, Indiana
46802-2125, USA

GEPA
Talstrasse 20
D-5830 Schwelm
Germany

Handelsfront
Drottning gatan 73C
11136 Stockholm
Sweden

IFAT
P.O. Box 2703
1000 CS Amsterdam
The Netherlands

Last Hope International
P.O. Box 119
Okpala P.O. Via Aba
Imo State, Nigeria

Mantis
P.O. Box 72229
Windhoek 9000
Namibia

MCCH
Avda Cardenal de la Torre
MZ "A" junto Iglesia
Quito
Ecuador

Minka
P.O. Box 14-0359
Lima
Peru

North Western Bee Products
P.O. Box 140096
Kabombo
Zambia

Shared Earth
17 Goodramgate
York YO1 2LW
UK

OS3
Bijfangstrasse 19
CH-2552 Orpund
Switzerland

Oxfam America
115 Broadway
Boston
MA 02116, USA

Oxfam Trading
Murdoch Road
Bicester OX2 7DZ
UK

Oxfam Wereldwinkels
Nieuwland 35-37
9000 Gent
Belgium

Preda
Upper Kalaklan
Olongapo City
Philippines

Press Alternative
Central Meguro-Ku 102
7-10, Meguro-Ku, Tokyo
Japan 153

Pueblo to People
1616 Montrose Street
Houston, Texas
77006, USA

Radicom
Rue 43bd Gl. de Gaulle
Dakar
Senegal

Refugees International Japan
c/o Showa Shell Sekiya K.K.
C.P.O. Box 1239
Tokyo 100-91
Japan

Sackeus
Tellusborgsvagen 67 B
126 37 Hagersten
Sweden

Self-help Crafts
704 Mainstreet Box L
Akron
PA 17501, USA

SERVV Self-help Handicrafts
P.O. Box 365
New Windsor
MD 21776-0365, USA

Simon Levelt BV
Prins Hendrikkade 26
1012 TM Amsterdam
Netherlands

SIPA
5 H.D. Raja Street
Eldama Rd. Teynampet
Madras 600 018
India

SOS Wereldhandel
Beesdeweg 5
4104 AW Culemborg
Netherlands

Stichting Ideele Import
Strijkviertel 38
3454PM de Meern
Netherlands

Sur Norte
Jose Pardo 1198
Lima 18
Peru

Tanzania Import
P.O. Box 211
61301 Oselund
Sweden

Tampere
Kauppakatu 10
33210 Tampere
Finalnd

Trading Partners
101 Young Street
Annandale
NSW 2038
Australia

Trade Aid
P.O. Box 18620
Christchurch
New Zealand

Traidcraft plc
Kingsway
Gateshead NE11 0NE
UK

Traideireann Ltd
P.O. Box 20 Athlone
Co Westmeath
Ireland

Twin Trading
345 Goswell Road
London EC1V 7JT
UK

U-landsimporten
P.O. Box 7
7900 Nykobing M
Denmark

World Development Tea
Co-operative
P.O. Box A559
Sydney South
NSW 2000
Australia

# Notes

## Foreword

1. Developing countries exported $951 billion of goods and services in 1990, mostly to the North, compared with $64 billion received in development aid, although a straight comparison is of course not possible. See *Handbook of International Trade and Development Statistics, 1991*, New York: UNCTAD, 1991, TD/Stat/18, and *Financial Flows for Developing Countries, 1990 and Recent Trends*, Paris: OECD, 1992.
2. Myrdal, G. *The Challenge of World Poverty*, UK Pelican Books, 1970, p. 273.
3. See Holmberg, J., Bass, S., and Timberlake, L., *Defending the Future: A Guide to Sustainable Development*, London: Earthscan Publications, 1991.
4. The Group of 77 is the group of developing countries which first met at UNCTAD I in 1964 to discuss a joint negotiating position. Member countries now number 129. It is the counterpart of the Group of 7 (G7) major industrialized countries.
5. Morton, K., and Tulloch, P., *Trade and Developing Countries*, London: Croom Helm/ODI, 1977.
6. *World Development Report, 1991*, Washington: World Bank, pp. 204–5.

## Chapter 1

1. *Handbook of International Trade and Development Statistics, 1991*, op. cit., p. 13 and p. 254.
2. Compiled from *Handbook*, ibid., and from *UNCTAD Commodity Yearbook, 1991*, TD/B/C1/STAT.8, New York: United Nations, 1991, p. 78.
3. *Holy Bible*, New International Version, Hodder and Stoughton, 1979, 1 Kings, 10:22.
4. Ibid. See, for example, Isaiah 3:14–17; Jeremiah 22:3; Amos 2:6–8; 4:1.
5. See, for example, Chichilinsky, G., 'North-South trade and basic needs', *Journal of Development Planning Literature*, 1989, 4(4) pp. 180–221.
6. Seldon, A., and Pennance, F.G., *Everyman's Dictionary of Economics*, London: J. Dent & Sons Ltd, 1965, pp. 77–8.
7. Reproduced in *New Internationalist*, February 1990, p. 10–11.
8. Morton and Tulloch, op. cit., p. 18.

9. Quoted in the *Ecologist*, September/October 1990.
10. *Industrialized Countries Policies Affecting Foreign Direct Investment in Developing Countries*, Multilateral Investment Guarantee Agency, Washington: World Bank, 1991, p. 26.
11. Quoted in *Food First*, Frances Moore Lappé and Joseph Collins, London: Souvenir Press, 1980, p. 84.
12. *Handbook of International Trade and Development Statistics, 1989*, UNCTAD, New York: United Nations, p. 48.
13. In economic terms, many export crops have a low income elasticity of demand.
14. *World Development Report, 1991*, op. cit., p. 105.
15. Harris, N., *The End of the Third World: newly industrializing countries and the decline of an ideology*, UK Penguin, 1986, p. 67.
16. Quoted in *Adverse Impact of Export-Orientated Industrialization on Third World Environment and Economy*, Walden Bello, Penang Malaysia: Third World Features Network, January 1992.
17. Chichilinsky, op. cit., p. 200.
18. Ibid., p. 191.
19. Ibid., p. 192.
20. Myrdal, G., op. cit., p. 275.
21. Chichilinsky, op. cit., p. 201.
22. Sider, R., *Rich Christians in an Age of Hunger*, London: Hodder and Stoughton, 1990, p. 134.
23. *Global Economic Prospects and the Developing Countries, 1992*, Washington: World Bank, 1992, p. 2.
24. *Human Development Report, 1992*, New York: UNDP, 1992, p. 48.
25. A community in southern Chile is reported to be charging outsiders $2000 per potato plant.
26. Discussion with author, April 1992.
27. See Cooper, D., Vellvé, R., and Hobbelink, H., *Growing Diversity: genetic resources and local food security*, London: Intermediate Technology Publications, 1992.
28. The other key proposal calls for an increase in development aid.
29. See Samir Amin, *Delinking: Towards a Polycentric World*, London: Zed Books, 1990.
30. *IFDA Dossier*, No. 69, Nyon, Switzerland, 1988, p. 52.

## Chapter 2

1. Mooneyham, W. Stanley, *What Do You Say to a Hungry World?* Waco, USA: World Books, p. 117.
2. Conversation with author, January 1988.
3. See *International Agricultural Development*, September/October 1989.
4. See Sement, G., *Cotton*, The Tropical Agriculturalist series, The Netherlands: CTA/MacMillan, 1988.
5. Information based on discussions with development workers at Selly Oak Colleges, Birmingham.
6. Dinham, B., *Production and Trade in Dangerous Chemicals*, paper presented to CIIR Conference, London, January 1992.
7. Presented to the FAO Committee on Fisheries, April 1992, FAO, Rome.
8. Ibid.

9. *What does the future hold for world fisheries*, Samudra Report No. 3, Belgium: International Collective in Support of Fishworkers, 1990.
10. The description might be compared with one nineteenth century writer's description of boys, who worked a 12–14-hour day in the dark satanic cotton mills built to facilitate Britain's industrial revolution, as 'lively elves'.
11. Eisold, E., *Young women in export industries – the case of the semi-conductor industry in Southeast Asia*, Geneva: ILO, 1984.
12. Information supplied by the Asia-Pacific People's Environment Network, Penang, Malaysia.
13. Conversation with development worker at Selly Oak Colleges.
14. Walden Bello, op. cit., *'Behind the success of Asia's export-orientated industrialization'*, Malaysia: Third World Features Network, January 1992.
15. Fourth EC-ACP Lomé Convention, Protocol 5. See *The Courier*, Brussels, March-April 1990.
16. *Our Common Future*, Report of the World Commission on Environment and Development, Oxford: OUP, 1987, p. 79.
17. FAO Secretariat note to the Committee on Forestry, September 1990, COFO 90/12, Rome: FAO.
18. See, for example, *'No Timber Without Trees'*, by Poore, D., Earthscan, 1989; this was the result of a study carried out by the ITTO. See also review by Marcus Colchester of the book in *Appropriate Technology*, September 1990.
19. Meeting in London, October 1988.
20. Goodland, Robert J.A., Watson, C., and Ledec, G., *Environmental Management in Tropical Agriculture*, Boulder, CO: Westview Press, 1984, p. 65.
21. Ibid., p. 51
22. Ibid., p. 35
23. Ibid., p. 71
24. Samudra Report, op. cit.
25. *Handbook of World Development, the guide to the Brandt Report*, London: Longman, 1981, p. 157.
26. Walden Bello, op. cit., *'Behind the success of Asia's export-orientated industrialization'*.
27. *Trade and the Environment*, Geneva: GATT, March 1992, p. 2.
28. Calculations based on BP Statistical Review of World Energy, London: BP, 1991, and discussions with energy analysts, April 1992.

## Chapter 3

1. *North-South: a programme for survival*. Report of the independent commission on international development issues, London: Pan Books, 1980, p. 142.
2. *Trade and Development Report, 1991*, Geneva: UNCTAD, p. 33.
3. UNCTAD paper, UNCTAD/PSM/CAS/380/Add.12, 1992, Geneva.
4. International Coffee Organization estimates.
5. *Financial Times*, 23 January 1992.
6. *Commodity Review and Outlook*, 1990–91, Rome: FAO, 1991.
7. *Cocoa Prices to the Year 2005*, Geneva: UNCTAD/International Cocoa Organization, 1990.

8. *Financial Times*, op. cit.
9. *Financial Times*, 1 August 1991.
10. *Tea: market developments in 1991*, Rome: FAO, 1992.
11. Figures supplied by FAO.
12. Study by the University of Waterloo by W.E. Forbes and M.E. Thompson.
13. Omar, S., *The Economic Consequences of Smoking in Egypt*, Cancer Institute, Cairo University, 1987.
14. *Commodity Review and Outlook*, op. cit.
15. *Timber from the South Seas: An analysis of Japan's Tropical Timber Trade and its Environmental Impact*, WWF, UK, 1989.
16. Akiyama, T., and Varangis, P.N., *The impact of the International Coffee Agreement on producing countries*, World Bank Economic Review, 1990, 4–2, p. 158.
17. *Sustainable Tropical Forest Management*, Gland, Switzerland: World Wide Fund for Nature, 1990.
18. *Report of the UN Conference on Trade and Development, Fourth Session*, UNCTAD Report TD/217, July 1976, Geneva: UNCTAD, p. 4.
19. *Third World Pressures at Nairobi*, 'Round Table', John Madeley, The Round Table Ltd, October 1976, pp. 342–9.
20. *New Compact for Co-operation*, New York: United Nations, 1991.

## Chapter 4

1. Compiled from UNCTAD trade and development statistics.
2. Figures supplied by UNIDO, Vienna.
3. *North-South: a programme for survival*, op. cit., p. 142.
4. Quoted in Lester R. Brown et al., *State of the World, 1990*, New York: Norton, 1990, p. 144.
5. The way that international trade statistics are calculated makes it difficult to compile overall figures. An example of escalating tariffs can be seen from UNCTAD figures on cocoa and chocolate. Whereas cocoa beans exported into Japan attract no tariff, cocoa paste attracts a 15 per cent tariff and chocolate 26.7 per cent. See *Uruguay Round: Papers on Selected Issues*, Geneva: UNCTAD, 1989.
6. See *UNCTAD VIII: Analytical report by the UNCTAD secretariat to the Conference*, TD/358, New York: United Nations, 1992.
7. *Who Did What?* London: Mitchell Beazley, 1974, p. 73.
8. Curzon, G., et al., *MFA Forever?* Trade Policy Research Centre, 1981. pp. 13-15. See also Madeley, J., 'Why a tighter MFA is short-sighted', *Guardian*, 8 February 1978.
9. Silverstone, A., *The Future of the MFA: implications of the UK economy*, HMSO, 1989.
10. Wood, A., 'What do Developing-country Manufactured Exports Consist of?', *Development Policy Review*, Vol. 9, London: ODI/Sage, 1991, p. 179.
11. *Adjustment or Protection*, Ed. Abby Rubin Riddell, London: CIIR, 1980, p. 5.
12. *The Generalized System of Preferences: Review of the First Decade*, Paris: OECD, 1983, p. 14.
13. Hameed, K., *Preferences – a better deal for the World's Poor?* London: World Development Movement, 1972, p. 13.

14. Report of the Special Committee on Preferences, 17th Session, May 1990, TD/B/1263, Geneva: UNCTAD.
15. *UNCTAD Bulletin* No. 10, July/August 1991, Geneva: UNCTAD.
16. OECD, op. cit., p. 51.
17. UNCTAD op. cit., p. 58.
18. Report of the Special Committee on Preferences, 17th Session, op. cit.
19. Quoted in *Development Co-operation*, December 1991, Paris: OECD, p. 18.
20. *Negotiating the Fourth Lomé Convention*, Briefing Paper, London: ODI, October 1989.
21. See, for example, *Liberalizing Foreign Trade in Developing Countries: the lessons of experience.* Papapeorgiou, D., Choksi A.M., and Michaely, M. Washington: World Bank, 1990.
22. *Finance and Development*, September 1991, Washington: IMF. p. 43.
23. *Accelerating the Development Process*, UNCTAD Report TD/354, August 1991, Geneva: UNCTAD, p. 50.
24. *Investing in Free Export Processing Zones*, Basile, A., and Germids, D., Paris: OECD, 1984, p. 20.
25. Walden Bello, op. cit.
26. *Multinational Enterprises and Employment*, Kreye, O., Heinrichs, J., and Frobel, F. Geneva: ILO, Starnberg Institute, 1988.
27. Ibid.
28. Ibid.
29. *Export Processing Zones for Growth and Development*, Rolf Alter, IMF Working Paper, WP/90/122, Washington: IMF, 1990.
30. *Adjustment to structural change in manufacturing in a North-South perspective: the case of the clothing export sector of Mauritius*, Roland Lamusse, WEP Working Paper No. 27, Geneva: ILO, 1990.
31. Ibid.

## Chapter 5

1. *Handbook of International Trade and Development Statistics, 1991*, Geneva: UNCTAD, 1992.
2. Briefing Paper, November 1990, Geneva: GATT.
3. *The Challenge to the South*, report of the South Commission, Oxford: OUP, 1990, p. 249.
4. See, for example, *GATT Briefing*, Trade in Services, the Uruguay Round and the GATT, No. 3, October 1990, European NGO Network on Agriculture and Development.
5. *The Challenge to the South*, op. cit., p. 250.
6. *GATT Briefing*, op. cit.
7. UNCTAD, 1991, op. cit., 144
8. UNCTAD, 1990, op. cit., pviii
9. *The Challenge to the South*, op. cit., p. 249.
10. See *Review of Maritime Transport*, Geneva: UNCTAD, 1989.
11. Ibid., p. 51.
12. Ibid., p. 49.
13. *Human Development Report, 1992*, Oxford: UNDP/OUP, April 1992.
14. *The Challenge to the South*, op. cit., p.251.
15. *Human Development Report, 1992*, op. cit., p.258.

16. Booth, A., 'The Tourism Boom in Indonesia', *Bulletin of Indonesia Economic Studies*, Vol. 26, No. 3, 1990.
17. *Conditions of work in the hotel, catering and tourism sector*, Geneva: ILO, 1989.
18. Included in information presented to a conference on tourism and Third World peoples at Bad Boll, Germany, March 1986.
19. Encik Zulfigar, quoted in the Malaysia newspaper, *Uttusan Konsumer*, mid-September 1991.
20. Bad Boll, op. cit.
21. See 'The Gambia tries to cash in on its Roots', *Panoscope, PS*. London: Panos Institute, London, January 1992.
22. Bad Boll, op. cit.
23. *The Great Escape? An Examination of North-South Tourism*, E.Philip English, Ottawa: North-South Institute.
24. Britton, S., *Tourism and Under-development in Fiji*, The Australian National University, 1987.
25. Address to Development Journalists Group meeting, London, July 1989.
26. Bad Boll, op. cit.
27. *Tourism Concern*, London: Spring 1991.
28. *Accelerating the Development Process*, UNCTAD, TD/354, August 1991, Geneva: UNCTAD, p. 69.

## Chapter 6

1. *The Triad in Foreign Direct Investment*, New York: United Nations Centre on Transnational Corporations, 1991.
2. *Agribusiness TNCs and Impact on the Rural Poor in Asia*, CCA-RM Consultation Report, Malaysia,1988.
3. *North–South: a programme for survival*, op. cit., p.187.
4. See *Transnational Corporations in World Development, Trends and Prospects*, New York: UNCTC, 1988.
5. Estimate of Richard Tapper of the World Wide Fund for Nature, quoted in The *Guardian*, 8 May 1992.
6. *Towards a New International Economic Order*, London: Commonwealth Secretariat, 1977, p. 61.
7. *Industrialized Countries Policies Affecting Foreign Direct Investment in Developing Countries*, op. cit.
8. *North–South: a programme for survival*, op. cit., p. 188.
9. See Adams, S., *Roche versus Adams*, London: Jonathan Cape, 1984, p. 220.
10. See Hay, D., 'International Socio-Economic Political Order and our Lifestyles' in *Lifestyle in the Eighties;* ed: Ronald Sider, Philadelphia: Westminster Press, 1982, p. 113.
11. *Multinational Enterprises and Employment*, op. cit.
12. Leaflet: *Transnational Corporations*, New York: UN Publications.
13. UNCTC leaflet, DESI E. 130, 1986, New York: UNCTC.
14. *International Arrangements and Agreements relating to Transnational Corporations*, UN Economic and Social Council, E/C.10/1992/8, New York: UN, February 1992.
15. Ibid.
16. E. von Bern, *The Infiltration of the UN System by Multinational Corporations*, Zurich, 1978.

17. *Transnational Corporations in World Development*, UNCTC 1988 Report, New York: UNCTC, 1989.
18. 'Transnationals led the way', *Development Forum*, New York: United Nations, September/October 1991.
19. 'Benchmark Survey', New York: UNCTC, 1991.
20. Dinham, B., 'Transnational Corporations: in debt to the poor?' Christian Action Journal, London, Winter 1990.
21. See Fowler, G., and Mooney, P., *The Threatened Gene: food, politics and the loss of genetic diversity*, Cambridge, UK: Lutterworth Press, 1991.
22. I am indebted to The Rural Advancement Fund International of Beresford, Canada for these points.
23. Nectoux, F., and Dudley, N., *A Hardwood Story*, London: Friends of the Earth, 1987, p. 48.
24. *Observer*, 15 December 1991.
25. *'Plunder in Ghana's Rainforest for illegal profit'*, London: Friends of the Earth, March 1992.
26. Nectoux and Dudley, op. cit., p. 53.
27. Tickell, O., 'Honduran chop logic', *Guardian*, 14 February 1992.
28. Chetley, A., *A Healthy Business?*, London: Zed Books, 1990, p. 73.

## Chapter 7

1. Armament exports are also in the 'deadly' category, although with little involvement of TNCs. These are considered in the Appendix.
2. *Public Health Impact of Pesticides used in Agriculture.* Report of WHO/UNEP working party, Geneva, 1990.
3. Jeyaratnam, J., 'Acute pesticide poisoning: a major problem', *World Health Statistics Quarterly*, 43, 1990, pp. 139-144.
4. British Agrochemicals Association, *Annual Review and Handbook*, 1991.
5. Figures included in a speech given by Barbara Dinham of the Pesticides Trust to a CIIR Seminar, January 1992.
6. Weir, D., and Schapiro, M., *The Circle of Poison*, San Francisco: Institute for Food and Development Policy, 1981, p. 3.
7. Bull, D., *A Growing Problem: pesticides and the Third World poor*, Oxford: Oxfam, 1982.
8. Dinham, op. cit.
9. *Financial Times*, 9 May 1991.
10. Dinham, op. cit.
11. Janice King Jensen, 'Pesticide Donations and the Disposal Crisis in Africa', *Pesticide News*, Journal of The Pesticide Trust, December 1991.
12. 'Dealing with Obsolete Pesticides', *Pesticide News*, Journal of The Pesticide Trust, December 1991.
13. 'Essential drugs' are those which are considered vital for health needs. Diana Melrose says that of the 'thousands of different drugs sold, WHO has identified a selection of approximately 200 which experts consider essential'. Melrose, D., *Bitter Pills*, Oxford: Oxfam, 1982, p. 15.
14. *Exposed: Deadly Exports. The Story of European Community Exports of banned or withdrawn drugs to the Third World.* WEMOS/Pharma pro-

ject, June 1991, WEMOS, P.O. Box 40066, 1009 BB Amsterdam, The Netherlands. This section draws on the project's findings.
15. Several other clioquinol products, made by local producers, were also on sale.
16. See 'EC frowns on dried milk's baby smiles', *Daily Telegraph*, 8 April 1992.
17. UNICEF report, *The State of the World's Children, 1991*, New York: UNICEF, December 1990.
18. Ibid., p. 26.
19. 'Action Now on Baby Foods', *New Internationalist*, August 1973.
20. Muller, M., *The Baby Killer*, London: War on Want, 1973.
21. Palmer, G., *The Politics of Breast-feeding*, London: Pandora Press, 1988, p. 206.
22. Ibid., p. 207.
23. Ibid., p. 208.
24. Ibid., p. 223.
25. Ibid., p. 237
26. Ibid., p. 240.
27. UNICEF Executive Board resolution 1991/22, 1991.
28. The letter was sent following a motion passed at the Church of England parliament, the General Synod, in July 1991, calling on Nestlé to end the promotion of breast milk substitutes, and endorsing a boycott of Nescafé.
29. *Breaking the Rules*, Cambridge, UK: IBFAN, 1991.
30. *International Waste Trade*, London: Greenpeace, 1991.
31. Ibid.
32. The Basle Convention, a global agreement to stop the export of toxic wastes, came into force in May 1992; countries are asked to sign up voluntarily.
33. *Waste Trade Update*, London: Greenpeace, 1991.
34. Conversation between author and Greenpeace official, April 1992.
35. *Economist*, 8 February 1992.
36. *Handbook of International Trade and Development Statistics, 1992*, op. cit.
37. Wilkinson, J., *Tobacco*, U.K. Penguin, 1986, p. 125.
38. Paper given to the Fifth World Conference on Smoking and Health, Winnipeg, July 1983.

*Chapter 8*

1. *Basic facts about the United Nations*, New York: United Nations, 1974.
2. Stewart, F., 'Are Adjustment Policies in Africa consistent with long-run development needs?' *Development Policy Review*, Vol.9 No.4, December 1991, London: ODI.
3. Ibid.
4. Ibid.
5. Torado, M., *Economic Development in the Third World*, New York: Longman, 1989, p. 421.
6. *New Compact for Co-operation*, op. cit.
7. World Debt Tables 1991-92, Washington: World Bank, 1991, p. 120
8. Ibid.
9. Ibid., p. 3.

10. Financial Resources for Developing Countries, 1990 and recent trends. Paris: OCED, October 1991.
11. Vallely, P., *Bad Samaritans*, London: Hodder and Stoughton, 1990, pp. 169-170.
12. *New Compact for Co-operation*, op. cit., p. 21.
13. World Bank, op. cit., p. 60.
14. Ibid., p. 123.
15. *New Compact for Co-operation*, op. cit.
16. Sachs, J., *Foreign Affairs*, USA, Summer 1989, p. 91.
17. World Debt Tables, op. cit.
18. *Human Development Report, 1992*, op. cit., p. 49.
19. See Halbach, A.J., and Osterkamp, R., *Countertrade with Developing Countries: New Opportunities for North-South Trade?*, Intereconomics, January/February 1989.
20. Chaldeans Mensah, *Countertrade in the Third World: some notes*, Ifda Dossier, 1989, Nyon, Switzerland.
21. Jones, S., *Third World countertrade: Analysis of 1350 deals involving developing countries 1980-87*; Newbury, UK: Produce Studies, 1988.
22. *Countertrade with Developing Countries: New Opportunities for North-South Trade?*, op. cit., p. 18.
23. Ibid, p. 23.
24. *State of the World's Children Report, 1990*, New York: UNICEF, 1990.
25. Much of the world's gold is buried deep in the ground in vaults at Fort Knox, USA. Gold is dug out of the ground in one part of the world, buried in another, and this gives confidence to the whole world trading system.
26. *Challenge to the South*, op. cit., p. 237.

## Chapter 9

1. *GATT: What it is, what it does*, Geneva: GATT, 1990.
2. Ibid.
3. *The Draft Final Act Embodying the Results of the Uruguay Round of Multilateral Trade Negotiations*, MTN.TNC/W/FA, GATT, Geneva, 1991.
4. *Sub-Saharan Africa: From Crisis to Sustainable Growth*, Washington: World Bank, 1989, p. 106.
5. ODI meeting, London, February 1991.
6. Page, S., Davenport, M., and Hewitt, A., *The GATT Uruguay Round: Effects on developing countries*, London: ODI, 1991.
7. Watkins, K., *Fixing the Rules: North-South issues in international trade and the GATT Uruguay Round*, London: CIIR, April 1992, p. 12.
8. Ibid., p. 90.
9. *The Draft Final Act Embodying the Results of the Uruguay Round of Multilateral Trade Negotiations*, op. cit., p. N.2.
10. See, for example, the *Ecologist*, November/December 1990.
11. *Trade and the Environment*, op. cit., p. 28.
12. Ibid., p. 34.
13. Ibid., p. 35.
14. Discussion with author, March 1992.
15. 'Environmental rules set stage for GATT conflicts', London: *Financial Times*, 5 December 1991.

16. For a detailed critique of the GATT and the Uruguay Round, see Watkins, op. cit.
17. Morton and Tulloch, op. cit., p. 63.
18. See the *Observer*, London, 9 May 1976.
19. *Report of UNCTAD IV*, TD/217, July 1976, Geneva: UNCTAD.
20. Ibid.
21. 'The West Missed Again', *South China Morning Post*, Hong Kong, 22 June 1979.
22. A number of other organizations are also involved with international trade issues. The Geneva-based International Trade Centre, for instance, set up by GATT and UNCTAD in 1964, undertakes marketing studies for countries or for groups of products. As part of its work, the International Labour Office conducts studies of the impact of TNCs on economies (see Chapter 4).

## Chapter 10

1. This example comes from material supplied by Traidcraft.
2. Agreed at an IFAT conference. Quoted in 'Fair Trading', *New Internationalist*, February 1990.
3. Ibid. *New Internationalist*.
4. Ibid.
5. Whittaker, B., *A Bridge of People*, London: Heinemann, 1983, p. 145.
6. Coote, B., *The Trade Trap*, Oxford: Oxfam, 1992, p. 166.
7. Letter to author, 22 April 1992.
8. *New Internationalist*, op.cit.
9. Traidcraft leaflet, 1990.
10. Traidcraft Financial Statements, 1991, p. 5
11. Communication with author, April 1992.
12. *The Network*, January 1988, London: TWIN.
13. TWIN Annual Report, 1991, London: TWIN.
14. Press statement, 1991.
15. Coote, op. cit., p. 180.
16. Based on information supplied by The Body Shop, March 1992.
17. Press Release, February 1989.
18. Wells, P., and Jetter, M., *The Global Consumer: Best buys to help the Third World*, London: Gollancz, 1991.
19. Ibid. p. 223.
20. 'Of Mickey Mouse and Hunger', *New Internationalist*, February 1992.
21. Conversation with the author, March 1992.

## Chapter 11

1. Calculated from *Handbook of International Trade and Development Statistics, 1991*, op. cit.
2. Ibid.
3. June Kronholz, *Wall St. Journal*, 30 July 1981.
4. *Challenge to the South*, op. cit., p. 171.
5. Ibid., p. 172.
6. *Financial Times*, 20 April 1988.
7. Press Bulletin on completion of second summit meeting, Caracas, Summit Level of Developing Countries, Geneva, November 1991.

8. Ibid.
9. Ibid.
10. *Challenge to the South*, op. cit., p. 177.
11. *African Employment Report 1990*, Addis Ababa: Jobs and Skills Programme for Africa, 1991.
12. Ibid.
13. *Handbook of International Trade and Development Statistics, 1991*, op. cit., p. 39.
14. Statistics derived from SADCC publications, Gaborone, Botswana: SADCC.
15. In August 1992 the SADCC countries signed The Treaty of the Southern African Development Community. They are now part of a 'community; rather than only an association of countries.
16. *Handbook of International Trade and Development Statistics, 1990*, op. cit., p. 37.
17. See, for example, *Financial Times* report 6 February 1991 'Mahathirs brain child proves problem for partners'.
18. Ibid., p. 37.
19. *African Employment Report 1990.*, op. cit.
20. See Madeley, J., 'The Bitter Taste of Fluctuating Coffee Prices', *Africa*, July 1978.
21. *Export Taxes on Primary Products*, Commonwealth paper no. 9, London: Commonwealth Secretariat, 1984.
22. See *New Internationalist*, August 1975.
23. *The Challenge to the South*, op. cit., p. 179.
24. *End of an Illusion – Verdict on UNCTAD 3*, London: WDM, 1972.
25. *Handbook of International Trade and Development Statistics, 1990*, op. cit., p. 254.
26. *Delinking: Towards a Polycentric World*, op. cit.

## Appendix 1

1. *Handbook of International Trade and Development Statistics, 1990*, New York: UN, 1991; *Global Economic Prospects and the Developing Countries*, Washington D.C.: World Bank, 1992.

## Appendix 2

1. Klare, M.T., 'The Arms Trade: changing patterns in the 1980s'. *Third World Quarterly*, 1987, 9(4).
2. Ibid.
3. Stockholm International Peace Research Institute yearbooks, London and Philadelphia: Taylor and Francis.
4. *Financial Times* defence survey, 17 January 1990.
5. *Disarmament and World Development*, Oxford: Pergamon Press, 1978, p. 3.
6. See *SIRPI Yearbook, 1985*, London and Philadelphia: Taylor and Francis.
7. Conversation with CAAT official, November 1991.
8. Aburish, Said K., *Pay-Off: Wheeling and dealing in the Arab world*, London: Unwin.
9. Klare, op. cit.

# Bibliography

Aburish, Said K., *Pay-Off: Wheeling and dealing in the Arab world*, London: Unwin.

Adams, Stanley, *Roche versus Adams*, London: Jonathan Cape, 1984.

*African Employment Report 1990*, Addis Ababa: ILO Jobs and Skills Programme for Africa, 1991.

*Agribusiness TNCs and Impact on the Rural Poor in Asia*, CCA-RM Consultation Report, Malaysia,1988.

Akiyama, T., and Varangis, P.N., *The impact of the International Coffee Agreement on producing countries*. Washington D.C.: World Bank Economic Review, 1990.

Amin, Samir, *Delinking: Towards a Polycentric World*, London: Zed Books, 1990.

Basile, A., and Germids, D., *Investing in Free Export Processing Zones*, Paris: OECD, 1984.

Booth, Anne, 'The Tourism Boom in Indonesia', *Bulletin of Indonesia Economic Studies*, Vol.26, No.3, 1990.

Britton, Steve, *Tourism and Under-development in Fiji*, The Australian National University, 1987.

Bull, David, *A Growing Problem: pesticides and the Third World poor*, Oxford: Oxfam, 1982.

Chetley, Andrew, *A Healthy Business?*, London: Zed Books,1990.

Chichilinsky, G., 'North-South trade and basic needs', *Journal of Development Planning Literature*, 1989, 4(4).

*Cocoa prices to the Year 2005*, Geneva: UNCTAD/International Cocoa Organization, 1990.

*Commodity Review and Outlook*, 1990-91, Rome: FAO, 1991.

*Conditions of work in the hotel, catering and tourism sector.* Geneva: ILO, 1989.

Cooper, D., Vellvé, R., and Hobbelink, H., *Growing Diversity: genetic resources and local food security*, London: IT Publications, 1992.

Coote, Belinda, *The Trade Trap*, Oxford: Oxfam, 1992.

Dinham, Barbara, *Production and Trade in Dangerous Chemicals*, paper presented to CIIR Conference, London, January 1992.

Dinham, Barbara, 'Transnational Corporations: in debt to the poor?' *Christian Action Journal*, Winter 1990.

*Disarmament and World Development*, Oxford: Pergamon Press, 1978.

Eisold, Elizabeth, *Young women in export industries – the case of the semi-conductor industry in Southeast Asia*, Geneva: ILO, 1984.

*Exposed: Deadly Exports. The Story of European Community Exports of banned or withdrawn drugs to the Third World*. WEMOS/Pharma project, The Netherlands, 1991.

*Export Processing Zones for Growth and Development*, Rolf Alter, IMF Working Paper, WP/90/122, Washington: IMF, 1990.

Fowler, Gary and Mooney, Pat, *The Threatened Gene: food, politics and the loss of genetic diversity*, Cambridge: Lutterworth Press, 1991.

*GATT: What it is, what it does*, Geneva: GATT, 1990.

*Global Economic Prospects and the Developing Countries, 1992*, Washington: World Bank, 1992.

Goodland, R.J.A., Watson, C., and Ledec, G., *Environmental Management in Tropical Agriculture*, Boulder, CO: Westview Press, 1984.

Halbach, Alex J., and Osterkamp, Rigmar, *Countertrade with Developing Countries: New Opportunities for North-South Trade?*, Intereconomics, January/February 1989.

*Handbook of International Trade and Development Statistics, 1991*, New York: UNCTAD, 1991.

*Handbook of International Trade and Development Statistics, 1992*, New York: UNCTAD, 1992.

Harris, Nigel, *The End of the Third World: newly industrializing countries and the decline of an ideology*, UK: Penguin, 1986.

Holmberg, J., Bass, S., and Timberlake, L., *Defending the Future: A Guide to Sustainable Development*, London: Earthscan Publications, 1991.

*Human Development Report, 1992*, New York: UNDP, 1992.

*Industrialized Countries Policies Affecting Foreign Direct Investment in Developing Countries*, Multilateral Investment Guarantee Agency, Washington: World Bank, 1991.

*International Waste Trade*, London: Greenpeace, 1991.

Jensen, Janice King, 'Pesticide Donations and the Disposal Crisis in Africa', *Pesticide News*, Journal of The Pesticide Trust, December 1991.

Jeyaratnam, J., 'Acute pesticide poisoning: a major problem', *World Health Statistics Quarterly*, 1990, 43.

Klare, Michael T., 'The Arms Trade: changing patterns in the 1980s', *Third World Quarterly*, 1987, 9(4).

Kreye, O., Heinrichs, J., and Frobel F., *Multinational Enterprises and Employment*, Geneva: ILO, 1988.

Lamusse, Roland, *Adjustment to structural change in manufacturing in a North-South perspective: the case of the clothing export sector of Mauritius*, Roland Lamusse, WEP Working Paper No. 27, Geneva: ILO, 1990.

*Liberalizing Foreign Trade in Developing Countries: the lessons of experience*, Papapeorgiou, D., Choksi, A.M., and Michaely, M., Washington: World Bank, 1990.

Madden, Peter, *A Raw Deal: trade and the world's poor*, Christian Aid, 1992.

Melrose, Diana, *Bitter Pills*, Oxford: Oxfam, 1982.

Mensah, Chaldeans, *Countertrade in the Third World: some notes*, Ifda Dossier, Nyon, Switzerland, 1989.

Morton, Kathryn and Tulloch, Peter, *Trade and Developing Countries*, London: Croom Helm/ODI, 1977.

Muller, Mike, *The Baby Killer*, London: War on Want, 1973.

*Multinational Enterprises and Employment*, Kreye, O., Heinricks, J., and Frobel, F., Geneva: Starnberg Institute, ILO, 1987.

Myrdal, Gunnar, *The Challenge of World Poverty*, UK: Pelican Books, 1970.

Nectoux, Francois and Dudley, Nigel, *A Hardwood Story*, London: Friends of the Earth, 1987.

*Negotiating the Fourth Lomé Convention*, Briefing Paper, London: Overseas Development Institute, October 1989.

*New Compact for Co-operation*, New York: United Nations, 1991.

Financial Resources for Developing Countries, 1990 and recent trends. Paris: OECD, October 1991.

*New Internationalist* magazine, February 1992.

*North-South: a programme for survival*. (The Brandt Report). Report of the independent commission on international development issues, London: Pan Books, 1980.

Omar, Sherif, *The Economic Consequences of Smoking in Egypt*, Cancer Institute, Cairo University, 1987.

Page, Sheila, Davenport, Michael, Hewitt, Adrian, *The GATT Uruguay Round: Effects on developing countries*, London: ODI, 1991.

Palmer, Gabrielle, *The Politics of Breast-feeding*, London: Pandora Press, 1988.

*Plunder in Ghana's rainforest for illegal profit*, London: Friends of the Earth, March 1992.

*Public Health Impact of Pesticides used in Agriculture*. Report of WHO/UNEP working party, Geneva, 1990.

*Review of Maritime Transport*, Geneva: UNCTAD, 1989.

Riddell, Abby Rubin (Ed.), *Adjustment or Protection*, London: CIIR, 1980.

Sachs, Jeffrey, *Foreign Affairs*, USA, Summer 1989.

Sement, Gerard, *Cotton*, The Tropical Agriculturalist series, The Netherlands: CTA/MacMillan, 1988.

Sider, Ronald, *Rich Christians in an Age of Hunger*, London: Hodder and Stoughton, 1990.

*State of the World's Children Report, 1990*, UNICEF, New York.

Stephen, Jones, *Third World countertrade: Analysis of 1350 deals involving developing countries 1980-87;* Newbury: Produce Studies, 1988.

Stewart, Frances, 'Are Adjustment Policies in Africa consistent with long-run development needs?', *Development Policy Review,* Vol.9 No.4, December 1991, London: ODI.

Stockholm International Peace Research Institute yearbooks, London and Philadelphia: Taylor and Francis.

*Sub-Saharan Africa: From Crisis to Sustainable Growth,* Washington: World Bank, 1989.

*Sustainable Tropical Forest Management,* Gland, Switzerland: World Wide Fund for Nature, 1990.

*Tea: market developments in 1991,* Rome: FAO, 1992.

*The Challenge to the South,* report of the South Commission, Oxford: OUP, 1990.

*The Courier* magazine, March-April 1990, Fourth EC-ACP Lomé Convention, Protocol 5, Brussels, 1990.

*The Draft Final Act Embodying the Results of the Uruguay Round of Multilateral Trade Negotiations,* MTN.TNC/W/FA, Geneva: GATT, 1991.

*The Generalized System of Preferences: Review of the First Decade,* Paris: OECD, 1983.

*The Network,* London: TWIN, January 1988.

*The Triad in Foreign Direct Investment,* New York: United Nations Centre on Transnational Corporations, 1991.

*Timber from the South Seas: An analysis of Japan's Tropical Timber Trade and its Environmental Impact,* WWF, UK, 1989.

Torado, Michael, *Economic Development in the Third World,* New York: Longman, 1989

*Trade and Development Report, 1991,* Geneva: UNCTAD.

*Trade and the Environment,* Geneva: GATT, March 1992.

*Transnational Corporations in World Development, Trends and Prospects,* New York: UNCTC, 1988.

*Transnational Corporations in World Development,* UNCTC 1988 Report, New York: UNCTC, 1989.

Tweeten, Luther, *Agricultural Trade, principles and policies,* Boulder, CO: Westview Press/IT Publications, 1992.

*UNCTAD VIII: Analytical report by the UNCTAD secretariat to the Conference,* TD/358, New York: United Nations, 1992.

UNICEF report, *The State of the World's Children, 1991,* New York: UNICEF, December 1990.

*Uruguay Round: Papers on Selected Issues,* Geneva: UNCTAD, 1989.

Vallely, Paul, *Bad Samaritans,* London: Hodder and Stoughton, 1990.

Watkins, Kevin, *Fixing the Rules: North-South issues in international trade and the GATT Uruguay Round,* London: CIIR, April 1992.

Weir, David and Schapiro, Mark, *The Circle of Poison*, San Fransisco: Institute for Food and Development Policy, 1981.

Wells, Phil and Jetter, Mandy, *The Global Consumer: Best buys to help the Third World*, London: Gollancz, 1991.

*What does the future hold for world fisheries*, Samudra Report No. 3, Belguim: International Collective in Support of Fishworkers, 1990.

Whittaker, Ben, *A Bridge of People*, London: Heinemann, 1983.

Wilkinson, James, *Tobacco*, London: Penguin, 1986.

Wood, Adrian, 'What do Developing-country Manufactured Exports Consist of?', *Development Policy Review*, London: ODI/Sage, Vol 9, 1991.

# Index

OPEC *see* Organization of Petroleum
    Exporting Countries
Organization of Petroleum Exporting
    Countries (OPEC) 50–1
Overseas Development Institute 65,
    136, 137
Oxfam Trading 150–1

painkillers (analgesics) 108–9
Pakistan 41, 162
Paraguay 167
Paris Club 125
patents *see* Trips
'perfect market' 8, 9, 34
Peru 167
pesticides 23–4, 51–2, 96, 116
Pesticides Action Network
    (PAN) 105, 106
pharmaceutical industries 101
    *see also* drugs, TNCs
Philippines 22, 32, 44, 70, 112, 121,
    123
plant breeding 13–14, 96–8
pollution 32, 114, 116
poverty 12, 18, 54, 173
Preferential Trade Area for Eastern
    and Southern Africa (PTA)
    166
prices 34
    cocoa 38–9
    coffee 37–8
primary commodities 1, 2, 34–7, 57,
    119, 143–4, 169–72, 173–4
producer co-operation 169–72
protectionism 9, 132
    *see also* trade barriers

quota systems 27, 45, 56, 57–8
    coffee 45–6
    cocoa 48
    *see also* buffer stock systems
        protectionism, tariffs

regional trade 163–9
remittances 77
resources 3–4, 6, 13–14
    demands on 10–14
rubber 36, 40–1, 48–9
rules-of-origin 61

sea farming *see* fishing
services 37, 72–5
shipping 76–7
soil damage 30, 31
South *see* developing countries
South Africa 165–6
South Commission report 73, 75,
    160–1, 172

South African Development Co-
    ordination Conference
    (SADCC) 165
South African Transport and
    Communications Commission
    (SATCC) 165
South Korea 1, 25, 59–60, 70
South-South trade 158–63, 168,
    172
Special Drawings Rights (SDRs)
    129–30
Sri Lanka 17–18, 40–1, 70
structural adjustment
    programmes 120–1, 128
subsidiary companies 89–90
    *see also* TNCs
sugar 39–40, 137
Swaziland 45

Taiwan 1, 27, 32, 56–7, 59–60
Tanzania 41, 106
tariffs 12, 132, 134, 167
    *see also* trade barriers
tea 17–18, 30–1, 34, 36, 41–2
Tea Research Institute 23
technology
    and TNCs 102
telecommunications 72
textiles 55, 56, 58–61, 137
    *see also* MFA
Thailand 39–41, 47
theory of comparative advantage 4–10
Third World 2, 17–20, 22, 24–5,
    56–8, 58–61, 65–8
    alternative trade 156
    debts 122–8
    government policies 22, 29–30,
        65–8
    TNCs 87, 90–2, 102, 105, 107–9,
        109–14
Third World Cotton Association 41
Third World Information Network
    (TWIN) 73, 152–3, 162
timber trade 28, 43, 48, 140
    *see also* forests, TNCs
tin 46–7
TNC *see* transnational companies
tobacco 30, 42–3, 117–18
tourism 28, 32, 77–86
Trade Aid 150
trade barriers 12–13, 56, 63–5, 132,
    133–7, 166
trade liberalization 65, 72, 133–7,
    140–1
trade-related aspects of property rights
    (Trips) 137
Traidcraft 151–2
transfer pricing 89–90

208